"The Father of Baseball"

"The Father of Baseball"

A Biography of Henry Chadwick

ANDREW J. SCHIFF

McFarland & Company, Inc., Publishers

Jefferson, North Carolina, and London

LIBRARY OF CONGRESS CATALOGUING-IN-PUBLICATION DATA

Schiff, Andrew J.
    "The father of baseball" : a biography of Henry Chadwick /
Andrew J. Schiff.
      p.   cm.
    Includes bibliographical references and index.

    ISBN 978-0-7864-3216-5
    softcover : 50# alkaline paper

    1. Chadwick, Henry, 1824–1908.   2. Sportswriters —
United States — Biography. I. Title.
GV742.42.C44S35   2008
796.357092 — dc22   2007044734
[B]

British Library cataloguing data are available

On the cover: Chadwick's scorecard for the June 17, 1869, match between
the Red Stockings and Eckfords; cricket and baseball writer Henry
Chadwick, 1857 (Transcendental Graphics); *The American National
Game of Base Ball* (yahoo.com). Cover design by Andrew J. Schiff and
Elyakeem Kinstlinger.

Manufactured in the United States of America

*McFarland & Company, Inc., Publishers
  Box 611, Jefferson, North Carolina 28640
  www.mcfarlandpub.com*

Contents

Preface

The origins of this work came when I first heard the name Henry Chadwick from a friend, and fellow Brooklyn College student, David Trachter. I was eighteen years old and I began to develop a keen interest in Chadwick's role in shaping baseball in its early years.

The idea for a biography of Chadwick came from a history class at Brooklyn College. Professor Edwin Burrows, who later won the Pulitzer Prize for *Gotham*, encouraged me to write a mini-biography on Chadwick because of my interest in New York and Brooklyn history and nineteenth-century baseball. Although the paper was only five pages long, the professor warmly received it, and I was able to gain confidence in my ability to develop ideas.

As a graduate student in history at the State University of New York, Albany, from 1993 to 1995, I was interested in writing a master's thesis. I tossed around several ideas and realized that my best option would be to expand on my earlier work on Chadwick and write an in-depth biography of the man known as "the Father of Baseball." Several professors were excited by the idea, but one in particular, Ivan Steen, showed incredible enthusiasm. I wrote an 85-page biography and received my master's degree. The work entitled "The Father of Baseball: Henry Chadwick, the Man and His Times" was not only a biography of Chadwick; it was an examination of his life as it reflected the era in which he wrote. Writing the thesis was hard work, but it was also great fun.

In 2000, I was working as an adjunct professor when my colleague Joe Dorinson, a man who had written numerous books on baseball,

1

suggested that I write Chadwick's full biography. Several months later I found a publisher.

During my research I relied on several libraries. The New York State Library in Albany was among the first libraries I used. Its collection of old newspapers, on microfilm, proved invaluable. The New York Public Library, too, was important. The Research Library on 42nd Street contained the Chadwick scrapbooks on microfilm and the Performance Library at Lincoln Center contained the *New York Clipper* on microfilm. Thanks and appreciation go to the Brooklyn Public Library. Grand Army Plaza and their numerous librarians were important for information on early Brooklyn and as a source for the *Brooklyn Eagle*. It also contained Chadwick's 1867 *The Ball Players' Chronicle*.

Other libraries proved invaluable, also. The SABR lending library and the National Baseball Hall of Fame Library and Museum were important sources of information that were vital to the writing of this biography. Thanks and special appreciation goes to the Hall of Fame's Gabriel Schechter, John Horne, Jr., and Tim Wiles for their passion and assistance in the research and writing of this book. Other helpful libraries and organizations were the Brooklyn Historical Society and the Chicago Historical Society. In New Jersey, the Hoboken Public Library and the New Jersey Room, located in Jersey City, assisted me greatly with information related to Elysian Fields.

The Chicago Historical Society was especially helpful with information on William Hulbert and the Chicago White Stockings. I owe a great thanks to Walter Wilson, who tirelessly and thoroughly read through Hulbert's letters, took Hulbert's hard-to-read script and rewrote Hulbert's words in legible English. Also, I thank my close friend Bill Clinger for his hard work doing research at the New York Public Library and his support for this project.

Special thanks also go to several people who supported me with encouragement, kind words and suggestions. Peter Nash supplied me with numerous sources of information that were extremely valuable to the biography. Peter's passion for Henry Chadwick is unparalleled. I also thank Henry Chadwick's descendant, Fran Henry, who supplied Peter with valuable information that he graciously shared with me.

Many thanks also go out to Harry Higham and Fred Ivor-Campbell for their support and feedback. Both men took the time to read my manuscript and offer suggestions on how it could be improved. Thanks are also given to Bob Schaeffer for his support. All three men are important members of the Society for American Baseball Research.

Many thanks also go to Professor Edwin Burrows of Brooklyn College and Professor Ivan Steen of the State University of New York, Albany, for their enthusiasm for this book. More thanks goes to Professor Allen Ballard for influencing my life with his brilliance when I took his course on the Civil Rights Movement in graduate school. Much thanks also goes to my closest friend, David Trachter, for his feedback, his critique of my writing style and support for this project.

I would like to thank the following people who also gave their support for this biography: retired professor Robert Muccigrosso, Elizabeth Berney, Tom Melville, Elyakeem Kinslinger, Mitchell Levine, Tzvi and Naomi Padeh, Jill Kaplan, Jordana Miller, Fred Feirstein, Ethan and Andrea Ries, Anna Tsepilovan, Harlan Schiff, Craig and Georgina Schiff and many others too numerous to name.

Introduction

He never played organized baseball. He never donned the uniform of a particular team, nor wore the cap of a particular club. He never was a professional athlete of any kind, never was a star of the diamond. And though he played baseball only sporadically, he never was remembered for hitting a home run, catching a searing liner, chewing tobacco, or even bunting a base runner into scoring position. Yet British-born Henry Chadwick, the man known in his time as the "Father of Baseball," sparked a cultural revolution in America that changed the face of his adopted country and revolutionized sports throughout the world.

Henry Chadwick was baseball's first real reporter, correspondent and writer. As baseball grew during the late 1850s, and throughout the 1890s, Chadwick used the latest American technological innovations, such as the railroad and telegraph steamboat, the penny press, and the electric light, to cover the game. Since baseball was America's earliest athletic pastime, Chadwick invented sports journalism and, as a result, fostered the growth and development of the game as it evolved.[1] The multi-faceted Chadwick also served and sometimes presided over baseball's rules committee during the crucial period of the game's development, reported as a journalist for the weeklies and dailies of New York, and invented the game's statistics. Because of his incredible impact on the game, Chadwick was inducted into the Baseball Hall of Fame in 1938.

Chadwick was not simply a journalist, statistician and rule maker. He was also a pivotal figure in American thought during the mid- to late 1800s. Chadwick advocated sobriety, morality and the health benefits of sports and games in digests, newspapers and books that were read across the country. His opinions had an enduring influence on baseball and other competitive sports still felt today, and they placed him decades ahead of his contemporaries in sports journalism. One of Chadwick's fellow writers from the *Sporting News* wrote that he was:

> 25 years before the dozens who [were] pointing out the advantage of clean sports to the young. He realized it at the start and single-handed he fought the battles of sport, trying all the whole to make the country realize that in sport it had one of the mightiest agencies for good.[2]

Throughout the five decades he covered the game, Chadwick was baseball's moral conscience. He advocated fairness, truth and honest play. And when faced with moral dilemmas, when he attempted to rectify impurities in the game, when he spoke of the "best interests of the game" to combat its social ills like gambling, alcohol, and illegal drugs, Chadwick laid the foundation of baseball's traditional ethics.

Although Chadwick never really played organized baseball, he did more to promote and develop the sport than anyone in its history. Harry Wright, Chadwick's contemporary and friend, could have claimed this title for himself. Wright invented baseball managing, developed in-game strategy, and put together the first all-professional team. Wright was a member of the New York Knickerbockers in the late 1850s, and he participated in baseball's first "All-Star Game," the Fashion Course Games of 1858. But Wright proffered the gift title to Chadwick. Wright stated, "It has always been a pleasure to me to do what I could to make the game of base ball interesting and worthy of the support of the public [however].... There is a gentleman in New York, *Henry Chadwick*, Esq. *who is richly deserving of the title*, 'father of the game,' for 'the pen is mighty' and he has ... used it for the best interest of the game, as you know."[3]

Chadwick modestly maintained that "base ball never had a father but like Topsey, the game just *growed*."[4] "But," he added, "I suppose they call me its father because in the days when it was attracting little or no attention, except among a mere handful, I became interested in it and did what I could to make it popular."

While Chadwick insisted baseball did not have a father who invented the game, he enjoyed the paternal role of nurturing baseball during its maturation. Recalling his youth in England, Chadwick wrote:

> Little did I dream when playing "rounder" in Plymouth in the decade of the thirties that I should afterward become the chief *gardener*, so to speak,

who from the little English acorn of "rounder," helped to cultivate the giant American oak of baseball [emphasis added].[5]

Other titles have also been used to describe Chadwick's role in sculpting baseball. Noted baseball historian David Quentin Voigt, for example, analogized Chadwick to Moses, "destined to show baseball leaders how to fulfill the game's promise as America's national field sport."[6]

Chadwick was clearly a giant in his time. And since baseball is the sport of America, the game most identified with American culture, Henry Chadwick was the man who helped America discover its identity. Though the nation was founded in the in the late eighteenth century, it wasn't until well in the nineteenth century that it began developing, on a more sophisticated level, its own writers, poets, and overall artistic identity. It took many decade before it found its own games and culture. Because Chadwick identified baseball early on and helped to develop the game, he must be given credit for helping to create our country as we know it today.

In the days when Chadwick was a leading figure in sports, he was easily identifiable. First, Chadwick's iron-gray beard and his sparkling blue eyes made him recognizable to the public. "Then others identified him by his prominently donned turban cap, winged overcoat, an umbrella made of India rubber, which he carried under one arm, and a thick stick, which he could make into a three-legged stool just by opening several compartments."[7] Standing six feet tall and of a heavy build, Chadwick, during the heyday of early baseball, was often larger than many ballplayers he encountered.[8]

Chadwick first established himself as a respected sports journalist at the *New York Times* as a cricket reporter in the 1850s. Athletes and fans deeply admired Chadwick's expertise and encyclopedic knowledge of the game's rules. His following among cricket enthusiasts facilitated Chadwick's role in the small but growing baseball community of the mid-nineteenth century as well. Many early players knew of Chadwick because they also played cricket. Chadwick was even an amateur cricket player, and his participation as both a journalist and athlete enabled him to easily to make the transition from cricket to baseball and become an important person in the rising baseball community.

In the days before radio and television, Henry Chadwick's writings were the descriptive link between the playing action and the fans. Later, as baseball and other sports became more accepted, Chadwick wrote about football, boxing, ice skating, yachting, sailing, and tennis. Chadwick was also an avid card player and was especially fond of chess. He wrote and edited several chess guides and even wrote an instructional book for chess beginners in the early 1900s.[9]

Although Chadwick wrote about many sports and games, he is most remembered for his pioneering work in baseball. Chadwick's numerous writings on baseball led to the perception of sports as news. Before Chadwick's contribution, newspapers only sporadically mentioned games with an occasional nod to a cricket match via a game summary and box score. However, within a decade after the appearance of Chadwick's first articles in the late 1850s, dailies routinely covered sporting events, and by the 1880s, sports pages had been developed. In 1895, the first sports section was launched after newspaper editors recognized the public's great appetite for sports coverage.

What made Henry Chadwick interested in sports and games? Why did he gravitate toward journalism? How did his family and the era in which he lived shape Chadwick's philosophy? How did Chadwick's love for and deep knowledge of English games both help and later skew his vision of baseball? How did Chadwick's vision in some ways sabotage the career of a man who devoted his entire career to the promotion of this game? In this biography, we will answer all these questions and reveal further insights into the psyche of Henry Chadwick and the game he helped make an institution.

We shall see how, when the sport became more business-oriented and appealing to working class masses, the average reader would receive both Chadwick's written style and approach to the game differently. Some came to view him as a curmudgeon regardless of his great achievement as the man who defined sports journalism in an earlier era.

In the end, despite his prickly ways, old-fashioned views, and tendency to over-moralize, most of his friends and followers still had the highest respect for his work. Those who knew Chadwick ultimately perceived him as a visionary, a great man who aggressively drew the game he loved to the forefront of the public consciousness like no journalist ever had before or since. They understood that his writings in the dailies and weeklies, the yearly guidebooks and other publications stimulated the evolution of baseball; there was indeed widespread admiration for the man who called baseball America's National Pastime.

While it would be foolish to say that his journalism alone precipitated the popularity of baseball and sports in general, without Chadwick's statistics, there would be no thorough understanding of America's oldest and most historical sport. There would be nothing for the fans to read, nothing to aid their comprehension of each individual player's performance. Though football and basketball have recently equaled if not eclipsed baseball in popularity, it was baseball that gave the United States its first sporting culture through the introduction of statistics.

Baseball was the first organized game ordinary Americans played, paid to see, and read about all at once. Horse racing, though it antedated baseball, never developed into an athletic pastime as baseball did. And it was the work of Henry Chadwick, a cricket writer–turned–baseball journalist who adapted some of cricket's stats and invented others for baseball, who was responsible for the phenomenon. Chadwick's contribution was enormous. Consider what America would be without baseball. Think about how synonymous baseball is with America, particularly how synonymous it was with America during the twentieth century. Think about how important Babe Ruth, Lou Gehrig, Joe DiMaggio, Sandy Koufax and Jackie Robinson were to Americans in their respective eras. Where would these men be, and more important where their sport be, if not for statistics? Statistics quantatively demonstrated the extent of the legendary capabilities of these iconic ballplayers. Without the advent of that tool, it would have been difficult to compare their relative prowess. And as America's most prominent game, what would this country be like without baseball? And, most critically, what would baseball be without Henry Chadwick? Let us begin our journey and discover Henry Chadwick, the father of baseball.

CHAPTER 1

Hoboken

Early one afternoon in the fall of 1856, a thirty-two-year-old journalist for the *New York Times* left the Fox Hill cricket field at Elysian Fields in West Hoboken, New Jersey, after a match had just ended. As he departed the grounds, he saw something in the distance that fascinated him. He crossed over to the old Knickerbocker club field and began to watch something strangely familiar. He had seen this sport numerous times previously — he had even participated in earlier versions of the game — but was now watching with greater interest than he had before.[1] It was a closely contested match between two rival nines of New York, the Gotham and Eagle clubs; a particularly spirited contest that typified early baseball.

This cricket journalist, who had been born in England and had a deep interest in health, came away from the contest a changed man. Later, he said what fascinated him about the game was that it was both fast and rugged and "suited to the American temperament."[2] While the game may have reminded him of the past, what he saw was the future.

This young cricket journalist, who had bypassed baseball to and from cricket matches played on the grassy meadow of Hoboken's Elysian Fields, would no longer walk the same path he had strode for decades. For years now, *New York Times* cricket journalist Henry Chadwick had been riding the ferry to New Jersey to watch cricket matches. Not only were ballplayers and sports writers attracted to the open, verdant Elysian Fields, but New Yorkers looking to escape the hectic city were drawn to it as well. The plush grounds of Elysian Fields were conveniently located only "a mile from the Hudson River ferry dock" and were frequented by New

VIEW OF HUDSON RIVER, FROM ELYSIAN FIELDS, HOBOKEN, NEW JERSEY.

The entrance to Elysian Fields in 1852, with a view of the Hudson River. Illustration from ***Gleason's Pictorial Drawing-Room Companion*** **(Hoboken Public Library).**

Yorkers as "a recreational destiny."[3] Perhaps the person most responsible for these events was Hoboken resident John Cox Stevens, the first Commodore of the New York City Yacht Club.[4] Stevens had donated the spacious five-acre grounds that hosted ball games, parades and other community events, and set up the ferries that transported reporters like Chadwick, spectators and players alike from lower Manhattan to Hoboken.[5]

Now that Chadwick had experienced baseball in a different light — he had perceived "base ball" previously as being "too juvenile and uninspiring," much like the rounders of his youth — he was struck with an idea. Chadwick believed that he could make baseball "the national game in word and in truth."[6] And, even as important, Henry Chadwick believed that he could make baseball "a powerful lever ... by which [the American] people could be lifted into a position" and devote more time "to physical exercise and healthful out-door recreation that they had hitherto, as a people, been noted for."[7] Chadwick's schemed to educate the American public on "out-door recreation" and make it part of America's cultural structure, like it had been in England, where his brother Edwin Chadwick had supported this same idea.[8]

Despite Chadwick's objectives, there already was one baseball journalist in 1856, William Cauldwell of the weekly *New York Sunday Mercury*. Cauldwell had been publishing results of baseball games along with box scores as early as 1853. But Chadwick had greater ambition and a greater vision for baseball than Cauldwell. Chadwick not only sought more coverage of "base ball," he sought to make baseball the national game. And with his vision of making baseball the national pastime, he would need to get the game covered more religiously than it had been before. In doing so, he was laying the groundwork for the future of sports journalism by instituting serious coverage of sporting events in the metropolitan dailies. His actions placed Chadwick decades ahead of any sports journalist. During the 1850s, newspapers had no sports sections and there was no daily coverage of athletic events.

Knowing that publicity would help baseball's growth, Chadwick tried to convince the editors of several dailies to publish the results of all "match" games. He talked "the ears off the city-editors in an honest effort to sell his own stories" and to boost baseball's popularity. Chadwick offered to send in results of the games, free of charge, but he failed to arouse enthusiasm, for the editors believed there was little interest in baseball and that coverage of the game would only be a waste of time and effort.

Part of the problem lay in the metropolitan dailies' greater faith in cricket since the British game seemed so well entrenched in the United States. As historian Jules Tygiel points out, for the last twenty years, cricket had become his adopted county's most popular game, with "clubs appear[ing] in at least twenty-two states and more than 125 cities and towns."[9] During the 1850s, cricket in its organized forms attracted more participants and bigger crowds to its more competitive events. The baseball-cricket rivalry was also reflected in the frustration baseball enthusiasts showed when "landscape architects for New York's new Central Park dubbed the land allocated for ball games the Cricket Ground" in 1858.[10] The issue was rather controversial. Even the *New York Clipper*, the most prominent sports and entertainment weekly in New York, had its own ideas about the snub:

> We stated some time since that efforts were making, by the Base Ball
> Clubs in this locality, to obtain a spot of ground in the Central Park, to
> be used as a play ground for the game of Base Ball. We are sorry to learn
> that these efforts are not likely to meet with success. Why, we cannot say

from our own personal knowledge, but we have heard it whispered that a certain party, *seemingly* interested in the success of the application, has played a game not strictly in accordance with the rules of fair and manly dealing, and the members of the clubs referred to will probably lose the expected grant in consequence.[11]

Despite cricket's popularity and despite his own affinity for his mother country's most popular game, Chadwick understood deeply that Americans really wanted speed and action in their ballgames, not the slow-paced game of cricket:

Americans do not care to dawdle over a sleep-inspiring game all through the heat of a June or July day. What they do, they want to do in a hurry. In baseball, all is lightning; every action is swift as a seabird's flight.[12]

Despite Chadwick's insight into the American temperament and his passion for making baseball the national game, he realized that it would be difficult, at least in the beginning, for baseball or any sport to be covered by the dailies. Even though the *New York Daily Times*, on July 10, 1856, printed baseball summaries, the paper required that he condense it to its "smallest possible limit." The summary read:

On Tuesday a match of Base Ball was played between the first nine members of the "Gotham" and nine members of the "Baltic" Clubs, at their ground at the Red House [located in Harlem]. Play commenced at 4 o'clock and ended at 5, the "Gothams" beating easily, the "Baltics" making but two aces.[13]

Though he had a game published in the *New York Times*, it was a popular weekly entertainment journal that would provide Chadwick with an opportunity to shine. Chadwick established consistent coverage for baseball when Frank Queen, co-founder of the weekly entertainment journal, the *New York Clipper*, hired him and agreed to publish game summaries in the early summer of 1857. The paper began publishing his summaries on June 20th and named him baseball and cricket editor.[14] By having the reports published in a sports/entertainment journal, Chadwick and the *Clipper* not only fed an audience that already was interested in sports and games, but also helped to create a following for baseball by exposing it to a new audience. The more positive exposure baseball received, the better known it became, thereby increasing the chance that baseball reporting would find its way to metropolitan dailies, which would lead to increased interest. More importantly, the *Clipper* was not a news-weekly read only by New Yorkers; it was read throughout the country,

Cricket and baseball writer Henry Chadwick had already established himself as an authority on bat-and-ball games when he was hired by the *Clipper* in 1857 (Transcendental Graphics).

enabling readers both north and south to become familiar with the New York version of baseball.

One might ask, considering his substantial presence in the athletic community of New York, Brooklyn, and New Jersey, what took Chadwick so long to realize baseball's potential? After all, he had participated in baseball matches back in the late 1840s. However, those games had left a sour taste for the sport. Chadwick's main recollection from a game played on a field, not far from the grounds where he walked hundreds of times to cover ball games, in Hoboken, was when he was "soaked"—hit in the ribs on his way to first base, the customary way that base runners in early baseball were put out before more "scientific" rules were universally put to use. The Knickerbocker Club of New York, which also played games at Elysian Fields, had done away "soaking," although this change was not widely applied until the early 1850s when the Gothams and Eagles agreed to play with this new rule. In fact, Chadwick held on to a baseball that he used in a game with the New York Knickerbockers in 1847, and may have been familiar with the rule change, but was not applied universally. On one particular game the next year, in a later recollection, Chadwick often remembered having played with a ball that was "ten inches in circumference, weighed six ounces, and was composed of two and one half ounces of rubber covered with yarn," Chadwick fielded the shortstop position at that time (which alternated between where the current shortstop plays and where the modern day second baseman plays) and thought the game was too much like the rounders he played back in Devonshire, England, where he was born on October 5, 1824, at Jessamine Cottage in St. Thomas, Exeter.[15]

Chadwick's recollections of his youth in England often centered on those early ball-playing years. It was traditional for young English boys to play rounders, and Chadwick was no exception. Reflecting on his youth, Chadwick remembered how he and his school-mates "would go to the nearest playing field, select a smooth portion of it, and lay out the ground for a contest. This was easily done by placing four stones, or posts in position as base stations, and by digging a hole in the ground where the batsman had to stand." As rounders had no set or established rules as cricket had, guidelines were established by custom.[16]

Chadwick remembered other aspects of the game while recalling those early ball-playing years. In many of his early baseball manuals, for which he later became nationally famous, he would always bring up rounders, for the game reminded him of early baseball. Here Chadwick describes in greater depth some of the events that would take place in a typical rounders match:

> When the ball tosser, or "feeder," sent a ball to the bat, and it was hit into the field, the player running round the bases at once became the target of the fielders, their efforts, if the ball was not caught, being directed to hitting him with the ball, in which case he was out, and, failing to do this, they would try and toss the ball into the hole at "home," provided there was no one to take the bat, and if they were successful, the side at the bat had to retire. When all of the side were put out — each man retiring from play as he was put out — then the field side took the bat, and so the game went on until a certain number of runs were reached — mutually agreed upon — and the party first scoring the required number won the game.[17]

Naturally, Chadwick outgrew rounders and began to play cricket. Unlike baseball and rounders, which had a one-bounce accommodation, cricket required catching the ball in the air to record an out, a game that necessitated great skill and real "manly" abilities. Like many Englishmen before and since, Chadwick had a natural affinity for cricket, a sport that had been America's favorite bat and ball game for 140 years. In cricket, Chadwick found a game that was "most scientific," the "most attractive game in existence." To be a successful "cricketer," wrote Chadwick, required courage to catch or stop a ball at full speed.[18] To Chadwick, cricket was a game for the sophisticated, as the sport "forms no debasing habits ... it is suited to the softer feelings of a refined age." But more than that, cricket is a game where all can be equal. Chadwick explained:

> Society has it rank and classes; these distinctions, we believe, are not artificial, but natural, even as the very courses and strata of the earth itself. Lines there are nicely graduated, ordained to separate, what [Robert] Burns call, the tropics of affluence, from the temperate zones of a comfortable independence, and the arctic circles of poverty; but these lines are nowhere less marked, because nowhere less wanted, than on the cricketfield."[19]

Chadwick, as both a cricket writer and amateur player, developed an encyclopedic knowledge of the game's rules as well as its history.[20] His involvement in the cricket community as both a journalist and an amateur player allowed him to make the transition to baseball journalist, which eventually led him to become a member of the baseball community of New York. After all, many of the players who played baseball were also playing cricket. Cricket, which had been brought over in a more primitive form during the colonial days, had been reintroduced to the American public by a new wave of British immigrants part of a larger wave of immigration of Western Europeans to the United States during the 1820s and 1830s. It was this wave of immigration that Henry Chadwick and his family were brought to this country during the late 1830s.

Henry Chadwick was almost thirteen years old when he arrived in Manhattan on Thursday, September 21, 1837. Chadwick migrated with his parents, Teresa and James, and younger sister, Rosa, and eventually settled in Brooklyn. It is Brooklyn where Chadwick spent the bulk of his life and where he was later honored as a member of the society of old Brooklynites for his fifty years of residing in the city that by 1898 became a borough of greater New York.

Henry, the rest of the Chadwick family and other English families had been transported by the packet ship *Philadelphia*. Like most arrivals that had migrated to the United States whose ships were docked in lower Manhattan, the immigrants must have been intimidated by the entire process.[21]

When the *Philadelphia* docked at the lower tip of Manhattan, the scene was typically chaotic. There was no system established to process Henry and his family and the other immigrants who were coming to America at the time. "Runners" or "agents" representing boarding houses near the docks or transportation lines offering to carry immigrants to inland areas swooped down on families coming off the boat.[22] Perhaps that is why the Chadwicks spent their first night in the United States in the cabins of the ship that brought them to America.

Like many anxious arrivals to this new land, as the ship pushed its way through the cold oceans of the Narrows, Henry may have scanned the vast harbor of New York. Though it may have intrigued the Chadwicks and excited them as they finally began to see the place that they would soon call home, New York and its surrounding areas in the 1800s would be strange to modern-day New Yorkers and those familiar with the city's makeup of tall buildings and connecting bridges. Back in 1837, the entire metropolitan area was a simple landscape. There was no Statue of Liberty to greet the passengers from their long journey, and Ellis Island was several decades from becoming the gateway for new arrivals from foreign lands. There were no towering bridges crossing over and connecting different parts of New York, nor were there skyscrapers that stood like giant steel redwoods soaring above the landscape of the metropolis. The cities of New York consisted of rural landscapes dotted with quiet cottages and church spires that dominated the thrilling view of Manhattan's skyline.[23]

America in 1837 was raw and full of promise. A relatively new nation that was built on the principles of enlightenment, the United States was a democracy that only a half-century earlier had broken away from the British monarchy. Perhaps that is what drew Henry's father, the radical journalist James Chadwick, a man who supported the French Revolution and the ideas it espoused, to America. Whatever his reasons, Chadwick, who in addition to being an outspoken political writer was also an amateur scientist and music teacher, decided to take his small family to start anew.[24] Perhaps New York reminded them of London, the city in which Edwin Chadwick, Henry's older half-brother, was carving out a career in public health.

Henry and the rest of the Chadwick clan had to have been a tad nervous coming to this relatively new nation, which had been led until recently by the popular, if controversial, Andrew Jackson. Many felt that President Jackson's destruction of the National Bank in 1836 had resulted in the Panic of 1837. Actually, there were other more complex explanations for the economic instability. Some saw the Bank of the United States' undoing as a consequence of excessive land speculation and a lack of adequate specie backing by the state banks. Others blamed the collapse of the New Orleans cotton market that bankrupted one of the largest New York dealers in domestic exchanges with connections to a variety of commercial and mercantile enterprises and banks.[25]

Despite the new administration, now led by the "Little Magician," former governor of New York Martin Van Buren, practically everyone was affected by the great economic downturn of '37. The great American writer Washington Irving complained that his own "means ... [were] hampered and locked up." During the Panic, Irving coined the famous phrase, "*the almighty dollar,* that great object of universal devotion throughout our land."[26] While the new country was going through a transition with a new president, New York, the city the Chadwicks encountered when they arrived in 1836, was also going through change.

If the Chadwicks were looking for lodgings in lower New York, near the ports, the area was mostly a commercial center, thanks to the construction of the Erie Canal in 1825. Tiffany's, then a bric-a-brac store, was one of the businesses featured in this vicinity.[27] And as Manhattan's main residential area reached further and further uptown, Brooklyn, particularly Brooklyn Heights, with its proximity to lower Manhattan, "became an attractive place to live."

Given Theresa Chadwick's background, it would seem highly unlikely that she would want to live in a place like Manhattan. Henry's mother lived most of her life outside of the city, having come from the bucolic Burton-upon-Trent. Rather than living in London, she and James raised Rosa and Henry in Exeter, in the county of Devonshire, in southwestern England.[28] And when Henry went to visit his brother and father in London in the summer of 1836, Theresa Chadwick wrote a revealing letter tinged with fear and emotion, typical of a protecting, yet loving, mother that conveyed her fears about his being in the big city.

> My Darling Child
>   ... I have trembled for your safety ever since you have been separated from me, never go out by yourself, you are not aware of the dangers of London, listen to no one in the street should any stranger speak to you whether male or female under any protest whatever and never ramble out of an evening or you will be decoyed away by some designing wretch and be for ever deprived of seeing your Ma keep in mind should any misfortune or disgrace befall you through your own conduct or neglect of my advice your Ma would die brokenhearted!...[29]

Perhaps that is why James Chadwick decided he would take his family and settle in Brooklyn.

After remaining on board the *Philadelphia* for the first night, the Chadwicks found a home at a Brooklyn boarding house on Fulton Street, opposite York Street, in Brooklyn Heights.[30] In a recollection of his first days in America recorded in the *Brooklyn Eagle* on May 11, 1888, Henry Chadwick remembered that an English gentleman who lived in the house befriended him and took him fishing on the freshly built docks at the foot of Cranberry Street. He also recalled how he and his family, along with fellow Brooklynites, relied on pump water from street wells, on whale oil for their table lamps and in the street lamps for light, not to mention the absence of sewers and all other means of sanitary living.[31]

Young Henry and his family were among many thousands of immigrants arriving to New York each year. A total of 58,000 German, British and Irish immigrants had already flooded New York in 1836, and more were on the way. At the time the city could count on two daily newspapers, *The Sun*, founded in 1833 by Benjamin Day, and the *New York Herald*, begun in 1835 by James Gordon Bennet, and one evening paper known as the *Transcript*. When Chadwick and other rivals came to New York from their long transatlantic journey, they came to a city in transition. In 1837, New York had elected a new mayor, the nativist Aaron Clark, the city's first Whig elected to the post. Clark's successful campaign was based on being simultaneously anti–Irish and anti–Catholic.[32]

That year the city approved a plan for a new water system that would bring water from upstate New York; the well water used by many Manhattanites had become a disgusting shade of brownish yellow that was simply undrinkable. The only way for most New Yorkers to get fresh water was by purchasing it from street vendors.

Manhattan had become an extremely dangerous or, at the other extreme, too expensive for a middle-class family like the Chadwicks. That may have been the reason they settled in Brooklyn. For instance, lower Manhattan's environment was corrupted by the dreadfulness of Five Points. Named because it was an intersection of five streets, Five Points was for the first fifteen to twenty years of the 1800s a decent section, a community filled with mixed ethnicities. But by 1820 it had begun to disintegrate. Built on landfill that had not been packed solidly enough, buildings began "to sink into the moist soil, their doors springing on hinges and their facades cracking into wooden grins." The most prominent landmark of that section was the Old Brewery, and as the tavern and the community become synonymous with the Irish as well as violence, prostitution, perversion, drunkenness and every other negative vice imaginable, "respectable" people began to move out in droves.

After living as boarders for a year, the Chadwick finally moved into their first apartment at 39 Pineapple Street, in Brooklyn Heights, in 1838.[33] That fall James Chadwick, who began earning a living as a music teacher, took Henry on a long hike into the country, which was only a few minutes from where they lived.[34]

Brooklyn in those days was a natural habitat for fishing, hunting and hiking, and Henry discovered the various ponds and open areas best for those hobbies. One area, known as Denton's Mill Pond, became a favorite spot for fishing. Henry would visit the locality with his school-boy companions and would come home with flounders, eels and tomcods. He caught larger fish by wandering along the shore road adjoining the creek (about where Bond Street now runs) down to Luquer's old mill.[35]

Not only did he fish, he would venture into Brooklyn's wilderness to go bird hunting. Pursuing fowl was a common practice in England, something Chadwick had participated in when he lived back in Exeter. Having migrated to America, Chadwick continued the practice of hunting birds. Armed with a rifle, he recalled having successfully downed robins along with some catbirds and a chippy or two. Henry remembered how after one particular hunting excursion he walked along the road that went beside a farm owned by a local family and spotted an apricot tree "well loaded down with ripe fruit, standing near the roadside edge, as far as any public right to the fruit was concerned." Henry made sure "by military observation" that no one was looking. All of a sudden, as he described, there was a "mysterious" dropping of apricots from the tree. Henry, determined not to see those stranded apricots go to waste, pocketed the fallen fruit, "his conscience being lightened of the burden of an alleged theft by the fact of a lucky find." Not surprisingly, Henry made several visits that month to that immediate neighborhood for a constantly decreasing crop of apricots on that lonely wayside tree, for it was just out of sight of the farm house.[36]

During the winters of his Brooklyn boyhood, Chadwick would go sledding and ice-skating. He and his friends would make their own skating ponds by pumping water into the gutters of a cold night. When Henry became competent enough as a skater, he would accompany his friends to the skating ponds in the outskirts of Brooklyn, one of which was located in a vacant lot at the junction of Court Street and Hamilton Avenue.[37]

Brooklyn was filled with nature for places to hunt and fish, but it had games, too. Henry loved watching sports and would go over to the rough, turfy field located on the vacant lots adjoining Smith and Bergen streets in Brooklyn Heights and watch the great cricket matches taking place.[38] The contestants in these matches, as with most cricket matches in the United States at that time, consisted of his fellow British immigrants who had made their home in the metropolitan area.

One particular match, which took place on September 20, 1838, pitted an eleven from New York against an eleven from Brooklyn. It happened to feature men who hailed originally from the English towns of Sheffield and Nottingham. Henry, who was on his way home after fishing at the Gowanus Creek Mill, stopped to watch the game in progress. One particular play remained etched in Chadwick's mind forever. A fly ball was hit out to the wicket keeper, who put his hands directly over his head to make the catch. However, as the ball hit his hands, it slid through his fingers and landed on his face, blackening one of his eyes.[39]

James Chadwick encouraged his son's love of the outdoors and sports, and he supported his son's curiosity in other ways. Naturally, like all good fathers, James played a significant role in shaping Henry as a person. He taught Henry how to play the piano, and brought out his inner curiosities by teaching him all he knew about the sciences, whether the subject was astronomy, biology or even physics.[40] James Chadwick's instructions, particularly his scientific instructions, had an enormous impact on

Henry, as he was to write numerous articles on the scientific aspects of baseball.

But more important, it was James Chadwick who imbued his son Henry with the spirit of reform. It was this same spirit which ultimately led to Henry's development and promotion of baseball statistics, the improvement of baseball's rules, his protests against gambling and alcohol, and his advocacy of sports and games in the newspapers as a means of fostering better health.

These reform instincts can be traced to Henry's paternal grandfather, "good old Andrew Chadwick," of Manchester, England. Henry's grandfather was a tall and venerable man and was remembered by another grandson, Henry's older brother Edwin, as being "white headed" and "wearing blue stockings and silver-buckled shoes."[41] Andrew Chadwick lived an extremely long and full life — 96 years — and played a significant role in this famous English city known as "the cradle of the Industrial Revolution."[42]

Andrew Chadwick descended from successive generations of Chadwicks who hailed from Lancashire. The Chadwick lineage can be traced to a city just northeast of Manchester called Rochdale. The Chadwick name derives from a hamlet named Chadwick, located in Spotland, a subdivision of Rochdale.[43]

There are two theories how the Chadwick name came to be. The first theory is that Chadwick was named after a "noted Saxon warrior" called Cadde, who settled and built a "rude fortification and dwelling on an eminence at the confluence of two streams about a mile above the present town of Rochdale."[44] Cadde's reputation as a soldier was so remarkable that even though his people, the Saxons, had been crushed by the invading Angles (the "war like hordes" dispatched by William the Conqueror, the man who led the Normans to victory at the battle of Hastings in 1066 A.D.), "he was permitted to wear a crest and achievement of arms." This "distinction then and for six centuries afterwards was limited to Gentlemen by descent, or to soldiers of distinction allowed, noticed by, or reported to the King on the field of battle."[45]

Due to Cadde's fortress and his greatness on the battlefield, the area was literally named after him. The name Chadwick comes from a patronymic of "Cadde and weig, vyck, vyke, or wyke, meaning a fortification, hamlet or dwelling." Thus the name actually means the fortification, hamlet or dwelling of Cadde. Just after the conquest, Cadde adopted the Norman usage of referring to himself after his possessions by utilizing "the Norman-French 'de' to go along with Caddewyck was henceforth the designation of the Saxon chief."[46] Variations of the spelling of the surname evolved over the centuries. Over time the "de" was omitted and the modern spelling of Chadwick came into existence. This change occurred in the fifteenth century.[47]

The second theory was that it was named after St. Chad, "a missionary to the Saxons of Mercia, which comprised a large eastern and middle part of England, who became Bishop of York and afterwards of Lichfield." The name of the area was "anciently called St. Chad's Wick." In fact, the "parish church of Rochdale, a fine old church of the Twelfth Century ... bears the name of St. Chad's."[48]

Regardless of the roots of the family's last name, Lancashire, which includes Rochdale and Manchester (along with another famous British city, Liverpool), would feel the importance of the Chadwick name in a variety of different ways. This area would certainly experience the impact of the Chadwick name for many decades, thanks in part to the contributions of Andrew Chadwick.

A native of Longsight, Andrew Chadwick was good friends and an admirer of preacher John Wesley, the founder of the Wesleyan Church of Methodism. Chadwick was highly influenced by John Wesley's teachings and was present when Wesley uttered, "If after I am dead it be discovered that one hundred pounds belongs to my estate, after all my just debts are paid, let any man call me a rogue."[49] Chadwick, inspired by Wesley's teachings, established the first four Methodist Sunday schools in Lancashire.[50]

A Wesleyan Methodist's worldview, as espoused by Wesley, was both strict and reform-minded in its attempts to universally uplift the working poor, those affected most by the Industrial Revolution.[51] Though members were "expelled for levity, for profanity and swearing, for lax attendance at class meetings," they were instilled with a sense of self worth. Methodist preachers taught converts that their souls were as good as the aristocratic or bourgeois souls that oppressed them. More importantly, the Methodist philosophy, as taught by John Wesley, was to imbue its followers with education. Science, literature and philosophy were taught to converts to elevate their moral character. Wesleyan Methodism was not a movement that required only pure spiritual feeling; Wesleyan Methodists also emphasized the intellectual development of their followers. Their schools stressed education beyond the religious teachings, focusing their energies on a wide array of subjects like medicine, electricity, and natural history. Students read a variety of classic authors like Shakespeare, Milton, Spenser and Locke.[52]

Andrew Chadwick, as a disciple of the Wesleyan Methodist philosophy, was a man of great morality and social consciousness that was best demonstrated when he refused to invest in real estate speculation that would have allowed him to make a fortune on the backs of the poor.[53] In fact, Chadwick, again in the tradition of John Wesley, so believed that to save money was to do wrong, he even "refused on principle" when "it was proposed to him, on good grounds, to contest the claim of succession to Sir Andrew Chadwick," the London millionaire worth 7 million pounds, "after whom he was named."[54] This social consciousness reflected not only Andrew Chadwick's view of the poor, but also begins to explain the radical political philosophy of his son, journalist James Chadwick.

Born in Manchester, on December 2, 1771, the eleventh child of his father and mother, James Chadwick became "a prominent figure in regional, intellectual and cultural circles.[55] Chadwick was a staunch adherent of the French Revolution, so much so that he was in Paris during this time, and later was in the company of Joel Barlow, an American-born writer and radical, when he stood in the Champ de Mars to witness Napoleon Bonaparte, as first consul, holding a military review. Not only was James Chadwick a believer of the French Revolution, particularly its core doctrine, *The Declaration of the Rights of Man*, he also was a follower of Thomas Paine and British Enlightenment philosophy.[56] Chadwick was influenced by his own father's social consciousness, but not necessarily his devotion to his religious teachings. However, given Andrew Chadwick's philosophies as a Methodist, it was natural that James would gravitate toward radical political beliefs, since Methodist philosophies led into those ideas espoused by *The Declaration of the Rights of Man*.[57]

In fact, the reason for James Chadwick's migration to America may have been his political inclinations. With its democratic government established on enlightenment ideals, such as those espoused by Paine, the United States suited his more "radical" tastes.[58] American democracy certainly contrasted with England's more conservative government, which stood opposed to the French Revolution and the ideals espoused by it.[59]

Chadwick attempted to convey these liberal views while tutoring his teenage son, Henry. While in Manchester, James Chadwick, a cellist and pianist, had taught botany and music to a young John Dalton, who became a great scientist in chemistry and physics. Dalton was the man who discovered the atomic theory.[60] James Chadwick most likely tutored his first son, Edwin, and was certainly qualified to influence his younger son, Henry, in his studies. In fact, there is evidence in his diaries that James

Chadwick had guided Henry in his formative years, imparting some delicate words of wisdom, words that were doubtlessly engrained in his psyche from his own father, Andrew Chadwick, and were a reflection both of his father's Methodist teaching and his own enlightenment beliefs:

> As you grow in years [you] will perceive that all men are, in the order of nature, to be considered equal. That is, there are no natural distinctions in birth, blood and the characters of men, but those which are produced by different degrees of moral and intellectual education.[61]

James Chadwick would also stress the importance of education in developing this inner moral code that was influenced by John Locke and David Hume.

> To live is not merely to breathe, but it is to act to make a proper use of those mental faculties with which you are endowed, so as to form an effective barrier against the all prevailing ... and ... seductive influence of vicious example. As the sun throws a genial glow of light over the physical world, so does learning over the intellectual powers: the latter will enable you to distinguish truth from error to combat the evil propensities of our nature and prepare you for enjoying the felicities of life, without adopting its follies. "I consider a human soul without education," says the elegant [Joseph] Addison, "like marble in a quarry, which shows none of its inherent qualities until the skill of the polisher fleshes out the colors, makes the surface shine, and discovers every ornamental beauty which lay concealed in the mine." So will education draw forth the latent perfections of the mind, and give to the enjoyment of life a luster more solid, and more lasting that all the fictitious pomp which fortune and wealth can, without it, bestow.[62]

These writings reflect the lofty ideals that were engrained in Henry Chadwick. Henry's education was not typical of many English, or even American, children. He was not brought up to value possessions or with an understanding of commerce and trade; rather he received an education that was drenched in moral philosophy and science. From his father he learned the value of education in its development of the human mind and unleashing of man's great potential. And when James Chadwick quoted the great British enlightenment poet and playwright, Joseph Addison, whose *tabla rasa* philosophies reflected the influence of John Locke, we see what James Chadwick was doing for his child: he had every intention, through education, like the polisher in Addison's analogy, to bring out Henry's potential as a human being.

James Chadwick may not have been able to endow Henry with great sums of money, but he was able to bestow his son with the values and teachings of the enlightenment's moral philosophy. As a result, Henry was taught a wide range of subjects. Of particular emphasis were the sciences: botany, astronomy, physics and physiology. His background in science gave rise to Henry's philosophies and worldview. He did not promote baseball only for the sake of the game; he promoted the game to improve the moral well-being of the individual. Henry's education, as we shall see, would also express itself in what he liked or disliked about the game and would serve in his later years to make him seem anachronistic.

At this point in his life, Henry was young and his education had yet to bear fruit. However, these philosophies were already having a significant impact on Henry's older half-brother, Edwin. Born on January 24, 1800, at Longsight, a small town near Manchester, Edwin received his early education at his city of birth and in Stockport. He moved with his father (his mother died while Edwin was young) to London in 1810.[63] To make ends meet during his legal studies, Edwin worked as a journalist in London and wrote for the *Morning Herald* and other papers. His experience as a journalist developed "his techniques of enquiry, precise thought and his flair for writing."[64] Edwin, who by thirty-eight had earned a law degree, began to carve a career in government as a civil servant, disappointing his friends who "prophesied the woolsack" for him had he stayed in law.[65]

Edwin's transformation from law student

Edwin Chadwick (circa 1848) had a strong interest in public health that influenced his younger brother.

to civil servant began in 1829 when he contributed an article to the *London Review* entitled "Prevent Police." This article caught the attention of England's greatest political philosopher, Jeremy Bentham. Sixty-two years Edwin's senior, "Bentham had devoted most of his life to writing stinging critical analyses of England's archaic political, legal and administrative institutions" that were based on aristocratic tradition. Knowing that England was fast developing into a nation-based modern capitalism, Bentham and his followers wanted to change British government into one that was centered on the philosophical ideas derived from Hume, Locke and Voltaire. Since Bentham had no use for England's tradition and aristocratic rule, he "devised elaborate codes for the wholesale reorganization of English government according to the canons of reason, efficiency, and utilitarianism."[66]

Already intoxicated by his own father's radicalism, Edwin Chadwick became a disciple of Bentham. As such he became, with Bentham at the center, a member of a group of intellectuals known as the "philosophic radicals." Bentham wanted Edwin to become "the systematic and permanent expounder of the Benthamite philosophy, and on that condition offered him an income for life."[67] Though he declined, Edwin Chadwick became Bentham's literary secretary and lived with the great master until his death in 1832.

Edwin's main interest, as a Benthamite, became sanitation. Initially, though, he turned his attention to improving the physical and moral health of the poor, those who were most adversely affected by the industrial revolution in England. In 1834, Edwin became secretary to the royal commission on the reform of the poor laws and helped to adopt legislation "prohibiting the employment of children in factories under a certain age, along with limiting the time of their work."[68]

While he had developed the "sanitary idea" as early as 1828 with the publishing of "The Means of Insurance Against Accidents" in the *Westminster Review*, he turned to improving the sanitary condition of the poor. Edwin believed that his mother, though she died very early in his life (perhaps he was talking about his stepmother, Henry's mother, Theresa), influenced his choice of career.

> Well I started in life as a barrister: but then you must remember that I was the son of a mother who was by nature a sanitarian *pur et simple*, and so I gradually turned my attention to this great subject.[69]

In 1838, while his father, stepmother, brother and sister resided in America, Edwin Chadwick began the first sanitary reform movement in

London after a fatal epidemic broke out in the east end of that city close to some stagnant pools. He quickly ordered an inquiry that found the causes of the epidemic, and then established a national sanitary commission, eventually helping to solve the problems of sanitation among the poor.

With Henry's grandfather, father and brother dedicating their interests to reform of one kind or another, whether of a religious or secular nature, it is easy to see how Henry would be inclined to approach his career in a similar manner. Henry's brother walked in some impressive social circles, men who set out, particularly after the death of Bentham in 1832, to change British government for the better. Men like John Stuart Mill, Francis Place and Thomas Maltus were all colleagues and associates of Edwin, as were Robert Peel, Palmerston and Russell.[70] And with a brother so famous in one part of the world, it certainly would seem that Henry would have plenty of motivation to have a similar impact in another part.

When he was not playing ball, catching fish, ice-skating, bird hunting or stealing fruit, Henry Chadwick was playing music. Since his pianist and cellist father taught Henry music, it was natural that he gravitate toward the music scene in Brooklyn. Not only did Henry play piano, he also played guitar, and would accompany his piano playing with his own singing voice. In fact, in the winter of 1838, he combined his singing talents with his interest in social causes when "he sang at a concert for the benefit of the Brooklyn Orphan Asylum, given in the old Brooklyn Institute Hall on Washington Street."[71]

Chadwick's interest in keeping records and organization led to his employment in 1840 as an assistant librarian at the Brooklyn Institute, where he became among the youngest librarians there.[72] When Chadwick turned eighteen, he began his professional career with something he knew best — music. Chadwick taught piano and later dabbled in composing music, specializing in waltzes.[73]

But music was not his greatest passion. Not surprisingly, given his father and brother's attraction toward journalism, Henry also gravitated toward that same career. Interestingly, Chadwick's father protested his son's entrance into journalism. Perhaps James Chadwick, toward the end of his years in England, had had a difficult time with the conservative British government while expressing his radical views, and his experiences may have turned him off to journalism. This would explain why he became a music teacher in the United States. Or perhaps James felt that journalism was too unsteady financially to support a family.

Chadwick was both a prolific journalist and avid composer of music. This piece, for guitar and piano, was written in honor of Winfield Scott, who in 1847 led the Siege of Veracruz, taking that city and eventually Mexico City during the Mexican-American War (Library of Congress, Music Division).

It was perhaps the right time to get into the world of newspaper writing. During this era, many technological changes were taking place that would revolutionize the world of newspaper production. In 1845 Richard March Hoe invented the revolving, or rotary press. This invention quadrupled the speed at which newspapers could be printed. The *New York Sun*, the pioneer of cheap modern newspapers, had made its debut in 1833. Printed by hand, it was able to produce only four hundred impressions an hour. When these new innovations and other publications were created, journalism, as we know it today, came into existence. Beginning with the *Long Island Star*, Henry Chadwick went on to write for numerous periodicals, and eventually landed with the *New York Times*, where he became the lead cricket writer during the 1850s. This was the atmosphere that Henry Chadwick encountered when he was suddenly struck with the idea to make baseball America's national game.[74]

It was in 1843, and against his father's advice, when Chadwick began his career, starting when the *Long Island Star* of Brooklyn published some articles he had written. The *Star* was one of three newspapers published in that city at the time, along with the *Brooklyn Daily News* and the *Brooklyn Eagle*.[75] Chadwick wrote news articles for the *Star*, but he was really drawn to the burgeoning sports scene in the cities of New York and Brooklyn, and even New Jersey, and wrote several articles on cricket. Despite his increasing attraction to journalism, Chadwick continued as a music teacher for a number of years, perhaps to supplement his income or even to please his father. After all, the sports scene in New York was still in its infancy.

Chadwick's entrance into journalism coincided with the most important development of the first half of the nineteenth century regarding the dissemination of information: the invention of the telegraph in 1844. The railroads, the police, and the Stock Exchange used Samuel Morse's device, but its greatest impact was felt in journalism. New York City's newspapers became the telegraph's most crucial supporters because of its speed in transmitting information. Chadwick was one of the benefitting pioneers of the telegraph.[76]

During the decade of the 1840s, there were many important events that occurred in Chadwick's life. Among the most important was his wedding on August 19, 1848, to Jane Botts at Trinity Church in Manhattan, near Wall Street. Originally from Richmond, Virginia, Jane was the eldest daughter of Alexander L. Botts, former president of the Virginia State Council and a close friend of John C. Calhoun.[77]

Though they had become residents of Brooklyn, Jane's family had played a leading part in the affairs of Virginia for generations. Her uncle, John Minor Botts, was a prominent member of the Whig Party, and served in the House of Representatives during the 1840s. Botts was a staunch supporter of Speaker of the House Henry Clay and Clay's American System.[78] Later, John Minor Botts became a controversial figure in the South. Though respected by secessionists, he was suspected of writing a secret history of the Civil War and was arrested. The suspicion was well founded, though no one located the manuscript after a thorough search of his home. Actually, Botts had given the manuscript to the Count de Merier, French minister at Washington, D.C., and it became Botts' book, finished in 1866, *The Great Rebellion: Its Secret History, Rise, Progress, and Disastrous Failure!* published by Harper & Brothers and edited by his gifted nephew, Henry Chadwick.[79] Not only was Jane's father side of the family relevant figures in American history, Jane's mother, the former Susan Randolph, was a descendant of John Randolph of Roanoke.

In 1833, at the age of fifteen, Jane arrived in New York when her father, because of failing health, moved his family to Corzine Farm in Jamaica, Long Island, then owned by Aaron Burr. Burr's association with the Botts family went back to Jane's grandfather, attorney Benjamin Botts. Jane's grandfather served as counsel for Vice President Aaron Burr during his trial for treason before the United States Supreme Court, led at that time by Chief Justice John Marshall, during the Jefferson administration.[80] Alexander Botts purchased the Union Race Course, at the time the most famous trotting course in the country, which adjoined Burr's farm. Mr. Botts had recently lost $30,000 by the defalcation of a public official on whose bond he had invested. Wishing to purchase Burr's farm, Botts went to visit him and stated his case. Burr's response was positive.[81]

"Anything I can do to oblige or advance a son of Benjamin Botts shall be done most heartily," said Colonel Burr, grasping his hand warmly. "That farm at no distant day will be very valuable. You have recently met with reverses, I know."[82]

Jane's father purchased the remaining property from Burr, the agreement consisting of a $500 annuity that would be paid to Burr until his death; at that point the farm would officially be turned over to the Botts family. The newly enlarged Union Race Course was formed and it was through Alexander Botts that a racing organization was begun.[83] Jane later recalled as a young girl seeing Burr. By then, the former vice president was an old man of 77. He had come to the Botts' family home to visit Jane's father on business. Jane recalled the anticipation she felt of seeing such a famous man and was "especially curious as to his wonderful black eyes, of which so much had been said." Remembering the moment when she saw him, "of course, the beauty and ardor of his youth had gone, but the piercing black eyes remained, and I shall never forget their intensity and power as he turned them for a moment on me."

Jane's family was politically well connected, and not only did the family know Aaron Burr, they knew Chief Justice Marshall as well. Jane Botts remembered Marshall as a man "of simple tastes, in both dress and manner of living." Jane's father also developed a close and intimate friendship with Governor John A. King of New York, with Jane becoming close with the governor's daughter, Cornelia.[84]

With his marriage to Jane and his gravitation to journalism, Chadwick experienced a pivotal decade in his professional and private life during the 1840s. Henry's marriage to Jane turned out to be his greatest personal decision, as Jane became a solid mate for Chadwick, someone who supported her husband through the hard economic times, particularly since journalists did not earn a significant income. Botts was five years older than Henry, and prior to the wedding, received a letter regarding the pending wedding plans.

> I immediately ... went to Trinity Church. Saw the minister, had our names registered, and we are to be married to morrow morning after services. Service commences at 9 o'clock and we are to be mated, after which you will come with us to Brooklyn and after partaking of some little refreshment we are to proceed to Park Richmond where I hope to stay until Monday where I shall return to town on business. Dearest Jenny, meet me to morrow with a cheerful face, and forget all but the devoted love of your dear.[85]
>
> Henry.
>
> P. S. I have purchased the ring — an English one — of Mr. Westlake. Remember dearest — a cheerful face for our wedding day.
>
> God in heaven bless and protect us on our future career. All at home send their best love.

After two years of marriage Chadwick's wife bore their first child, Richard Westlake Chadwick.[86] Two other children followed: daughters Susan, in 1851, and Rosa, in 1854. A third daughter, Jane, died shortly after birth in January 1855. Chadwick doted on his wife and children and, as his parents did with him, wrote love letters and poems to them.

To Richard Westlake Chadwick

My bright eyed boy — my darling child
My first born, only son.
Thy merry laugh, and actions wild
Give joy to more than one.
I love to hear thy prattling voice,
So joyous, sweet and free
Loved almost as my hearts first choice,
Thou art most dear to me.
From all that's evil Love and Truth
Thy faithful guides will be
did throughout the days of youth
Bring happiness to thee.
Then blessings on thy steps attend,
My darling dearest boy
bright child my heart would send
From almost every joy[87]

Henry and his new family remained with his father until his death in 1853 at the age of 82. Only a year earlier, James Chadwick had celebrated a birthday with a diary entrance which recounted the day he was born, describing the actions of those closest to him upon his birth. James Chadwick wrote a poem in celebration of his birthday, his last on earth.

When first I breathed my native air,
In England's proudly favored Isle;
And fostered with a mother's care,
Charmed with my new born infant smile,
Her own reflected image there;
When sweet affections tender sigh,
Breathed forth a blessing and a prayer;
Amy they devoted head and hear,
Thro' varying scenes of weal of woe,
No sorrow to they give impart,
Nor cause a Mother's tear to flow.[88]

Given James Chadwick's love of words, his passion for creativity and writing, it was easy to see how Henry would gravitate toward a career of words. James Chadwick lived a great life and had the bravery to migrate to a new nation with his young wife and two children to start anew. Henry Chadwick's career as a baseball journalist was only years away, and one wonders how proud the eminent journalist from England would have reacted to knowing what an impact his second son was going to have on his adopted country.

But there were other factors at play that influenced Henry Chadwick. While his family molded his mind and world outlook, his early years in his new home may have shaped him as well.

New York and Brooklyn, after 1837, the year Henry Chadwick came to America, were changing. Thanks to the influx of immigrants from Germany, Ireland and England, the populations of New York and Brooklyn combined to increase by 747,000 people between 1840 and 1860. In that twenty-year period, Brooklyn's population soared from a meager 11,000 to 267,000 people. A big reason for Brooklyn's growth came from consolidation. On January 1, 1854, Brooklyn was the seventh-largest city in the country; however, on January 1, 1855, Brooklyn became third-largest city when the Consolidation Act of 1854 added Bushwick and Williamsburgh to Brooklyn. The addition of these two communities increased Brooklyn's population from 145,000 to 202,000.[89]

Though most immigrants left and migrated to other parts of the country, those who stayed in New York and Brooklyn virtually "transformed [these cities] in every aspect of life in the metropolis — its patterns of work, housing, religion, politics, and gender — and nowhere would the impact be more dramatic than in the arena of class relationships."[90] With a greater influx of immigrants, new pressures were added to the growing rift between rich and poor, between wealthy Protestant Victorian culture and the hard-drinking, hard-fighting squalor of the Bowery B'hoy culture in the lower east side of Manhattan.

During the decades of the 1840s and 1850s, many parts of New York disgusted and frustrated the wealthy class of the city. As hotbeds of Catholicism, Unionism and even fighting, these sections were considered unsafe, both physically and socially. The city, legislators feared, was becoming rife with prostitutes, the homeless, vagabonds and beggars. By steamboats and railroads, these undesirables flooded toward the bucolic suburbs of Long Island, Staten Island and New Jersey.[91] At the root of these problems were poverty, disease and crime and Chadwick, being from a reform-minded family, was aware, given his interest in health, of the social tragedies taking place in New York, though the Chadwicks lived in Brooklyn, which had its own share of health problems. What Henry also must have been cognizant of were the measures taken to combat these problems. Unlike the official response to the depression of 1837, when both civic and city government failed to combat the difficulties of the poor (and in some cases restricted themselves to blaming the poor for their wretched condition), others began to more scientifically reconsider, in Edwin Chadwick-like fashion, "some cherished assumptions about the causes of poverty [and crime and disease] and the role of government in responding to it."[92]

What is more important and more directly related to Henry Chadwick's interest in outdoor sports was the environmentalist movement begun in the 1840s. The environmentalist movement had a dual approach: first, to make a connection between the living conditions of the poor with their behavior and health; second, to seek environmental solutions like the creations of parks, where people could play games; and finally, to solve the health and behavior problems of the population. Throughout the late 1840s and early 1850s, cholera and typhus spread through the tenements of New York City. Brooklyn, though more bucolic than Manhattan, was affected, too. In May 1849, Cholera hit that city and "remained throughout the summer." All told, 642 people died — 495 were adults and 147 were children. Brooklyn's hardest hit areas centered in the "well defined localities" of Hoyt, Bond, Butler and Douglas streets that consisted of densely populated rows of houses. Though the Cholera outbreak of 1849 was handled well by Brooklynites, a second outbreak in 1854 had similar costs to life as the one five years earlier. As in the first outbreak, most of the patients were immigrants who lived in filthy hovels, particularly along the East River.[93] Unlike New York City, however, Brooklyn did a better job at containing the spread of the illness. By 1856, "more New Yorkers were dying each year than were being born."[94]

Despite studies researched by civic-minded individuals who attempted to raise public awareness regarding the problems of the working-class poor, no legislation was adopted to ameliorate the problems of the poor and sick in both Manhattan and Brooklyn.[95]

In response to the health problems facing both cities, a solution, one supported by the wealthy (since it would benefit them and the poor) was the construction of parks for creating better ventilation. Brooklyn built two small parks between 1835 and 1850: City Park in 1835 and Washington Park in 1847. These parks predated New York City's construction of Central Park because Brooklyn's civic leaders recognized the need for maintaining open areas in a period when agricultural lands were being converted to home sites. Parks were considered necessary as ventilators in purifying the air.[96] The reasons for the construction of Brooklyn's two parks were in line with what many scientists in the 1840s and 1850s had believed they could do, which was to purify the air and alleviate the difficulties that took place inside the city tenements. After the 1850s, the parks were also part of the movement that led to people's interest in the wilderness for escape from the rough and tumble of the city and an indication of the need for even fresher air.[97] Since heading to the wilderness was a financial impossibility for the working poor, the construction of Central Park and the eventual construction of Brooklyn's "Central Park," Prospect Park, with its wilderness-like feel, were a cheaper and more convenient alternative for most. The original point of proposing this massively designed people's park in central New York City, one that would total more than five hundred acres and whose final location was established after much discussion, was primarily twofold: one, to bring greater social intercourse between rich and poor that would uplift the lower order; and two, "that the park's material as well as moral environment would be beneficial" to the masses.[98]

But there were other reasons as well. The construction of a public park would gentrify New York and would remove the boorish materialistic and restless reputation it had attained when foreigners had visited abroad, thus countering the charges leveled by the likes of Alexis de Tocqueville that Americans became involved in civic affairs more out of self-interest and greed than from pride or sense of civic duty.[99]

What motivated the interest in social intercourse between the classes was crowd control (another interest of Chadwick's in the 1870s and 1880s, even though it involved ball park attendance). Andrew Jackson Downing, a landscape artist and one of many prominent figures credited with proposing the Central Park project, was alarmed at the class-based revolution in the streets of Paris in 1848. The concept of the park, Downing hoped, would soften tensions that existed between rich and poor. "[W]ealthy New Yorkers worried much about the conditions of inequality that fostered new kinds of social disorder. Riots in the late 1840s spurred the wealthy to take action. In 1849 riots had broken out when native born merchants protested the appearance of an elite-backed British actor at the downtown Astor Place Theater." Twenty-two people were killed after troops, brought in to restore order, fired into the crowd.[100]

Another significant fact relating to the construction of Central Park was its connection to the sanitation movement and its simultaneous goal for better ventilation. The movement to improve ventilation and sanitary conditions in homes and in the cities actually grew stronger after the 1860s due to the microbiological discoveries in science that related the causes of illness and disease to bacteria and the creation of sanitary commissions based on the ones that were active during the Civil War.[101] There is a very good chance that Henry Chadwick's educational upbringing made him interested in these issues; his interest in science most likely led him to read about these facts and influenced his writing. Henry's keen interest in science led to an article he wrote for *Scientific American* on the physics of the curveball.

Henry's encouragement of outdoor athletics and games in general coincided with the public's growing knowledge on the nature of disease and ventilation and found receptive readers. As a result, the public became more open to heeding the advice from those like Chadwick. As early as 1858, he noted

> ... the physical degeneracy of the people and [how it can be] attributed it to the over-exertion of the intellect and the disuse of the muscular system ... leading to innumerable diseases of body and mind....
>   Something of the truth of these homilies seemed to impress itself on the popular mind; and all at once the rage — for it can hardly be called by a more sober term — for field sports seized on the male portion of the community; and base ball clubs sprang up with marvelous rapidity all over the city.

As Chadwick fought against alcoholism, gambling and disease, New Yorkers and Brooklynites battled these issues as well.

In an attempt to battle alcoholism, temperance societies, both Catholic and Protestant, began to spring up. The New York Temperance Society and the Roman Catholic Total Abstinence and Benevolent Society were two of note. The New York Association for the Suppression of Gambling was established to combat betting on billiards and cockfights as well as gambling in the shooting galleries. Like Chadwick in the decade of the 1860s and 1870s, the ASG "professed great concern about the impact of these establishments on vulnerable young men."[102]

Thus, it is easy to see how Chadwick, as an impressionable young man, was influenced both by his family and the intellectual, reformist and social milieu of New York and Brooklyn in the 1840s and 1850s. It is these influences that helped to shape Henry Chadwick as a journalist and sports reformer.

While the 1850s was a pivotal decade for Henry Chadwick, it was also tinged with tragedy. The Chadwick family felt the tremors of death twice within a week in early 1859. It was common in this era that children died, especially in the city. By this time Abraham Lincoln had already lost one son and would in the ensuing years lose two others, one during

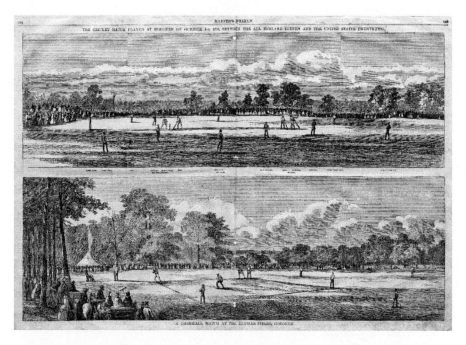

Past and future side by side: Cricket and baseball were often played in close proximity to one another in the relaxed setting of Hoboken's Elysian Fields, where Henry Chadwick was "struck" with a stunning idea (Hoboken Historical Museum; Paul Neshamkin Gift).

his presidency and another after his own death in 1865. Chadwick's family had a similar fate. On January 11, 1859, Henry's only son, Richard, tragically died of convulsions. Three days later, Chadwick's daughter, Rosa, succumbed to scarlet fever.[103] Despite their great though common suffering, the Chadwicks saw their eldest daughter survive childhood and live a full life. Henry and Jane, perhaps to make up for the loss of their two other children, adopted in 1861 a girl named Helen.

As the 1840s wore on, Chadwick continued teaching music, but he gradually moved closer to journalism, becoming more involved with the sporting scene in and around New York. By the 1850s he had become a full-time sports journalist and was headed on a collision course with a descendant of the game he played as a child that was fast becoming a popular pastime among white-collar men. Chadwick would bring his enlightenment education, his background in science, his training as an artist and his newly found passion for writing to help legitimize a fast growing sport in the fastest growing city in America.

CHAPTER 2

The Manly Pastime

It is not difficult to fathom what forces influenced the mind of Henry Chadwick as he departed the grounds of Elysian Fields in Hoboken, New Jersey, the very territory that the Knickerbocker Base Ball Club of New York had established as its own during the mid–1840s. Given Chadwick's upbringing and background, his family's illustrious history, his brother's burgeoning career in public heath, and the forces that were shaping the United States during Chadwick's formative years, one could easily understand why he would appreciate baseball's potential. Though Chadwick had largely ignored the primitive early game of baseball — it was always on the periphery of his vision as he walked across the ball fields of New Jersey and Brooklyn — it now would occupy a central part of his life. Henry Chadwick set his sights on making the game the National Pastime.

From the mid–1840s to the mid–1850s, significant changes had taken place in the social world of New York's athletic community. Much had happened to baseball in New York and much had happened to Henry Chadwick. The changes taking place in the athletic community in New York and in Henry Chadwick's life were being made amid the backdrop of some major transformations occurring in the United States.

This era saw the young nation expand westward after several territorial gains were made during the mid-to-late 1840s under the aggressive leadership of President James K. Polk. Polk had already inherited Texas after it had been annexed just prior to his inauguration, and the new leader sought to gain even more territory, either through war or peaceful negotiation. Polk opted to fight Mexico, with the war officially ending two years later with the Treaty of Guadalupe Hidalgo in 1848. The accord gave the United States California and the New Mexico Territory (present-day New Mexico and Arizona).

With Britain, Polk negotiated the Oregon Treaty, whereby Britain received Vancouver and the United States all what is present-day Washington, Idaho, Wyoming, Oregon and Montana. But with more territory came more problems. The slavery issue, whether to allow slavery into the new territories or not, became a heated debate between Southerners and Northerners, a question that nearly tore the country apart.

The Wilmot Proviso, a proposal put forth by Senator David Wilmot, a Democrat from Pennsylvania, set off a firestorm, for it proposed to exclude slavery from all the lands acquired from Mexico. The Compromise of 1850 avoided civil war between the North and South, but the fire was not extinguished completely and the next ten years would spark more debate and increased hostilities. The Kansas-Nebraska Act of 1854 ignited more sectional animosity and roused a sleeping giant. Former U.S. Congressman Abraham Lincoln of Illinois became interested in politics again when the Kansas-Nebraska Act was passed. Lincoln, like many northern Whigs, was against the act and wanted the restoration of the Missouri Compromise that contained the expansion of slavery.[1]

While the nation was expanding during the 1840s and 1850s, Chadwick spent much of that period gravitating toward journalism, a career his father had not encouraged his son to pursue. James had wanted his son to pursue teaching music, as he had done in America, with some exceptions. But journalism was in Henry's blood; it was his greatest passion, exceeding his love for music and composition.

Chadwick was clearly in his element going to ballgames at these grounds. It was there, in Hoboken, where he encountered the game that would make him famous like his brother, Edwin, back in England. It was there that he schemed to make baseball the national game. Elysian Fields was a special place for many reasons. Not only did it provide the grounds in which baseball and cricket could be played, it provided a way in which young white-collar professionals in America could begin to mimic their English cousins by playing sports for health reasons while also becoming passionate about a game all their own. Thus, Henry Chadwick realized that it was time for Americans to develop their own games as they began to cultivate a greater sense of national identity and consciously move further away, culturally and socially, from their British heritage.

After having spent close to twenty years in America, Henry Chadwick was also becoming more identified with his American nationality. As a sports journalist Henry was aware of such overtones pre-existing in harness racing. But because harness racing was a relatively non-athletic and non-participatory sport, it failed to become a symbol of an athletic movement or as an athletic pastime. It simply did not have the potential possessed by baseball to transform the nation from inert activity to wild passions about recreation and athletics.[2]

There may have been other motivations for Chadwick to promote baseball by the late 1850s. Coming from a reform-minded family, one that advocated moral change with the aid and assistance of science and health, Chadwick's desire to cover and promote baseball could have been based on a movement that he had come to advocate. Chadwick's foray into sports journalism in the 1850s reflected his interest as well as a general public's growing interest in sports and games. Like other journalists and educators during that decade, Chadwick implored his readers to take advantage of the fresh air by exercising.

In 1860 Henry Chadwick remarked that "the Game of Base Ball," owed much of "the high position which it now occupies, as the leading game of out-door sports," to the claim that it was "important and necessary as a branch of physical education."[3] Chadwick was part of the emergent physical health ideology that believed that exercise and games would lead to self-improvement and national betterment. Before the beginning of the Victorian Age, during the 1840s, sport was viewed with suspicion by middle-class American men. Sharing the views of their intellectual forbearers, the Puritans, these men perceived the sports of the day as a waste of time, immoral, illegal and debilitating. Sportsmen, when America was still an agrarian world, "were members of a traditionally oriented male bachelor subculture who lived on the frontier, in the South, or in a few crowded urban centers." Male competitions usually in the form of games were deemed "blood and gambling contests that were illegal and reprehensible, and more important, totally antithetical to the bourgeois ethos of early Victorians."[4]

Between 1840 and 1860, however, ideas regarding sport became more complex. As sports became more accepted, health advocates, such as Chadwick, began to differentiate between such clean sports as baseball, cricket and skating and unclean, unacceptable sport, like gambling and boxing (the kind, fought on the frontier, usually to the death).

Even if sport had not been accepted in America until mid-century, the physical health ideology of participating in ball games for both individual self-improvement and national betterment originated in the decade of the 1820s when German romantic intellectual Charles Fallen immigrated to the United States and brought with him the idea of merging education and exercise.[5] Taking their cue from Fallen, Harvard professors George Bancroft and Joseph Cogswell, who were "enthusiastic about German educational forms and theory and so disenchanted with the comparative lack of discipline at Harvard," founded the Round Hill School of Northampton, Massachusetts, in 1823, the first school in the nation devoted to the physical, mental and moral education of its students. Through their teachings, they inspired a philosophy utilized by teachers, doctors, political leaders, authors, journalists, and a "new generation of students to think and write about sports and exercise, and their importance for the future of the rapidly expanding nation."[6] However, since the United States was still largely a rural and agricultural nation and because Americans were philosophically closed-minded to sport, the physical health ideology failed to progress into a movement.

By the late 1850s, conditions that were once considered unfavorable for civilized sport in the United States became more favorable. The Industrial Revolution burst onto the American landscape and shattered traditional ways in which Americans labored and leisured by forming, among other things, a more clearly demarcated time between work and leisure. The revolution also fostered a "fast-growing commercial sector in cities which led to a growing sedentary population of office workers and professionals" that worked in cramped offices with poor ventilation, making them more vulnerable to disease and sickness. These circumstances dovetailed to nurture both an audience for spectator sports and, more importantly, men eager to get out on the field to play sports. The noted orator, the honorable Edward Everett, in 1856 described the problem of sedentary middle-class men. Everett remarked that:

> The Americans, as a people — at least, the professional and mercantile classes — have too little considered the importance of healthful, generous recreation. They have not learned the lesson contained in the very word to which teaches that the worn out man is recreated, made over again, by the seasonable relaxation of the strained faculties. The old world learned this lesson years ago, and found out that, as the bow always bent will at last break, so the man, forever on the strain of thought and action, will at least go mad or break down.... From morning to night, from January to December, brain and hands, eyes and fingers, the powers of the body and the powers of the mind are spasmodic, merciless activity. There is no lack of a few tasteless and soulless dissipations which are called amusement, but

noble athletic sports, manly out-door exercises are too little cultivated in town or country.[7]

In an 1858 edition of the *Atlantic Monthly*, Thomas Wentworth Higgins asked:

> Who in this community really takes exercise? Even the mechanic confines himself strength in his right arm, and the dancing teacher in his left leg. But the professional or business man, what muscles has he at all?[8]

Henry Chadwick joined the great thinkers of this era in promoting exercise. Chadwick in his own way addressed the phenomenon and responded to those who disagreed with his point of view on exercise:

> ... to the business men, literati, and the religious classes we have a few words.... To business men we would say, that experience has proved conclusively that better work and more of it is to be got out of employees who are allowed time to recuperate their physical powers by recreation than the most slave-worked laborer can yield.[9]

This ideology was similar to that of others who held that clean sport would improve public health. Others who supported the physical health movement included religious leaders such as "the Unitarian Reverend William Ellery Channing, Utopians like Robert Dale Owen, educators like Horace Mann, transcendentalists like Ralph Waldo Emerson, scientists like Dr. Lemuel Shattuck, physicians like Dr. Oliver Wendell Holmes, Sr., and health faddists like Sylvester Graham." Most of these men, like Chadwick, believed that clean sports, particularly clean outdoor sport "would improve public health, raise moral standards and build character; that sport would provide a substitute for the vile practices of the sporting fraternity, and that such rational recreations would encourage the development of sport among the sedentary middle class."[10]

As an example of his advocacy of outdoor sport, Chadwick describes the benefits of outdoor recreation on the human mind and the spirit:

> To literary people we would state that their learning has been of little avail if it has not taught them the policy of judiciously combining out-door exercise and recreation with study, if only to enable the mind more thoroughly to digest the mental food provided for it. And to the religious classes we would say, that they never interposed a greater barrier to the advancement and popularity, if we may so use the term, of the doctrines they advocated than when they fulminate anathemas upon the "waste of time" which the advocates of amusements and recreative exercises are guilty of.[11]

Not only was Henry Chadwick espousing these views, but someone he was close to — though not in distance — was doing so too. Edwin Chadwick, Henry's older half-brother, shared the same philosophy on the relationship between physical activity and the performance of the mind. In an article printed in 1860 by the *Brooklyn Eagle,* the periodical along with the *New York Clipper* that Henry Chadwick is most associated with, published a paper read by Edwin Chadwick at a social science meeting in Glasgow, Scotland, on the very subject. Edwin Chadwick's lecture brought up many of the same themes touched on by his younger brother:

> The Eton and Oxford students I have been assured by the collegiate authorities are greatly improved in health and strength, and in every way, by the common military drill, in addition to their common exercises.... As denoting the connection between body and mind, it may be mentioned that as a general rule, to which there are fewer exceptions than might be supposed, those who are foremost in drill and in bodily exercises are found in low schools and well as high, to be amongst the foremost in mental exercises.[12]

Thus, it is easy to see how Henry Chadwick, given the milieu in which he was writing, along with his influences, particularly his familial ones, would advocate these enlightenment influenced beliefs. Chadwick's reform sensibilities, which combined with his interest in athletics and journalism, would allow him to guide the game once he was able to involve himself in the growing yet wayward baseball community.

Though there were not many other entries in the *Times* following this particular summary, Chadwick began to write for other dailies. The *Brooklyn Daily Eagle*, Brooklyn's great newspaper, became Chadwick's home and the place where he honed his journalistic style. Initially, Chadwick's strategy for promoting the game was marked by attempts to reinforce its social aspects. Recounting a nine-inning match in 1858 between the Brooklyn Excelsiors and the Manhattan-based Eagle club, won by the Excelsiors, 32 to 13, Chadwick described how the game concluded with:

> tremendous cheering by the two parties ... in a congratulating and jovial spirit, which invariably indicates the gentleman, and gives evidence to our friends of the base-ball fraternity are possessors of noble and generous disposition, and know as well how to bear defeat, as how to wear the laurels of victory ... the gentlemen of the Eagle with their friends were escorted by their Brooklyn friends to Montague Hall, where a bountiful collation had been prepared....[13]

For Chadwick, the model for this kind of writing came from cricket. In these early years, Chadwick believed that baseball ought to model itself on England's sporting gentry and, therefore, wanted the players to behave like gentlemen. For the most part, the types of players playing baseball at this time were "gentlemen." Many of these players were also cricket players, and they had the types of jobs that "were flexible enough to permit a game." For instance, the original baseball teams of New York — the Knickerbockers, formed in the early 1840s, the New York Gothams (1850) and the Eagles (1851) of Brooklyn — "consisted of young lawyers, doctors, merchants, bank and insurance clerks and others who could get away twice a week to play ball."[14] Chadwick was also lucky to live in Brooklyn, a city blessed with so many teams.

The mid-to-late 1850s were a tempestuous time in the United States. The years leading up to the great American conflict, the Civil War, only inflamed the passions between the North and South. The Supreme Court decision in the Dred Scott Case, in *Dred Scott* v. *Sandford*, propelled the slavery issue once again into the forefront and created more sectional animosity. The decision to deny a slave, Dred Scott, his freedom nullified the Missouri Compromise of 1820. The ruling, with Chief Justice Roger B. Taney delivering the majority opinion, stated that the compromise was unconstitutional because Congress had no authority to exclude slavery from the federal territories.

Abraham Lincoln, a rising leader of a new political party, the Republicans, declared the decision "erroneous." In June 1858, Lincoln made his famous "House Divided" speech, declaring that the Union will "cease to be divided." He also suggested that it "will become all one thing or all the other. Either the opponents of slavery will arrest the further spread of it ... or its advocates will push it forward, till it shall become alike lawful in all the States, old as well as new, North as well as South."

While the late 1850s were a tempestuous time for American politics, it was also a period of tremendous growth for the New York version of baseball and Henry Chadwick's career. While 1856 saw the convergence of Henry Chadwick's journalism with baseball, it was the following year, 1857, that proved to be instrumental in creating a new calling for the cricket journalist-turned-baseball writer. Not only did Chadwick help spread baseball with his ever-so-important stint with the *Clipper*, along with other periodicals, he was appointed to a significant committee of the New York baseball community.

In the winter of 1857, in "the interest of uniformity, a convention of representatives of all the clubs was called to establish a permanent code of rules."[15] A convention of this nature was seriously needed because of the diversity of baseball being played in the metropolitan area of New York, in places such as Manhattan, Hoboken and Brooklyn. In fact, Brooklyn was fast becoming the true Mecca for baseball. While it has been said that "Base Ball" had its origins and growth in New York City largely due to the Knickerbockers' ties to New York, after 1857 baseball clubs in Brooklyn were more numerous than in Manhattan or New Jersey. By 1858, Brooklyn ball clubs outnumbered New York City teams by a ratio of at least three to one.[16]

With all the clubs spread through the "cities" of New York, a glue to cement the teams together under one set of rules was required, as baseball was by no means uniform. Though the Knicks had established rules in the 1840s and had forged an agreement with three other teams in 1854, other baseball clubs had, as Tom Melville points out, played with rules that differentiated themselves from the Knicks, Gothams, Eagles and Stars. For instance, Melville writes that some games were played with as little as seven to as many as eleven men per side "with time periods that varied from five to twelve innings." When the Knickerbockers or any of the clubs that had forged the agreement in 1854 had to play "non-agreement" teams, they sometimes had to conform the rules of other nines.[17]

This turned out to be a significant convention for baseball's future and equally important for baseball's great crusader, Henry Chadwick. Because of Chadwick's efforts in achieving popularity for the game, and due to his thorough knowledge of both cricket and baseball, he received an invitation to attend the meetings of the rules committee of the association, led at that time by Knickerbocker president Doc Adams. Chadwick could make suggestions in the way of various amendments because of his experience with the game while reporting it.[18] Imagine Chadwick, with brown beard, slightly receding hairline and self-confident blue eyes, sitting in on the rules committee, persistently raising his hand to offer his viewpoints.

While Chadwick's outspokenness in the press was helping baseball grow, his status in the baseball community, as reflected in his attendance at the convention and his invitation to join the rules committee, rose with it. At this particular stage only one other person, Dr. Daniel "Doc" Adams of the Knickerbockers, may have had more influence. Doc Adams was elected presiding officer of the first convention of baseball players and was credited with many of the game's early innovations. Adams was typical of most players of that era in that he was a "professional" who could afford to play a few times a week. Born in Mount Vernon, New Hampshire, in 1814, Adams was educated at Yale, and graduated from Harvard Medical School in 1838. Shortly thereafter he moved to New York and began playing baseball. In the early fall of 1845, Adams joined the New York Knickerbockers, a club comprised of men who had played for the defunct New York baseball club. Adams made a lasting impact with his invention of the shortstop position in 1848. His invention of the position was not an effort to create an extra infielder, but "to assist in relays from the outfield." This was needed because the ball used was so light and airy that it could not be thrown at a reasonable distance by any of the outfielders.[19] Later, when the ball was made heavier — but, obviously, not too heavy — the shortstop became an extra infielder and was positioned to cover the holes between second and third base, and second and first base. The custom in those days was for the first, second and third baseman to play on their respective bags.

With Adams working within the game as a player and as a member of the rules committee, he served an important purpose, especially given his long connection with the game, dating back to the 1840s. But it was also important to have someone like Chadwick, an observer from the outside looking in. That is where Chadwick's experience as a cricket journalist, someone well versed with the rules of other bat and ball games, could serve in helping to mold the game.

As stated earlier, the 1857 convention was important because it established a uniform code of playing rules made for all baseball clubs to follow.[20] The 1857 convention was crucial in establishing rules that are still in effect today. It was the Adams-led convention, with Chadwick in attendance, that established the bases being set at 90 feet apart, and "who fixed the distance of the pitcher's mound to home plate at 45 feet."[21] The distance between the pitcher's mound and home plate lasted until 1880, until it was moved back to fifty feet. They also established that the winner of a game would be determined at the conclusion of nine innings rather than the first team to score 21 runs.[22] Because of the uniformity established at this first convention in 1857, more clubs entered the fray and joined the baseball community.

The following year was an even greater example of the game's growth when in March a delegation of New York and Brooklyn clubs that included the Knickerbockers, Excelsiors, Gothams and Atlantics formed the National Association of Base Ball Players. The National Association was the first attempt to organize a league of baseball clubs. In 1858, the National

Association was declared a permanent organization and was held together with its bylaws. It consisted of 71 teams from Brooklyn and 25 clubs from Manhattan. As an indication of his growing stature within the small but growing baseball world, Chadwick was invited by William Cauldwell "to attend the meetings of the rules committee of the association where he was able to offer suggestions in the way of sundry amendments, on account of [his] experience of the game gained while reporting it."[23]

The great number of Brooklyn teams reflected the greater amount of open space that was available in that city. As early as 1854, three Brooklyn clubs had already sprung up. One of the more interesting clubs was the Eckfords of Brooklyn. This club took its name from one of the great shipbuilders of the early half of the century, Henry Eckford. He was famous for having built the vessels for the War of 1812, and as the builder of the *Robert Fulton*, the steamship that journeyed famously from New York to New Orleans and Havana.[24] During the 1863 campaign, amidst the height of the Civil War, the Eckfords won all of their nine match games and as a result became the acknowledged baseball champions for 1863.[25] The other two Brooklyn teams were the Atlantics and the most famous of the three, the Excelsiors, the first team organized in Brooklyn. Their games, as well as the contests of other organized clubs, were played on open multipurpose fields. The Atlantics, for one, would play their games on old lots on York Street, not far from the Brooklyn Navy Yard.[26]

With the pivotal creation of the National Association of Base Ball Clubs, 1858 proved to be an important year for baseball off the field. For Chadwick, it was only the beginning of his great contributions as a writer, statistician and rule maker. Naturally, without the ball players and the games there would be nothing to report. Ordinary games certainly played their role, but games of great importance obviously played a significant part in baseball's development. What made Chadwick such a valuable person, particularly in his latter years, was his presence at many of the important games of early baseball where he simply played the role of journalist.

His presence at the Fashion Course Games of late July 1858, a best-of-three series between an "All" New York nine and an "All" Brooklyn nine, was probably the first memorable games that Chadwick had the great fortune to attend. The matchup was etched in baseball history because it was the first series ever played that was half all-star game, half championship series. The games took place on Fashion Course racetrack in Flushing, Queens County, on Long Island, to accommodate the throngs of fans, reported to have been anywhere from three to ten thousand, that were expected to attend the match. The game itself was important for a variety of reasons, mostly in its promotion, but also because it featured a who's who of baseball notables, those that figured and were to figure in Henry Chadwick's life and those that figured and were to figure in the game of baseball. Acting as scorer was Justice William Van Cott, head of the National Association, the founder and first president of the Gotham Club of New York, whose brother, Thomas, starred as pitcher and who was on the mound pitching for the New York nine. A young center fielder represented New York by the name of Harry Wright, who like his father had made his reputation as a great cricket player, but had crossed over to play baseball. Then there was Dr. Joseph B. Jones, president of the Brooklyn Excelsior club, who had been instrumental in the formulation of the association rules along with Doc Adams and Henry Chadwick.

The series was important in many respects. It served as the first all-star game ever played and in some respects was like a modern championship series in that the teams had to play a best-of-three matchup. New York won the series, 2–1, which featured several memorable events important to baseball's development.

The downside of the Fashion Course series was that it highlighted gambling, the aspect of the game that would eventually plague the sport. Given Chadwick's later reputation as a crusader against this evil, it probably unnerved him when he overheard some men betting on whether John Holden, a second baseman for the Brooklyn side, would hit a home run. A man came up to Holden and made the following proposal: "Jack, I've bet $100 that you'll make a home run in this game, and if you do I'll give you $25."

"All right," Holden was supposed to have said, "I'll try my best."

Holden went to bat against pitcher Thomas Van Cott of the Gothams, representing New York, and crushed a ball to right-center, over the head of Harry Wright, clearing the fence.[27]

Later, in two instances, Chadwick had a much different recollection of the events that took place at the game regarding the bet and Holden's home run. First, in 1873, he wrote a retrospective published in the *Brooklyn Eagle* on July 16 entitled "The Fashion Course matches." Chadwick wrote:

> In the first game, in one of the innings, John Holden, just before going to the bat, bet $75 that he would make a home run, and hitting a ball to centre field he actually did score the coveted run and won his bet.[28]

His second recollection of the Holden home run was published in Albert Spalding's *America's National Game*:

> Two Brooklyn cranks had a wager of $100 a side on John Holden's making a home run. One was an Atlantic rooter, the other an Excelsior fan. In this game I noticed that when Holden went to bat he was very particular in selecting his bat. It appears that the man who had bet on him went to him and told him that he would give him $25 of his bet if he made the hit; so Jack was very anxious. Matt O'Brien was pitching, and Jack, after waiting for a good ball, got one to suit him, and sent it flying over Harry Wright's head at right center, and made the round of the bases before the ball was returned, thus winning the $25.[29]

Though the games were highly competitive — the gambling in and around the game served as an omen for the negative aspects that were to plague the game — much of the old camaraderie and sportsmanship still pervaded at these matches, as in earlier contests. After the first game, won by the side from New York, 22–18, those involved got to the "Committee room" where refreshments were served. Led by the venerable Judge Van Cott of the Gotham club, who proposed the toast, "Health, success and prosperity," to his opponents, the Brooklyn club, "which was received with all the honors and three times three and a tiger [hip-hip-hooray]." In response, Dr. Joseph B. Jones, one of the leading members of the rules committee and president of the Excelsior Base Ball Club of Brooklyn, "appropriately responded in like terms, and with much good taste, hoping that on the return match victory might favor Brooklyn. Three times three and a tiger."[30]

While Henry's attendance at some of the most critical games in baseball's early history was important, it was his influence on pivotal decisions that reflected the fatherly role he assumed in the 1850s and 1860s. Chadwick was involved in the many debates during the winter conventions (much of which he discussed publicly in his newspaper articles). The subject matter of these arguments ranged from the distance between the pitcher's mound and home plate to the number of balls and strikes allotted to each batter and to what determined a fair or foul ball. But the most controversial debate during this period was the elimination of catching the ball on the bound. Chadwick, several years after its implementation, remembered that the establishment of the fly-catch was "one of the toughest fights I had."[31]

The fly-catch proposal required a fielder to catch the ball in the air in order to record an out and would eliminate outs made on one bound.

The New York game, during the 1850s, allowed for a one-bounce accommodation rather than requiring the fielder to catch the ball on the fly, as is required in modern baseball. The fly-catch, already in use in cricket and the Massachusetts game, was introduced to baseball for debate in 1857.[32]

Shortly after the bound catch was made law, Chadwick wrote that to implement this rule, he:

> adopted [in the press] the feint of advocating the rule in one paper and opposing it in others, and had thereby created two influential parties, where but one had before existed, that I fully succeeded in my object. I only asked one season's trial of it at the hands of the Convention, to satisfy the fraternity that the fly rule was the correct one.[33]

Chadwick adopted this strategy, though not at the beginning. For instance, when the fly-rule failed to get approval by the delegates of the NABBP in 1859, Chadwick chastised association officials for not adopting the innovative rule, contending that the players themselves wanted a game with greater skillfulness.[34] Besides, various clubs experimented with the fly-rule as ball players improved their fielding, partly through simultaneous participation in cricket.

By 1860, however, he began to change his approach. Chadwick used the pages of the *Eagle* and later the *Clipper* to express his views. For example, in August 1860, Chadwick used the *Brooklyn Eagle* to discuss a matchup between the Excelsior and Putnam clubs, known as the "Fly Game" in "contradistinction to the regular game, the latter allowing players to be put out from balls caught on the bound." Chadwick described the game, despite the lopsided score of 23–7 in favor of the Excelsiors, to be "one of the most interesting and well played contests" he and the spectators taking in the game had "witnessed this season." In covering the game, Chadwick noted the "degree of skill in batting and fielding on both sides being shown such as does not often characterize our first-class matches" because of the "necessity of the fly catch to record an out." He added that between the types "of games we have hitherto seen, we certainly prefer the fly game of the two."[35]

While this article reflects Chadwick's support of the fly-catch and the elimination of the one bound accommodation, in a November 1860 edition of the *New York Clipper*, only three months after the *Eagle* article, Chadwick began "to modify [his] views somewhat" on the issue. Here, Chadwick started to put his strategy into effect.

Chadwick had been in Philadelphia to watch cricket and was impressed with the play of "young American cricketers of that city." The

THE EAGLE STAFF IN 1860.

FRANCIS A. MALLISON   JOHN STANTON   JAMES McCLOSKEY   HENRY CHADWICK   RICHARD McDERMOTT.
ALFRED G. HENMAN   JOS. HOWARD, JR.   ISAAC VAN ANDEN   THOMAS KINSELLA

The staff of the *Brooklyn Eagle*, circa 1860. Chadwick stands in the back row, second from the right (Brooklyn Public Library).

American cricketers were baseball players, too, and were praised for their fielding. Because baseball clubs had not adopted the fly-catch rule and still played with the bound catch allowance, Chadwick was led to reconsider his position of the elimination of the bound catch.

"Why," Chadwick asked, "is it that a party of base ball players can take part in a game of cricket, for the first time, and acquit themselves in the field as creditably as a similar class of youth who have practiced cricket for years?" Chadwick concluded, "the only reasonable answer is that base ball is a superior school of fielding to cricket," that a baseball player had to concern himself with three aspects of fielding — catching on the first bound, on the fly, and then the throw — whereas in cricket the fielder had to concern himself with only the fly-catch and the throw. In cricket, Chadwick observed, "it is not always required to return it in as fast as possible, as, provided the one run is saved by the stoppage of the ball, the ball can be leisurely fielded in to the wicket keeper."

Chadwick admitted that should the bound catch be allowed to continue in practice, it would not prevent "first class clubs from playing matches on the fly game," and that changing the rule to only the fly-catch and eliminating the bound-catch allowance would not lead to the improvement of the fielding, "which is now such a marked and credible feature of the manly pastime, that many people suppose it will."[36]

Chadwick's reassessment of the rule reveals he obviously implemented this plan of alternating between support of the fly-catch in one instance and against it in another, though he did this generally in one newspaper. Perhaps his strategy backfired, for that is why the game took another four years to adopt the fly-catch proposal, since many of the clubs and decision makers considered the strength and weakness of instituting the new rule that would make the game more like cricket and more like the Massachusetts game of townball. As a whole, however, Chadwick still advocated the adoption of the fly-catch, despite some thoughts to the contrary.

Chadwick was not alone in his support for the fly-catch. Doc Adams of the New York Knickerbockers supported this amendment and strongly believed that the fly-catch ought to be part of the game. The fly-catch rule appears in the 1857 laws of the Knickerbockers, seven years before the association adopted it.[37]

Despite the presence of two of the most influential men on the rules committee, the proposal took a while to pass. There were many arguments made against the adoption of the fly-catch. One argument against the adaptation of the rule was that "it would make the game," according to the *New York Evening Express*, "interminably long, that it could not be finished before dark." This idea proved to be totally unfounded, as games played with the fly-catch lasted a normal length of roughly two hours.[38] Perhaps many players feared that the sport would become too offensive oriented if the law was passed since requiring a player to catch the ball in the air was certainly more difficult to do, given the players did not have fielding gloves that would enable them to catch the ball more comfortably. The players also may not have wanted the sport to become too much like cricket, wanting baseball instead to remain separate and unique.

The idea that the game might become too much like cricket should not be overlooked. Chadwick's involvement in this sport, his first love, was to shape his views on what he liked or disliked about baseball at various stages in its development. To understand Chadwick, one must look to the game of cricket, a sport that requires skill and mental acuity. Chadwick describes what is needed to be an effective cricket player:

> Patience, fortitude, self-denial, order, obedience, and good humor, with an unruffled temper are indispensable.... In one word, there is no game in which amiability and an unruffled temper are so essential to success, as in cricket.... Cricket lies within the reach of average powers. A good head will compensate for hands and heels. It affords scope for a great diversity of talent: bowling, fielding, wicket keeping, free hitting, safe and judicious play, and good generalship, are all points of the game, in one of which many a man has earned a good name, though inferior in the rest.[39]

Cricket's rules are also important to understand. Cricket requires a ball to be caught on the fly and has no fair or foul ball, as everything hit is in play. There are no walks or strikeouts, nor is there a home run, *per se*; however, there is something akin to a home run in cricket called a "six." The name "six" comes from the amount of runs a batsman gets when he hits the ball entirely out of the park or playing area. Unlike the home run in baseball, where the hitter must run completely around the bases, the batsman in cricket does not have to run from wicket to wicket to complete the "six." In fact, the batsman does not move from the hitting area at all. One of Chadwick's critiques of the home run was centered on the energy spent on running around the bases. This very well could have factored into Chadwick's dislike for the home run.

Chadwick was able to see the differences that made baseball unique and appealing to players, spectators and even journalists. We shall see how this manifested itself over and over in his writings.

There are other fascinating aspects to the fly game versus the bound catch debate that reflect the Chadwick mind and personality. Chadwick's arguments regarding this rule change centered on three aspects of his personality: the artist in him, the composer of melodies and waltzes, the man who wrote poetry to his children and wife; the scientist, the man who discussed the scientific aspects of a thrown ball, the developer of baseball statistics; and the reformer, the man who argued that baseball and exercise improved mankind. As an artist, Chadwick believed that catching on the fly was without question the "prettiest mode of fielding."[40] He also used the "artistic" argument when discussing the type of pitching he preferred. For example, Chadwick wrote that good pitching was "based on the chances offered the fielders for outs because it is to the excellence in fielding that we are to look for the beauty of base ball."

Then, in his argument promoting the fly-catch on non-artistic reasons, Chadwick would suggest the game incorporate the fly-catch on the grounds that it made "the game more manly and scientific." Chadwick also used this argument in other aspects of the game. Chadwick believed that good hitting was "scientific" when it involved putting the ball in play rather than "slugging," which he felt required too much expenditure of energy. His entire argument, whether he was for or against the fly-catch, centered on his reform instincts, to improve the game in an effort to make it more appealing for participants and spectators alike.

Another aspect of his argument for the fly-catch involved his desire that the game needed to become more manly, for a bound catch is "a feat a boy ten years of age would scarcely be proud of."[41]

Whatever the motivations behind Chadwick's support for the fly-catch, he was clearly determined to facilitate its official entrance into baseball. Several weeks prior to the convention in December 1864, Chadwick wrote an entire column about the fly game versus the bound game debate with the hope of eliminating the bound catch. Chadwick warned that until the fly game rule "has been tried for one season as the 'regular game' it will continue to be the principal question the convention will have to discuss each year." Chadwick wrote that the bound rule "is unquestionably the one for amateurs, as it admits of easy catches." After making his initial points, Chadwick proceeded to attack the arguments made against the adoption of the fly-catch, namely that it would lengthen the game. Chadwick said that there was "reliable statistics" that "conclusively prove the very reverse to be the case." Granted, Chadwick said "that where the contestants in a match are not good players, the rule of the fly is very likely to lengthen the contest."[42] Overall, Chadwick stated that the average game with the fly-catch was shorter than the overage game that allowed catches on the bound.

> In the first place, we can conclusively prove that seven out of every ten bound catches made, which require any skill to take the ball, are made on foul balls or in the in-field, in the former instance being just as effectual in the fly game as in that of the bound, and in the latter case almost as much so, as such catches invariably lead to players being put out at first or second bases. In the second place, it can be also shown that the average time of all the fly games played this season is not less than the average time of all the games played on the bound, and that too during a season in which quicker bound games have been played than ever known before, but less that the average of a selection of the bound games in which the longest contests are excluded. The shortest bound game played — nine innings

being finished — was one hour and thirty minutes; the shortest fly game
played was fifty-eight minutes.[43]

In this article, published several weeks before the December 14 convention, Chadwick went on the offensive. All Chadwick was asking was that the bound rule get eliminated for one experimental season. Chadwick felt it was extremely important to adopt the fly rule, for it would force teams to more consistently play the game with this rule, arguing against the idea "that those clubs who like to play the game are permitted to play it by the present regulations...." Chadwick wrote that the Atlantic nine of Brooklyn, who were among the best clubs at the fly game, "openly refused to play it" one time because it "was not the *regular* game."[44]

During the season, as Chadwick pointed out, there were two clubs that played only the fly game, both the Excelsior and the Star club of South Brooklyn. There was obviously some momentum coming into the convention of the winter of 1864, where Chadwick felt he had to give one last push to finally get it through for good. His last bit of advice to those advocates of the fly-catch who were to vote in the upcoming convention was this:

> It will be requisite that the friends of the fly game, instead of depending upon their numerical strength in the next conventions for their success would be to make some effort to compromise matters with their adversaries with a view solely of having the fly game tried for one season ... and we have no doubt that ultimately all first class clubs will adopt the same rule, except such as are more ambitious of winning games that they are of playing their games in the most skillfull manner, for it should be distinctly remembered that matches are not always won by first class play only, or lost by general unskillfullness.[45]

Chadwick's persuasion and hard work finally did pay off. The bound catch was eliminated for the 1865 season at the December 14, 1864, convention by a vote of 32 in favor of the fly-catch and 19 for the old rule.[46] Chadwick would always cite this rule change, along with the elimination of "soaking," as one of the most important reforms made in baseball's evolution. Though a more physically challenging (and especially more painful) adaptation for the players, this rule was required of all competitive clubs, and since its "one-year experiment," baseball has never turned back. Whether Chadwick's strategy of "adopting the feint of advocating the rule in one paper and opposing it in others" worked as he claimed or whether it was his hard work on the rules committee or a combination of the two,

Chadwick certainly played a significant role in shaping the debate. This is unquestioned. As a member of the committee of rules and as a writer, he shaped the game from both an inside and outside prospective. But this was only one area in which he would help in sculpting the game. To Henry Chadwick, numbers and statistics would be another way he would lend his fatherly hand in constructing baseball to become the game of America.

CHAPTER 3

Scoring One
for the Records

The 1860s were a defining period in American history. Not only did a war consume the minds and bodies of Americans in the North and South, the decade also laid the foundation for the Industrial Revolution that would transform the United States. This decade also saw the growth of baseball, despite the interruption of war. If the 1840s and 1850s were an incubation period for baseball's foundation in New York, the 1860s saw the growth of the game outside of the nation's largest city.

One of the reasons why the game expanded was related to the pioneering work of journalist Henry Chadwick. Chadwick had already been contributing to the game as a member of the rules committee of the NABBP. Chadwick also helped promote an understanding of the game and its players through baseball's first guide, published in 1860, known as *Beadle's Dime Base Ball Player*. This guide, whose publishers consisted of Irwin Beadle and Robert Adams and whose offices were located on 141 William Street in Manhattan, was the first "publication of its kind yet issued" as Chadwick proudly stated. It established the yearly custom of a magazine or digest that promoted the game and gave its followers insight into the sport. Equally important, since New York was the hub of publishing, this particular version of baseball, as described by Chadwick, would be read by others across the country.[1]

And since the game was relatively new, Chadwick in the guide's first edition played historian, claiming that baseball derived from the English

BEADLE'S
DIME

BASE-BALL PLAYER:

A

COMPENDIUM OF THE GAME,

COMPRISING

ELEMENTARY INSTRUCTIONS

OF THIS

AMERICAN GAME OF BALL:

Together with the Revised Rules and Regulations for 1860:
Rules for the Formation of Clubs; Names of the Officers
and Delegates to the General Convention, &c.

BY HENRY CHADWICK.

NEW YORK:
IRWIN P. BEADLE, & CO., PUBLISHERS,
141 WILLIAM ST., CORNER OF FULTON.

ball game of rounders. Chadwick not only used the first edition of *Beadle's* guide to note the progress of the game from its origins, he deemed "it appropriate to introduce the rules for playing the English game." In fact, Chadwick was so certain of baseball's connection to rounders, he used the same introduction in the first twelve editions of the *Beadle's Dime Base Ball Player*, from 1860 to 1871.

Little did Chadwick realize what he was unleashing. At the time, however, Chadwick's claim that baseball derived from the British bat and ball game was acknowledged with ho-hum acceptance. Later, by the turn of the century, with the winds of nationalism sweeping across the country, his belief would be challenged with the kind of aggression that would be associated with ruthless American capitalism. Because no one gave much thought to baseball's history, Chadwick had free reign to espouse his ideas unchallenged. Considering Chadwick's writings on the subject in this book, one that would be read by thousands across the nation, it might be said that Chadwick's writings on baseball's ancestry would, in some ways, make him officially the game's first historian.

Though he felt strongly about baseball's British roots, Chadwick made it clear that the sport was an "invigorating exercise and manly pastime [that] may now be justly be termed the American game of ball," because it had "been so modified and improved of late years in this country as almost to deprive it of any of its original features beyond the mere groundwork of the game."[2]

Chadwick's use of this digest to discuss the game's origins was not without context. In fact, he may have been prompted by previous writings that had considered its roots. In 1856, *Porter's Spirit of the Times*, which was one of the periodicals in New York that covered baseball, implied that the founders of New York, the Dutch, had invented the game.[3] Then in 1858 and 1859, the *Atlantic Monthly* published two articles, one that claimed the game sprang up in America and the other that clamed it had, like Chadwick's belief, English origins.

Chadwick's concept that baseball evolved from rounders also may have been influenced by another source, one that had no connection at all to games or sports. Given Chadwick's interest in science, there is a good chance that he would have been impacted by a new book that had been published the year before: Charles Darwin's *Origin of Species*. Chadwick's

Opposite: Chadwick's first guide, the 1860 *Beadle's Dime Base Ball Player*, which included his scoring system and his now well-known theory about baseball's origins.

article in the game's first baseball digest, stating that baseball evolved from rounders, was to provide the framework for the baseball origins debate for the next one hundred and fifty years.

Chadwick's first manual was filled with additional bits of information aside from publishing the rules of rounders. Chadwick gave credit to the New York Knickerbocker club for starting the game's "progress" when it was formed in the autumn of 1845. Though he acknowledges the existence of the New York Club, which preceded the Knickerbockers, Chadwick still cited the latter with "pioneering" the game, emphasizing how the Knickerbockers were the club to do away with "soaking," or plucking a player between the bases to put the runner out, and replacing it with requiring a player "to be touched by the ball while in the hands of an adversary." This development was one that Chadwick seems to have been fixated with, for he believed that this rule was the first step in its departure from the more primitive style that made it appear close to the game of rounders.

While much of the guide had some interesting history, it also contained much filler. For example, several pages were used to print the rules laid down by the Knickerbockers and to list each existing club in the New York area, mostly situated in Brooklyn and Hoboken, along with the date of organization of each nine up to the time of the first convention held in New York in 1857.

Clubs.	Organized.	Location of Ground.
Knickerbocker	Sept. 1845	Hoboken
Gotham	1850	Hoboken
Eagle	April 1852	Hoboken
Empire	Oct. 12, 1854	Hoboken
Excelsior	Dec. 8, 1854	South Brooklyn
Putnam	May 1855	Williamsburgh
Newark	May 1, 1855	Newark
Baltic	June 4, 1855	New York
Eckford	June 27, 1855	Greenpoint
Union	July 17, 1855	Morrisiania
Continental	Oct. 1855	Williamsburgh
Atlantic	1855	Jamaica, L.I.
Harlem	March 1856	New York
Enterprise	June 28, 1856	Bedford
Atlantic	Aug. 14, 1856	Bedford
Star	Oct. 1856	South Brooklyn

(Clubs.)	(Organized.)	(Location of Ground.)
Independent	Jan. 1857	New York
Liberty	March 1857	New Brunswick, N.J.
Metropolitan	March 4, 1857	New York
Champion	March 14, 1857	New York
Hamilton	March 23, 1857	Brooklyn
St. Nicholas	April 28, 1857	Hoboken[4]

Once these introductory facts were finished, Chadwick then displayed his expertise on almost every facet of the game. He even included a description of how to make proper bases, suggesting that the bags be made of "the best heavy canvass, and of double thickness as there will be much jumping on them with spiked shoes."[5] Chadwick added that the best way to fill the bags would be with cotton or sawdust since sand would make it too heavy to carry out onto the field. Also described were the pitcher's point and home base, the rules and regulations on the proper bat, and some important pointers on the subject of hitting.

> Players have different modes, and adopt different styles of batting ... all give good reasons for their different styles. Practice with one bat, as a player thereby becomes more sure of striking than he would were he constantly to change his bat. In striking at the ball, do not try to hit it so hard that you throw yourself off your balance, but plant your feet firmly on the ground, and swing the bat in as natural a manner as possible. The secret of hard-hitting lies in the quick stroke and firm position of the batsman the moment the ball is struck. This will account for some small and light men being hard hitters.[6]

Chadwick then focused his attention on defense, entailing the duties for each position on the field. Perhaps the most intriguing was that of the catcher, because it included vital information on in-game leadership.

> This player is expected to catch or stop all balls pitched or thrown to the home base. He must be fully prepared to catch all foul balls, especially tips, and be able to throw the ball swiftly and accurately to the bases, and also keep a bright look-out over the whole field.... As the position occupied by the Catcher affords him the best view of the field, the person filling it is generally chosen captain, although the pitcher is sometimes selected for that honor. We suggest, however, that some other player than the pitcher be selected as captain [because] the physical labor attached to that position tends to increase the player's excitement, especially if the contest is a close one, and it is requisite that the captain should be as cool and collected as possible.[7]

Ending the first baseball guide, interestingly enough, was Chadwick's inclusion of the rules for the Massachusetts game of townball. In some sense, this seems again to be information that was needed to fill up space, especially compared with what would be added in the ensuing guides after 1860. Or, perhaps, Chadwick wanted to sincerely pay tribute to the other ballgame that was popular in the Northeast.

While the 1860 *Beadle's Guide* broke new ground as the first baseball manual, it was the following year's edition that may have made the most lasting impact. The 1861 *Beadle's Dime Base-Ball Player* was an issue that promoted one of Chadwick's true passions — statistics. Chadwick created a scoring system based on letters and numbers to identify how each player performed during an at-bat. Chadwick insisted that, "Every club should have its regularly appointed scorer," someone "who fully understands every point of the game." Chadwick clarified his mechanism in detail:

> It will be observed that each player is numbered on the score, from one to nine, and his position, in this respect, and also in reference to that he holds in the field, remains unchanged on the book throughout the game, no matter how many times his position in changed as a fielder... In order ... to record the movements of each player during the game, a series of abbreviation are adopted, those we use in scoring being as follows:

A for first base.	D for catch on the bound.
B for second base.	L for foul balls.
C for third base.	T for tips.
H for home base.	K for struck out.
F for catch on the fly.	R for run out between bases.

Double letters — HR, or hr, for home runs.
LF for foul ball on the fly.
LD for foul ball on the bound.
TF for tip on the fly.
TD for tip on the bound.[8]

Chadwick even provided a diagram of the first three innings of an imaginary contest between a hitting nine and a fielding nine.

FIELDING NINE.	BATTING NINE.
1 Leggett, catcher.	1 Masten, catcher.
2 M. O'Brien, pitcher.	2 Creighton, pitcher.
3 McKinstry, short stop.	3 Pearce, short stop.
4 Price, first base.	4 Pearsall, first base.
5 Brown, second base.	5 Oliver, second base.
6 Beach, third base.	6 Smith, third base.

(FIELDING NINE.)

7 P O'Brien, left field.
8 J. Oliver, center field.
9 Whiting, right field.

(BATTING NINE.)

7 Russell, left field.
8 Manolt, center field.
9 Grum, right field.

From this, Chadwick took the batting nine and drew up a hypothetical at-bat performance for the hitting nine.

DIAGRAM OF A SCORE BOOK.

_____*Base-Ball Club.*

INNINGS.

PLAYERS.	POS'S	1	2	3	4	5	6	7	8	9	TOT'L H.L.	TOT'L RUNS
1 Masten	C	8 F 1		*							1	1
2 Creig'ton	P	4 A 2		*							1	1
3 Pearce	SS	5 B 3		*							1	1
4 Pear	1B		6 L D 1	*							1	1
5 Oliver	2B		7 F 2	*							1	1
6 Smith	3B		1 T D 3	* .							1	1
7 Russell	LF			9 D 1*							1	1
8 Manolt	CF			3 F 2*							1	1
9 Grum	RF			K Hr * 3							1	1
Total runs in each Innings.		0	0	9							1	1⁹

Grand Total   0   0   9

Passed Balls_____

Umpire_____Winning Club_____

Date of Match_____Scorer.

Where Played_____[10]

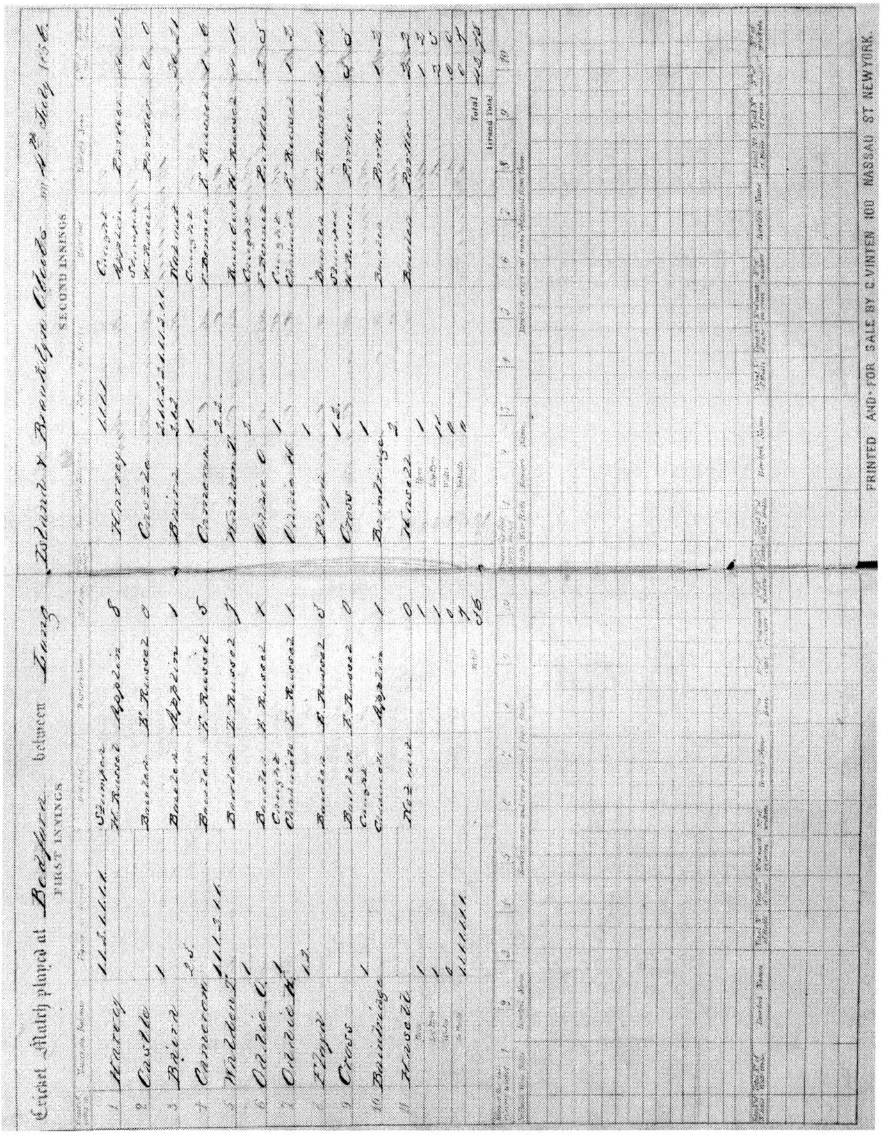
Cricket Match played at
between
FIRST INNINGS
SECOND INNINGS
PRINTED AND FOR SALE BY C VINTEN 100 NASSAU ST NEW YORK

A Cricket Match played at Montreal
on the 22d, 23rd & 24th Augt 1872
Gentlemen of England
vs
Montreal Cricket Club
First Innings   "England"

order of going in	Striker	Runs		How out	Bowler
1	W. G. Grace	3.1.1. 3.3.3. 1.1.1. 4. 2.2.2. 4. 2.3. ½ 1.1. 4. 1.2. .1. 4.1.2. .1.1.1.1.1. 2.1.3. 1.1.1.3.1.1.1.1.31.	81	"C" Benjamin overthro	A. Lang
2	C. J. Ottaway	1.1.1.1.2. 1.2. 1.1.1.1.1.1 3.2. 1.1.1	24	"B"	Hardman
3	A. N. Hornby	3.1.2.2. .1.1.1.3. .1.3.1.2.1.1.1. 2.2. 1.1. 5.1.1.2	39	L. B. W.	Green
4	A. Lubbock	1.1.2.1.11.	7	"B"	A. Lang
5	Hon J Harris	1.1.2	4	"B"	Green
6	C. K. Francis	2. 1.1.1.1.1 2.1.	11	"C" McKenzie	C. McLean
7	E. Lubbock	2.2. 1.1.1.1. 3.2.3.2.	18	"C" Jones	do
8	C. Appleby	3.1.2.1.2.	9	"C" Hardman	do
9	W. M. Rose	1.1.1. 2. 1.1.1.1. 2.4.	15	Not out	
10	F. Pickering	4.1.3. 4.1.2. 1.3.	19	"C" Mills	A. Lang
11	R. A. Fitzgerald	Sick	0		
	Byes	.1.1.2. 1.1.1.1.2. 2.1.	12		
	Leg Byes	1.1.1.1.1.1.1.1	8		
	Wide Balls	1.1.1.1.1.1.1.1	8		
	No Balls				
			255		

Opposite page and above: **These cricket score cards, from Chadwick's collection, served as models for his invention of the baseball scoring system (New York Public Library).**

In this box, Chadwick shows that Masten was retired with a fly out, as indicated by the letter "F" with the number "8," meaning the center fielder, J. Oliver of the fielding nine. The number below the "F" and "8" indicates the out, in this case the first out.

Chadwick explains the other development that occurred through the first three innings of the contest. After Creighton reached first base along with Pearce:

> But Pearsall, being the next striker, struck the ball to short field before Pearce had made his second base; the consequence was that Pearce was third hand out, the ball being sent to second base before Pearce reached it. In the second innings, Pearsall again too the bat, being the next striker to the third hand again too the bat, being the next striker to the third hand out — and was put out from a foul ball on the bound by the third baseman. Oliver was put out on the fly at the left field, and Smith tipped out on the bound. In the third innings, Russell was put out at right field on the bound, Manolt at short field on the fly, and Grum made a home run, the others following with runs until it was again Grum's turn to strike, when after striking at the ball three times and missing each time, he was put out by the catcher holding the ball on the bound after the third time of striking. Grum thus "striking out."[11]

If this particular section seems complicated and difficult to follow, then it would explain why the scoring system was simplified over the years. In fact, this arrangement, where letters and numbers were used to indicate the specific action on the field, was meant only for the scorers of the game, though much of it was adapted later for the fans to use when attending the ballgames. The most lasting and well known of all his lettered contributions was the letter "K" for strikeout. For the fans of 1861, Chadwick developed a much simpler version, one that he developed from cricket. This Chadwick introduced with his famous words that have been oft-quoted by many historians. Chadwick introduced his new device as such:

> In order to obtain an accurate estimate of a player's skill, an analysis, both of his play at the bat and in the field, should be made, inclusive of the way in which he was put out; and that this may be done, it is requisite that all first nine contests should be recorded in a uniform manner, and to facilitate matters, we give below a copy of the bland form we fill up in making out our reports for publication....[12]

With these few words, Chadwick unveiled his scoring system that allowed fans to record the match as it progressed. This scoring system would enable the masses of fans to follow the sport as the game progressed, actually making the fan feel a part of the game. Chadwick's attempts to create baseball as America's National Pastime required him to create a standardized, uniform, or "national" scoring system.[13] Though Chadwick's own scoring system did not survive due to its complexities, as Chadwick numbered the players by their position in the batting order rather than the modern system that has the fan number them by their position on the field, his invention was truly an important device that has stood the test of time. Chadwick's diagram for a scoring system looked like this:

_____Club. _____Club.

BATTING.

PLAYERS.	H.L.	R'NS	PLAYERS	H.L.	R'NS
1					
2					
3					
4					
5					
6					
7					
8					
9					

INNINGS.

CLUBS.	1	2	3	4	5	6	7	8	9	TOTALS.

FIELDING.

PLAYERS.	FLY.	BOUND.	BASES	TOTAL.	PLAYERS.	FLY.	BOUND	BASES	TOTAL.
1					1				
2					2				
3					3				
4					4				
5					5				
6					6				
7					7				
8					8				
9					9				
TOTALS.					TOTALS.				

HOW PUT OUT.

PLAYERS.	FLY.	BOUND.	BASES.			FOUL.	PLAYERS.	FLY.	BOUND	BASES.			FOUL.
			1	2	3					1	2	3	
1							1						
2							2						
3							3						
4							4						
5							5						
6							6						
7							7						
8							8						
9							9						
TOTALS,							TOTALS,						

Passed Balls, on which bases were run_____
Home Runs_____
Struck Out_____
Put Out at Home Base_____
Run out between Bases_____
Times left on Bases_____
Times of Game_____
Umpire, Mr._____of the_____Club.
Scorer for the _____Club, Mr._____
Scorer for the _____Club, Mr._____
Date of Match,_____1860.
Where played: on the grounds of the _____Club.

These forms, which were clearly a reflection of baseball in the early 1860s, were a simpler and more direct format than the convoluted setup Chadwick proposed for in-game scorers. What has been confusing is how most historians have claimed that the alphabet scoring system that Chadwick established initially was for the "cranks." Instead, the former system, as opposed to the latter, was originally meant for the in-game scorers. Chadwick, who played and wrote about cricket, clearly understood the power of this statistical device. The practice of recording cricket matches began in England, so Chadwick cleverly adopted a scoring system from cricket.

In the late 1860s, Chadwick simplified the scoring system to make it easier to use. This is the format Chadwick published in the 1869 *Beadle's Dime Base Ball Player*:

The Score of the _____ *Base-Ball Club, of* _____

BASE RUN-NING.		BASES ON ER'RS.		BASES ON HITS.		OUTS AND RUNS.		TIME PLAY CALLED.	WHEN PLAYED...........1869 .... SCORE OF INNINGS.									TIME GAME ENDED	FIELDING SCORE.							
H	L	B	M	T	1	O	R	BATSMEN.	1	2	3	4	5	6	7	8	9	FIELDERS.	B	F	L	F	K	R	T	A
								1										1								
								2										2								
								3										3								
								4										4								
								5										5								
								6										6								
								7										7								
								8										8								
								9										9								
								Totals,										Totals.								
								Grand Total,																		

Winning Club,_____ Scorer,_____

Umpire,_____   Time of Game,_____hours_____minutes.[14]

This new format made it easier to follow the game by simultaneously recording the fielding and hitting on a card. This grid also indicates what Chadwick specifically wanted to make note of during a game. In the hitting category, which is located to the right, Chadwick distinguishes between base runners who reach safely because of an error and those who reach on "clean" hits. Underneath the different categories for Base Running are the letters "H" for home runs and "L" for left on base. Under the category of bases on errors, the letter "B" is for called balls and "M" for runners getting on base by a muff. Chadwick believed that a walk was a reflection of bad pitching rather than good or effective selective hitting. There was some truth to what Chadwick believed, but of course his cricket background would never let him accept the fact that a hitter would allow himself to be on base unless by a clean ball hit into play. Chadwick wanted the ball in play, so it was up to the hitter to hit the ball and put it in play and, simultaneously, the pitcher to throw accurately enough for the batter to strike the ball and the fielders, either in the infield or the outfield, to make a play.

The other letters indicated in this scoring grid, under the title Bases on Hits, are the letter "T" for total bases and the numeral "1" for "first base hits" or singles. Under Outs and Runs are simply "O" for outs and "R" for runs. Since there are two opposing teams in baseball, there are two versions of this setup available so that each offense and defense of both clubs could have a contrasting accounting of what they did during the game.[15]

On the right side of the page is the recording of the fielders and under the rubric of the "Fielding Score" is an accounting of what happened per play. As the batsmen are numbered 1 through 9, the fielders are listed 1 through 9. Like the early scoring system in the first setup in 1862, Chadwick uses a letter scheme to describe the action by the fielders. The National Association of Professional Base Ball, he wrote, had endorsed this scoring grid that Chadwick developed. Here is the updated version presented in the 1869 *Base Ball Guide*.

A — put out on first base.   L F — put out by foul fly catches.

B   put out on second base.   L D   put out by bound catches.

C   put out on third base.   R O   put out between the bases.

H   put out on home base.   H R   home runs.

F   put out by fly catches.   K   put out by three strikes.[16]

Chadwick admitted in the 1869 guide that this setup looked like "complicated alphabet to remember," yet "when the key is applied it will be at once seen that a boy could easily impress it on his memory in a few minutes." Chadwick even provided an example, as he had in the 1861 guide. Chadwick took this scored game from a match held on October 12, 1868, between the Mutual and Atlantic clubs.

INNINGS.

BATSMAN.	1	2	3	4	5	6	7	8	9	FIELDERS.
1. Pearce,	9-6A 1		*	*		5 6 A 1	*		5-9 B 1	1. C. Hunt, c.f.
2. Smith,	2 6 A 2		*	*		6 A 2	*		*	2. Devyr, s.s.
3. Start,	*		*	*		3d	*		*	3. Wolters, p.
4. Chapman,	K 3		9-2 B 2	3d			7 L D 3		*	4. McMahon, l.f.
5. Crane,		6A 1	2d	7L D 3				7F 1	1F 2	5. Swandell, 3b.
6. Mills,		9-6 A 2	5-6 A 3		K 1	hr *		*	*	6. Mills, ib.
7. Ferguson,		*		*	*	LD 3		*	3d	7. Dockney, c.
8. Zeittlein,		7LD 3		5 6 A 1	7 L F 2		LF 1	2-9 B 2	}6 F	8. Jewett, r.f.
9. McDonald			K 1	6A 2	9F 3		6A 2	9-6 A 3	}6 F 3	9. Flanly, 2b.[17]
	1	1	3	4	1	4	2	2	4	
	2	5	9	10	14	16	18	22		

While Chadwick developed the scoring system for the "cranks" (the mid-nineteenth century word for fans) attending a match, simultaneously he began to manipulate another scoring device. Chadwick has often been credited with inventing the box score, but it was a tool already used in cricket matches by the press in the United States as early as the 1840s.[18] The box score was even in use in the earliest reports of baseball contests from the 1820s and was even utilized by baseball's first-known reporter, William Cauldwell. But those early systems contained only the most rudimentary points of the game, like runs scored and outs. For instance, one of the earlier box scores discovered, though by no means the earliest, in the last twenty years was one published by the *New York Times*. It featured a pre–Fashion Course matchup between New York and Brooklyn in 1845, originally printed in the *New York Morning News*. It read:

Base Ball Match.

A friendly match of the time-honored game of Base [sic] was played yester day at Elysian Fields, Hoboken, between eight members of the New York Ball Club and the same number of players from Brooklyn. . .

NEW YORK BALL CLUB.

	Runs.	Hands out.		Runs.	Hands out.
Davis.....	5		Case......	2	2
Tucker...	2	3	Vail.........	3	1
Miller.....	4	1	Kline........	2	3
Winslow..	4	2		–	–
Murphy...	2			24	12

BROOKLYN PLAYERS.

	Runs.	Hands out.		Runs.	Hands out.
Hunt . .		2	Sharp. . . .		1
Gilmore....	1	2	Whaley	1	1
Hardy......	1	2	Ayres		1
Forman....	1	1		–	–
Hine.........				4	12 [19]

By the early 1860s Chadwick developed a more advanced box score. This box score published in the *New York Sunday Mercury* in 1862 of a game between the Eckford and Atlantic clubs of Brooklyn is a good example of his innovativeness:

ECKFORD.	O.	R.	ATLANTIC	O.	R.
Campbell (1st b.)	4	2	Chapman (C.)	4	1
Munolt (l.f.)	1	5	Joe Oliver (r.f.)	3	2
Spence (r.f.)	3	3	C. Smith (3d. b.)	3	1
Beach (C.)	2	2	P. O'Brien (l.f.)	3	2
Mills (P.)	2	3	R. Pearce (s.s.)	1	3
Wood (2nd b)	3	3	A. Smith (P.)	4	1
Reach (3rd b.)	5	0	Crane (c.f.)	3	1
Josh Snyder (s.s.)	3	1	John Oliver (2nd b.)	4	1
John Snyder (c.f.)	4	1	Start (1st b.)	2	3

INNINGS	1	2	3	4	5	6	7	8	9
Eckford	4	3	0	2	0	1	5	3	2–20
Atlantic	4	1	6	2	1	0	0	0	0–14

ANALYSIS OF FIELD — HOW PUT OUT.

ECKFORD.	Fly	Bound	Bases	Total	ATLANTC.	Fly	Bound	Bases	Total
By Chapman..	1	2	0	3	By Campbell......	0	0	4	4
Joe Oliver....	1	0	0	0	Manolt..........	1	3	2	4
C. Smith......	3	1	0	4	Spence..........	0	1	0	1
P. O'Brien....	0	0	0	0	Beach...........	1	2	0	3
Pearce........	1	0	0	1	Mills..............	0	3	0	3
A. Smith.....	0	0	0	0	Wood...........	0	4	1	5
Crane........	0	1	0	1	Reach...........	2	1	0	3
John Oliver...	2	3	0	5	Josh Snyder...	1	1	0	2
Start..........	0	6	12	12	John Snyder...	1	1	0	2
Total.....	7	7	12	26	Total....	6	16	5	27

Struck out — Josh Snyder, 1.

Home Runs — P. O'Brien, 1.

Left on Third Base — Beach, 2. Mills, 1, Start 1.

Missed on Bound — Beach, 1; Wood, 1; John Snyder, 1;

John Snyder, 1; Joe Oliver, 2; Pearce, 1; Start, 1; Total, 9.

Missed on Bound — Beach, 1; Wood, 1; John Snyder,1; P. O'Brien, 2.

Balls Passed Catcher — Chapman, 9; Pearce, 5; Beach, 4.

Over Pitches — Smith, 1; Mills.

Scorers — Atlantic Club, M. O'Brien ; Eckford, D., J McAusland.

Umpire — A.R. Taylor, of Mutual Club of New York:

We cannot close our report without according due credit to Mr. Taylor, the umpire who was called to decide several very close hitches and did his duty promptly, justly, and, we believe, satisfactorily to all the players engaged.[20]

This box score demonstrates many things. Chadwick did not publish the types of numbers that today's readers would be accustomed to seeing. Chadwick's layout reveals much about how the game during his era differed from modern baseball. The defensive aspects of the game were showcased as much as the hitting. There are no pitching statistics. Although Chadwick admired talented pitchers, he believed that pitching was secondary to the action of the game, at this time, and not as important to calculate as fielding and hitting. Offense was not completely ignored, and of particular note was Chadwick's listing of home runs, which on some level he would later regret, along with a peculiar recording of which runners were left on third base. Even this statistic was significant, for it showed that early on how the man who would be called baseball's father was thinking about what was important in terms of tabulating statistics for hitters. Despite the additions made by Chadwick, the box score, at least from the side of the offense, still did not differ much from the 1845 entry. The main difference was that much of the offenses' summaries were placed after the fielding and not in the meat of the alignment, where outs and runs are tabulated. This was an early trend in Chadwick's ongoing thinking, centered on how to properly reward a player through a statistical category.

But where did Chadwick get the ideas on developing a box score uniquely for baseball? Was it built on a particular model? The answer to both of these questions is simply one word: cricket. Cricket was or course the game that Chadwick used as a cognitive blueprint in which he shaped the game. Chadwick applied the principles from cricket he felt best related to baseball as well as those areas he felt made baseball uniquely its own game, whether from a statistical standpoint or a playing perspective. Here is an example of a cricket box score taken from the *New York Clipper* in August of 1856:

ALL ENGLAND

First Innings.		Second Innings.	
1. J. Caesar c Grundy b Maringell	11	c and b Maringell	35
2. R. Marsham, run out	9	c Locklear b Lillywhite	25
3. J. Wisden b Grundy	4	b Gaffyn	39
4. G. Parr, at Lockyer, b Dean	31	c Lockyer b Lillywhite	0
5. E. Willsher b Grundy	8	c Walker b Dean	18
6. H. Stephenson c Grundy b Dean	7	c Lillywhite b Martingell	45
7. R C Tinley b Dean	3	b Tredcroft	50

(First Innings.)		(Second Innings.)	
8. C.D. Marsham c Lockyer b. Dean	8	lb w. b Dean	15
9. F. Bell b Dean	24	at Nicholson b Lillywhite	9
10. H. Perkins b Dean	11	b Martingell	24
11. T. Sherman not out	4	not out	12
Byes 1., leg byes 8	9	Byes 12; leg byes 9	21
No balls	6	No balls	2
Total	130		298
		First Innings	130
		Total of both innings	428

M.C.C. AND GROUND

First Innings.		Second Innings.	
1. W. Nicholson b Willsher	4	c and b. Willsher	13
2. J. Grundy c Stephenson b Wisden	4	b C.D. Marsham	13
3. W. Caffyn, c Caesar b Willsher	2	b C.D. Marhsam	0
4. Jn Lillywhite c Stephen- son b Wisden	4	b Willsher	26
5. C Marsham b Wisden	0	c R. Warsham b Wisen	2
6. E Tredcroft b Willsher	21	d Sherman b Willsher	0
7. R Broughton b Wisden	16	b Willsher	4
8. T. Lockyer c C.D. Marsham b. Willsher	52	not out	5
9. A. H. Walker b C.D Marsham	2	b. Wisden	4
10. J. Dean b Wisden	12	c. Tinley B Willsher	0
11. W. Matingale not out	0	c. Wisden b Willsher	5
Byes 16; leg byes 6	22	Byes 2; leg byes 5	7
Wide balls	1		
Total	140	Total	79

First Innings	140
Total of both Innings	219

ANALYSIS OF THE BOWLING.

England — *First Innings*

	Balls	Runs	Mdns.	Wkts	No bls.
Martingell	100	44	8	1	6
Grundy	108	41	10	2	0
Dean	60	26	4	6	0
Caffyn	20	4	3	0	0

Second Innings

	Balls	Runs	Mdns.	Wkts	No bls.
Martingell	119	69	9	3	2
Grundy	182	57	13	0	0
Dean	148	47	16	2	0
Caffyn	64	33	6	1	0
Lillywhite	64	36	4	3	0
Lockyer	36	24	3	0	0
E. Tredcroft	16	9	0	1	0

MARYLEBONE — *First Innings*

	Balls	Runs	Mdns.	Wkts	No bls.
Wisden	172	46	21	5	0
Willsher	168	43	21	4	1
Sherman	40	14	3	0	0
C.D. Marsham	28	14	1	0	0

Second Innings

	Balls	Runs	Mdns.	Wkts	No bls.
Wisden	69	19	6	2	0
Willsher	120	33	16	6	0
C.D. Marsham	56	20	9	2	0[21]

Given the similarities between this box score from this cricket match and the box score from a baseball game, it is easy to see how one was the model for the other. Each box score is concerned with runs scored by each player. Runs scored was considered an important statistic even in this early period. It figured in the worth of a batter in both games, as it would in the batting average that will be discussed later in this chapter.

But there are significant differences between the baseball and cricket box score that illustrate the disparities between the two games. As cricket is only a two-inning contest, the breakdown of the offensive contributions is boiled down to what each hitter has done in each inning. The only inning by inning tabulation for baseball is the runs scored per inning for each team. This is not to say these two box scores were typical examples presented in this era. In fact, most box scores from cricket and baseball did not always include information about the defense or the bowling. Nonetheless, these were excellent examples to what extent those who computed box scores and the length that journalists like Chadwick went in conveying a game through this device.

Later, however, by 1871, Chadwick did develop a box score that revealed more about the offensive side of the game. Here is a sample from a match between two of the National Association of Baseball Players' finest, the Boston Red Stockings and the Philadelphia Athletics.

BOSTON.	A.B	R.	1B	PO.	A.	ATHLETIC.	AB.	R.	1B	PO.	A.
G. Wright, s.s..	6	2	2	2	3	Cuthbert, lf..........	5	1	2	6	0
Barnes, 2d b..	6	4	4	1	4	McBride, p..........	5	2	1	1	1
Birdsall, r.f......	7	3	4	2	0	Radcliff, ss.........	5	0	2	0	6
McVey, c........	7	2	2	4	0	Malone, c...........	5	0	2	2	1
Spalding,[p].....	6	2	2	0	0	Fisler, 1st b.........	5	1	1	9	0
Gould, 1st b...	6	2	1	12	0	Reach, 2nd b.......	5	0	1	6	2
Schafer, 3d b...	6	1	3	2	2	Senaenderfer, cf..	4	2	2	1	1
Barrows, lf......	6	4	1	3	0	Heubel, rf.......	4	1	2	1	1
H. Wright, cf....	5	3	3	1	0	Bechtel, 3d b......	4	1	0	2	2
Totals......	55	23	22	27	9	Totals........	42	7	12	27	13

INNINGS — *Runs scored.*	1st	2nd	3rd	4th	5th	6th	7th	8th	9th
Boston	2	3	5	0	3	0	6	0	4 — 23
Athletic	0	1	1	0	0	0	0	0	5 — 7
Runs Earned.									
Boston	0	3	2	2	0	0	1	0	1 — 9
Athletic	0	0	0	0	0	0	0	0	4 — 4

Bases on errors — Boston, 3; Athletic, 2. Bases on called balls — Barnes, 1; Bectel, 1. Umpire — Theodore Bomeisler, of the Eureka of Newark, N.J. Scoreres — Mssrs. Cone and A.H. Wight. Time of game — 2 hours and 30 minutes.[22]

This box score would be more recognizable to the modern fan. By and large, this format had been around for several years with one new inclusion — the tabulation of at-bats. The box score had already been expanding, or in some cases contracting, during the 1860s, from the time it only tabulated outs and runs for offense. Since there had been more information about how the batter made outs than how many times he reached base, Chadwick understood why people were watching baseball and helped them understand what happened offensively in a game.

As the box progressed throughout the 1860s, a new offensive category was included: how many times a runner reached first base (as indicated by 1b). As the box score expanded to include this category, another part faded away. When the bound catch was eliminated, there was no longer a need to calculate the types of outs made on the fly or on the bound. As a result, the offensive categories began to take priority over the defense in the box score; defense was not eliminated altogether, but offense became more central to the system.

When the *New York Clipper*, under the guidance of Henry Chadwick, began to tabulate at-bats, beginning in 1871, a new era opened in box score formulations. Two years earlier, Chadwick, in the 1869 *Beadle Dime Base Ball Player*, had begun to recognize the value of getting on base with a clean hit as opposed to getting on base via an error.[23] This was an important distinction, as it separated and distinguished the way players were getting on base.

Thus, when the *Clipper* began to tabulate at-bats, and when Henry Chadwick wrote that the "only true estimate of a batsman's skill, is ... based on the number of times he makes his bases on hits, not by errors of the fielders," it was only a matter of time that a new statistic would appear.[24] Keeping at-bats and recording legitimate ways of getting on base were important because it led to one of the most vital and well-known statistical tabulations in the history of the game: the batting average.

Actually, Chadwick was not directly responsible for this invention. This honor belongs to H.A. Dobson of Washington. Dobson wrote to Chadwick about the idea of dividing at-bats into hits as the best way to determine a hitter's bating average. Chadwick graciously published the letter and over the next several years it became one of the most popular statistics in the game's history. This new method replaced some of the other techniques used to determine the efficacy of a hitter. As Dobson pointed out, one early method to determine a hitter's worth, one that was chiefly calculated by Chadwick, was simply using two categories: the fewest outs and the most runs. The average was figured "by dividing the total number of outs and runs by the number of games played." Therefore, the average runs per game determined the ability of the hitter, known as Analysis of Batting or Batting Analysis.

As a member of the *New York Clipper*, Chadwick proudly introduced this tabulation in 1860 and promised by 1861 that he would "have complete scores of the principal matches played by the leading clubs of New York and its immediate vicinity, and shall, therefore, at the close of the season, give the averages of each and all of them in full." Here is a sample of the statistics Chadwick presented in 1860. He reminded his readers that "the *Clipper* is the first paper to promote the welfare of the game by these analyses."

ANALYSIS OF BATTING.

Names.	Matches Played in.	Hands Lost.	Average and Over.	Runs.	Average and Over	Highest Score in a Match.	Clear Scores.	Matches in Which no Runs Were made.	Most Hands Lost.	Least Hands Lost.
GOTHAM CLUB.										
Anderson..........	3	7	2-1	10	3-1	4	0	0	3	1
Burtis..............	4	11	2-3	6	1-2	4	0	1	4	1
Curtis..............	5	12	2-2	14	2-4	4	0	0	3	1
Commerford.......	2	7	3-1	2	1-0	2	0	1	4	3
Cohen..............	4	11	2-3	11	2-3	6	0	0	4	2
Dupignac..........	3	12	4-0	5	1-2	3	0	0	4	4
Forsyth............	3	11	3-2	3	2-2	6	0	1	5	2
Griswold..........	1	2	2-0	1	1-0	1	0	0	2	2
Hacket.............	2	5	2-1	5	2-1	4	0	0	3	2
McCosker.........	3	10	3-1	7	2-1	4	0	0	3	4
McKeaver.........	5	16	3-0	10	2-0	4	0	1	5	2
Minne..............	1	4	4-0	2	2-0	2	0	0	4	4
Turner..............	4	13	3-1	10	2-2	4	0	0	5	2
Tucker.............	1	2	2-0	2	2-0	2	0	0	2	2
Van Cott, T........	4	11	2-3	7	1-8	2	0	0	4	1[25]

According to these calculations, the best hitter of the Gotham club was Anderson, with his average of three runs. To the modern fan, these calculations would seem strange or even ridiculous because of our understanding of how hitters are determined today. But Chadwick was writing to a mid-nineteenth century audience, an audience that did not understand baseball the way we understand it now. While these calculations may seem ridiculous or strange to modern audiences, mid — nineteenth century ball-playing fans understood these numbers from another game that was popular throughout the country — cricket — a sport that Henry Chadwick knew extremely well. Cricket, as discussed earlier, was the more established game and anybody reading the *Clipper* or other sports-related newspapers would be familiar with the calculation of runs as being central to the offensive game of Chadwick's mother country. Chadwick and other writers of the game in that era tried to make it easy for followers of the more established game of cricket to understand baseball by presenting a concept like the tabulation of runs as the method of determining the best offensive player. Cricket statisticians even used the term "Batsmen Averages." Here is an example of how the *Clipper*, in 1857, laid out the statistics for cricket players who came from Albany, New York:

	Matches	Innings	Runs	Average Over	Times not out.	Highest Scoe in one Inning
Austen	1	2	3	1–1	0	3
Beavington	1	2	14	7–0	0	14
Comery	2	4	76	19–0	0	23
Chapin	3	6	31	5–1	1	9
Cutler	3	6	19	3–1	0	14
Cramfiled	1	2	3	1–1	0	3
Crooper	1	2	5	2–1	0	5
Gillespie	2	4	21	5–1	1	17
Hobbs	3	6	32	5–2	0	10
Hole	3	6	22	3–4	0	9
Hadey	1	2	15	7–1	1	10
Hughes	1	2	4	2–0	0	3
Lacy	3	6	30	5–0	0	11
Lightfoot	1	2	2	1–0	0	2
Moore	2	4	26	6–2	0	10
Rich	1	2	1	0–1	0	1
Rose	2	4	38	9–2	0	28
Smith	1	2	4	2–0	0	4
Saunders	2	4	6	1–2	1	5
Slater	2	4	24	6–0	0	10
Sunderland	3	6	8	1–2	3	3
White	2	4	40	10–0	0	28
Warnum	1	2	2	1–0	1	2[26]

It is clear, just as in the case with the box score, that a hitter's worth was dependant on the number of runs scored. Chadwick's early thinking on a hitter's worth, as stated earlier, was based on runs scored, which was essential in cricket calculations. By these calculations, Comery's average is the highest because he scored 19 runs an inning, which is figured by dividing runs, in his case 76, by innings played, 4, netting the average of 19 runs. Since cricket served as the model for early baseball averages, runs scored became the original way to determine a player's worth.

Of course, there were many factors that contributed to a runner scoring in baseball, and much of it had to do with the batter at the plate determining whether a runner on base would score a run. Soon a different method to determine a hitter's talent was used, which divided the number of first base hits by games played. These methods were some of the original ways in which to tabulate a hitter's capabilities before the advent of the modern batting average. As a result, Chadwick's tabulations for baseball averages started to become more detailed. He was determined to reveal what each hitter was actually doing. Here is an analysis of the Atlantic club printed in January 1861:

> The Atlantic Club, of Brooklyn, having closed play for the season, we present below the season's averages of those of the members of the club who have taken part in [its] first nine matches

	Matches Played In	Hands Lost	Average Over	Runs	Average Over	Highest Score in a Match	Clear Scores	Matches Where No Runs Were Made	Most Hands Out	Least Hands Out	Home Runs	Struck Out
1. Boerum	1	1	1.0	6	6.0	6	0	0	1	1	0	0
2. Boughton	1	7	7.0	0	0.0	0	0	1	7	7	0	0
3. Babcock, A.	1	2	2.0	1	1.0	1	0	0	2	2	0	0
4. Colyer	1	2	2.2	5	5.0	5	0	0	2	2	0	0
5. Hawthorne	3	8	2.1	9	3.0	3	0	0	4	1	0	0
6. McMahon	2	5	2.1	5	2.1	3	0	0	3	2	0	0
7. Oliver, Jhn.	3	10	3.1	6	2.0	3	0	0	4	3	1	0
8. Oliver, Jos.	8	25	3.1	24	3.0	6	0	0	1	6	3	2
9. O'Brien, P.	7	21	3.0	19	2.5	5	0	0	4	2	0	0
10. O'Brien. M.	3	10	3.1	9	3.0	6	0	0	4	2	0	0
11. Pearce	10	27	2.7	37	3.7	6	0	0	4	1	0	0

	(Matches Played In)	(Hands Lost)	(Average Over)	(Runs)	(Average Over)	(Highest Score in a Match)	(Clear Scores)	(Matches Where No Runs Were Made)	(Most Hands Out)	(Least Hands Out)	(Home Runs)	(Struck Out)
12. Price	2	6	3.0	7	3.1	5	0	0	4	2	0	0
13. Ross	1	3	3.0	4	4.0	4	0	0	3	3	0	0
14. Smith, C.	9	22	2.4	33	3.6	6	0	0	3	1	1	0
15. Smith, A.	1	2	2.0	2	2.0	2	0	0	2	2	0	0
16. Seinsoth, F.	7	18	2.4	22	3.1	7	0	0	4	1	4	1
17. Seinsoth, G.	3	8	2.2	8	2.2	4	0	0	3	2	0	1
18. Seinsoth, R.	6	18	3.0	23	3.5	6	0	0	4	1	0	0
19. Seibert	1	5	5.0	0	0.0	0	0	1	5	5	0	0
20. Thwaites	2	5	2.1	7	3.1	4	0	0	4	1	0	0[27]

Chadwick certainly seemed to be trying different ways to assess hitting, yet never really established a system for batting averages that stuck. Nevertheless, his innovative listing of home runs and strikeouts, as well as the tabulation for runs scored, are important calculations that are still in use today. Was it Chadwick trying to fair, his sense of right and wrong dripping from the ink of his pen, or was he trying to tell a story? Perhaps it was a little of both. To say that Chadwick was trying to be precise is an understatement.

To understand what Chadwick was trying to do, we must first comprehend what statistics actually mean, particularly what they began to mean by the mid–1800s. Obviously, statistics like these were a way for Chadwick to promote the sport. If the game was worth quantifying, then it was worth playing or following as a spectator. But there was a deeper meaning for statistics. Statistics, in the middle of the nineteenth century, also began to represent something more than just mere quantification: it was a way of proving the truth. After 1790, statistics became defined as "authentic facts." If we go by this definition, we more accurately understand Chadwick as a person. Chadwick used statistics to tell the truth about a player's ability, as a way of proving which players were actually most productive. Rather than criticizing a player directly, which he rarely did, he let the statistics speak for themselves, for "facts were objective and indisputable."[28]

Statistics became a tool of reformers. They were used in England to help solve the social problems of the day. For instance, Chadwick's older brother used statistics in his *Report on the Sanitary Condition of the Labouring Population of Great Britain* in 1842. The *Report* "featured voluminous quantitative data supporting the opinions of doctors and public health officials."[29] The Chadwick brothers, like many nineteenth century thinkers, understood the effects of statistics and "quantification on social thought." The act of taking numbers, calculating them and making statistics "focused concern on an issue, accurately described its dimensions and suggested the proper course to be taken." Chadwick, in accordance with that belief, confidently boasted that statistics have "always proved ... the correctness of my views, and, in this, I have, of course, been greatly assisted by facts and figures derived from actual observation and from a statistical analysis of each season's play."[30] As ball players became workers employed by businesses, the usage of statistics greatly increased (as they did in other businesses) and became more sophisticated.[31] In the 1864 edition of *Beadle's Dime Base Ball Player*, Chadwick insisted that statistics, in general, were the only fair method of judging a player's skill:

> Many a dashing general player, who carries off a great deal of *éclat* in prominent matches, has all "the gilt taken off the gingerbread," as the saying is, by these matter-of-fact figures, given at the close of the season; and we are frequently surprised to find that the modest but efficient worker, who has played earnestly and steadily through the season, apparently unnoticed, has come in, at the close of the race, the real victor.[32]

In this photograph (ca. 1873), Chadwick reminds the baseball public that he was, above all, by the book (Baseball Hall of Fame Library, Cooperstown, N.Y.).

Here, of course, the value that Chadwick placed

on a worker's efficiency was the same as any modernizing business held. But his writings, which again predate professional baseball, were a way that fans, particularly white-collar, middle class fans, who themselves were becoming part of the bureaucratic corporate world, could understand and relate to the game.

Throughout his long association with baseball, Chadwick constantly voiced his thoughts about the way in which to reward a hitter for his contribution. Even in the late 1880s — as the game was still in its evolutionary stages — and new ways of rewarding a hitter kept appearing, Henry Chadwick was right in the middle of the action. Rewarding a player for forwarding runners was important to him and he felt, with deep conviction, that moving runners from base to base, especially driving runners home, was an important way to determine whether a hitter was doing his job. During the winter of 1887 Chadwick wrote an article for the *Sporting News* that dealt precisely with this issue.

> Look at the score of the game as recorded in the papers.... Is there the slightest record of the efforts made by batsmen to bring in runs? None at all. But special prominence is give(n) to the name of the batsman who makes two and three baggers, but there is not a figure to show what he did in the way of forwarding runners on bases or in bringing in runs by his hits. A batsman may send a runner home by a safe tap of the ball to short out field, or by a hit which forces the fielder to put him out at first base, or, he may forward a runner from first to second, or perhaps to third by just such hits, but not a figure does he get recorded in the score for such creditable work in batting. But if he makes base hits in a game yielding two or three baggers, down goes credit in the score for this so-called "splendid batting," while not a solitary run may be scored by such hits or even a runner forwarded on the bases.[33]

Chadwick touted an idea that would become one of the most important statistics in a hitter's evaluation: runs batted in. The RBI took a while to be taken seriously, but by 1891, the game's official scorers were ordered by the National League to count it as a legitimate statistic in the box score.[34]

With Chadwick laying the foundation for the tabulation of statistics and with his adaptation of the box score, he was helping baseball continue its growth. His statistical innovations helped to facilitate an understanding of a particular game, or a particular season for those who could not attend a match. A fan could be thousands of miles away from a game that took place in one part of the country and could fathom which contributions were made, or were not made, by a player in a winning or losing effort. Chadwick's adaptation of the box score to baseball was so effective that it has become even more synonymous to the American game than it has to any other sport, even the sport that he appropriated it from, the English game of cricket.

His success in making both baseball and the box score connect throughout history came from his meticulous emphasis on the unique character of the game's events. By developing the box score, Chadwick attempted to tell the true story of a contest, but even more importantly, this device worked as a type of advertisement for the game. As Chadwick began to wax poetic regarding the benefits of baseball as a "lever" to make Americans take up exercise, his detail-oriented box scores gave the game a certain validation to the public that bought the *New York Clipper* or any of the other dailies Chadwick wrote for. Unlike the older box scores, which only included the number of runs scored and the number of outs made by each hitter, Chadwick also incorporated at various times the hits, the number of balls pitched to each batter per-plate-appearance and runs batted in.

Chadwick's statistical innovations and adaptations had a purpose other than to simply tabulate cumulative numbers. Along with his promotion of the sport, Henry's calculations, through the usage of the scoring system and the box score and particularly in his specific tabulation of the fly catch, were another display of his reform inclinations. These tendencies reflected not only his family's influence, but the era's influence as well.[35] Chadwick's statistics held players accountable for their effectiveness and gave the spectators a deeper understanding of the players they were watching. While it has been argued that "[s]tatistics were developed [and] employed [so that] employers [could] measure the abilities of players they had never seen," many of Chadwick's statistics predated the official advent of professional baseball. Statistics at this early stage helped the fans identify the good players from the weaker ones, and helped to create a sense of connection between players they did not know personally. In this period of baseball there was a great deal of controversy among players and the fans as to who were truly the "ringers," the great players, and who were the "muffins," the lousy players.

While Chadwick contributed to the dailies, he continued to make his weekly contributions to the *Clipper*, where he found greater freedom in expressing his views on baseball, and discovered that he could expand his coverage of the game. Expounding on numerous games played over the previous several days, Chadwick provided in-depth and lengthy analysis of these contests, his reports resembling the baseball guides in a narrative and statistical sense rather than the basic box score and paragraph to which he was generally restricted in the daily newspapers. Not only did he include both offensive and defensive box scores, he described the fielding and hitting action taking place within the game and used language that today would seem unusual to the reader of modern baseball writing. In a contest between two of Brooklyn's best, the Atlantics and the Excelsiors, Chadwick wrote:

> Creighton was the ninth *striker* [emphasis added], and he was splendidly caught on the bound by M. O'Brien, the ball sent from the bat. This ended the first innings for the Excelsiors, and the Atlantics then went in to offset the lead of 5 runs their opponents had obtained.[36]

"Striker" was a nineteenth-century term used in cricket (as well as "batsman") to describe the hitter. The significance of this description demonstrates how baseball had not developed its own identity as a ball game and how cricket's dominance still influenced those writing about baseball, like Chadwick, in the early 1860s. It also shows how baseball's terminology had not evolved at this stage.

Though he still followed cricket and wrote about the sport, by 1860 Chadwick's main emphasis became baseball because the game, by this time, had exceeded cricket in popularity. Fans of the rising sport of baseball were eager to read about the game, thanks to Henry's writings and statistical innovations. Since the games were played during the day, next-day reporting of the events taking place on the fields of Brooklyn and Hoboken became a crucial must-read for fans. Not only could games be found in the *Eagle*, the *New York Times*, and the *Spirit of the Times*, but also in nationally illustrated publications like *Harper's Weekly* and *Frank Leslie's Illustrated Newspaper*. Thus Henry's role as a reporter was helping the game grow exponentially.

But early in 1861, the Civil War erupted, as the first shots fired at Fort Sumter in South Carolina reverberated throughout the country. Temporarily, the war affected Chadwick's life. In April 1861, Chadwick worked for the *New York Tribune* as a Civil War correspondent, in Richmond, Virginia, his wife's former home, but only briefly, "returning to Brooklyn and to baseball with prolific intensity. He began to publish his own weekly, the *American Chronicle of Sports and Pastimes*, though it only lasted thirteen months."[37]

Despite its effects on baseball activity in New York, the Civil War

actually helped to spread New York baseball throughout the country. While
the North won the war, it was also the New York game, which proved to
be the other victor in the great American conflict. During the war, enlisted
players from the New York and Brooklyn teams took their game with them
into the camps of Virginia and Tennessee. Whether in summer or fall,
when "the Federal armies rested for a week, someone was sure to take a
baseball out of his haversack and start a game." But it wasn't just any version of the game; it was the New York version that by now was becoming
more favored than the other styles played in other parts of the country.
More importantly to the game's growth, baseball was also played in the
Confederate prisons, where the Union soldiers taught it to their captors.
While not in battle, soldiers played baseball as a form of recreation. Those
soldiers who had not seen or played the sport had the opportunity to see
it and participate in it for the first time. Again, the version of the game
they saw was the New York version.

As a sportswriter, Henry had become an integral part of the sporting community in New York and one of the leading voices and thinkers
promoting outdoor sports and games. He and other sportswriters became
part of an intense public relations campaign waged by baseball magnates
and sportswriters who were willing to cooperate in any way to promote
the game. Baseball writers began to convince the public that participation
in the rituals of baseball contributed to both individual self-improvement
and national betterment.[38]

A devote moralist, like his grandfather before him, Chadwick directed
his ill will toward gamblers, crooks, drunks and those who disrupted games
with rowdiness. Though it was rare for Chadwick to name evildoers
directly, those he held hostility toward felt his ire by being omitted from
his columns. When baseball became a sport run by the owners in the late
1870s, Chadwick spoke out against management when he felt that own-
ership was not making baseball as great as he believed the game could
become.

Chadwick's baseball writing was not confined to a description of the
game. In addition to his baseball columns, Chadwick wrote a type of commentary not found in today's newspapers. In it he conveyed what he considered to be the model player in attitude and temperament. In one of
these columns, written in the *New York Clipper* in 1861, Chadwick
described the model player as one who comports:

> himself like a gentleman [as] he abstains from profanity, always has his
> temper under control, and takes matters good humoredly; or, if angered,

keeps silent.... He never disputes the decision of an umpire, either by his words or actions; but, when a judgment has been rendered, he silently accepts the decision.... Regarding the game as a healthful exercise, and a manly and exciting recreation, he plays it solely for the pleasure it affords him, and if victory crowns his efforts in a contest, well and good; but should defeat ensue he is equally ready to applaud the success obtained by his opponents.[39]

Chadwick used his columns to advocate social reform, but his writings also reflected definitions of early Victorian manhood. To Chadwick, and to many of his readers, this was the essence of manliness. It was not the brash exhibitionism and competitiveness that the sport (and the culture itself) in the latter part of the century came to be identified with. It was, rather, the man who kept his temper under control, who enjoyed the success of his opponents as much as his own, and who found joy in the simple participation in the outdoor activity that determined the "manliness" of the adult male.

Chadwick's genteel essay also held significance for another reason. In describing the proper etiquette of a ballplayer, his suggestions resembled the advice given in the etiquette manuals that were popular in this period. These manuals voiced a concern with establishing an American code of manners that would "regulate social interchange and temper" in an increasingly urban and heterogeneous population, from which, of course, baseball players and crowds were drawn.

Despite his eloquent essays that promoted and reflected the genteel aspects of baseball, Chadwick's approach would be challenged. As the 1860s witnessed the growth of baseball, the country was changing drastically. The Civil War forever altered the landscape of the country as the North and South clashed for supremacy. As the battles were fought on American soil, baseball continued its growth, moving outside the confines of New York to the rest of the country. More importantly, different people began to play baseball. Not only did the game grow outside of New York, it also began to take hold with people outside of white-collar workers. How would Henry Chadwick, given his education and his background, respond to these changes?

As we shall see, Chadwick's reactions to the revolution in American society would be varied and complex; they would reflect the temperament of a baseball genius.

CHAPTER 4

On Tour with
Mr. Chadwick

The bitter years from 1861 to 1865 saw the United States torn asunder by violence. The Civil War raged on the battlefields of Gettysburg, Antietam, Manassas and Chickamauga, as the war symbolically represented America's struggle to redefine itself. The country had been heading in that direction for decades, with negotiation and compromise by its great political leaders preventing conflict. Henry Clay, Daniel Webster, John C. Calhoun, and even Stephen Douglass were names synonymous with keeping the Union sewn together by the great Compromise of 1850. But the threads that kept the nation from being ripped apart over the slavery issue would not hold together. By the next decade, the nation was on the verge of violence between the North and South. March 1861 saw the swearing in of a new president, Abraham Lincoln of Illinois, whom the South held with great mistrust, and whatever ties that had previously held the nation together began to seriously unravel. After Lincoln sent in munitions and food to a fort in South Carolina, the South fired the first shots of war, and Fort Sumter became synonymous with the start of the Civil War, shaking the nation to its very core. The great American conflict would soon determine the fate of the millions of black slaves held in bondage.

Temporarily, the war affected the life of Henry Chadwick. When the war began, Chadwick was in Richmond, Virginia — his wife's former home — working for the *New York Tribune* as a Civil War correspondent. Chadwick, perhaps preferring to stick with sports or simply out of fear, returned to Brooklyn and to baseball with prolific intensity. Chadwick remained entrenched in the New York baseball scene during the great American conflict, as the game seemed to flourish despite the country's preoccupation with war. For instance, Chadwick arranged on October 21, 1861, three months after the Battle of Bull Run, a contest between select nines of Brooklyn and New York. The game, known as the "Silver Ball Match" due to the prize, a "*facsimile* of a base ball" coated with silver contributed by Chadwick's employer, Mr. Frank Queen of the *New York Clipper*, drew more than ten thousand people at Elysian Fields, in Hoboken, New Jersey. The crowd saw Brooklyn, powered by players from the Excelsiors, Atlantics and Eckfords, defeat the New York nine, 18 to 6.[1] The game, like the Fashion Course games before it, featured some of baseball's most prominent players, among them Harry Wright of the Knickerbockers representing New York, Al Reach of the Eckfords and a young hurler named James Creighton of the Excelsiors representing the city of Brooklyn. The Atlantic club took the trophy because "their three members ... made the greatest number of runs."[2] Though this seemed to be a novel way to reward a club, this recognition was an early indication of Chadwick's belief in rewarding a club for a statistical contribution. As established in the last chapter, runs were an important part of early baseball statistics because of their importance in cricket, and early baseball was seen through the eyes of Chadwick and others who were more familiar with the older, more established game.

Indeed baseball and similar games grew so much in popularity during that time that even politicians began taking up the sport. Legend had it that even President Abraham Lincoln participated in bat and ball games similar to baseball, like town ball. In 1904, Frank P. Blair recalled in a work entitled "*Abe*" *Lincoln's Yarns and Stories* that Lincoln "would join ardently in the sport." He remembered "vividly how he ran with the children; how long were his strides, and how far his coat-tails stuck out behind, and how we tried to hit him with the ball, as he ran the bases."[3] Whether the story was true or not — it really wasn't — or whether Lincoln actually had played the game, there was no question that the beleaguered leader enjoyed his time away from his duties as leader of a nation torn apart by civil war. One of the things that Lincoln enjoyed most was attending theater.[4] Henry Chadwick, like the president, enjoyed seeing plays, stemming from his background in musical composition, poetry and singing. In fact, in 1864, the dean of baseball writers was actually in Washington, D.C., at a play at the same time as the president. In an eerie foreshadowing of what was to take place in the spring of 1865 at Ford's Theatre, Chadwick recounted in some correspondence dated November 19, 1864, the experience of being in the same building as President Lincoln:

> I visited Grover's new theatre the other night to see ... Hamlet. It was the night the President occupied a private box, accompanied by Major-General Hunter and his wife. Mr. Lincoln was evidently an interested and attentive spectator of the performance throughout, as he sat leaning his arm on the edge of the box with his chin on his hand in true Western style. I must confess I was not taken by the appearance of his profile with view him in this position. Though he gave an attentive ear to the play, it was not till the grave digger's scene in the fourth act was presented that his particular fancy seem to have been struck by the occurrences of the drama. You may probably have seen that caricature that Strong of New York used during the late presidential campaign, in which [George B.] McClellan is represented as Hamlet with Lincoln's head in his hand in the place of Yorick's skull, an Irishman being the grave digger, and Seymour, Horatio. McClellan is made to remark: "I knew him, Horatio, a fellow of infinite jest, where be now you jibes?" From the manner in which Mr. Lincoln enjoyed this whole scene, it was manifest to me he had seen this witty publication; certainly there were others in the house who had. It is well that the occupant of the White House possess this mental safety valve of humor, or otherwise the immense weight of cares incident to his position must have long since caused him to succumb to the great pressure....[5]

It was truly a great moment in Chadwick's life to have been in the same place as the president, who shortly thereafter delivered his famous second inaugural speech after winning reelection. In fact, Chadwick's encounter in 1864 with the president was sandwiched by two of Lincoln's great speeches. The first was Lincoln's Gettysburg Address, delivered in 1863 on the site of the famous battle that took place in the state of Pennsylvania. The speech paid homage to those soldiers who perished in the famous battle, but, more importantly, redefined the meaning of freedom. Later, in his second inaugural address, given on March 4, 1865, with the end of war in sight, the president spoke about the "peculiar" institution of slavery, eloquently reciting the words of his address: "Fondly do we hope — fervently do we pray — that this mighty scourge of war may speedily pass away."[6] Lincoln ended his speech by offering an olive branch of sorts to the South:

> With malice toward none, with charity for all, with firmness in the right as God gives us to see the right ... to do all which may achieve a just and lasting peace among ourselves and with all nations.[7]

During the war years, another transformation was taking place in America, one that would shape and forever alter baseball and affect Henry Chadwick's career in baseball journalism. The nation's transformation from an agrarian society to an industrial one was underway while the ethos of commercial competition began to etch itself into the minds of Americans. The concept of a paid employee, one who worked for a boss in a factory or in an office setting, became an emerging phenomenon. As a result of the changing tide in the working life of Americans during the war years, the period between 1865 and 1870 was revolutionary. While the post-war years in America began with reconstruction, baseball faced its share of changes, too.

Between 1865 and 1870, baseball clubs had begun to be classified into two categories: amateur and professional. This was a profound and fundamental shift in the baseball world. The professional clubs participated in championship matches, took competition more seriously than the amateurs, and geared themselves toward making money. Because of the greater intensity of competition, baseball fans, noted Henry Chadwick, began to attend only "those matches wherein the clubs, aspiring to the championships are interested, thinking that these matches are the only exhibitions of good play."[8] Chadwick seemed alarmed with the idea that fans, or cranks as they were called in those days, would be concerned with this idea. He disagreed with the notion that the more important games were the ones that were played for titles. Chadwick did not equate the quest for championship and competitiveness with manliness.

> ... let those clubs which propose to win the championship, at the risk of honor and respect, notify the Association, that they are candidates for the championship; and those clubs which propose to make base ball the game of the gentlemanly youth of America, say that they will play the game in its purity; not for gate money, not for the empty honors of championship, but for the honor, the reputation and manliness of the players themselves....[9]

But times were changing. In the postbellum era athletics came to mean serious, commercial competition. Furthermore, it was not enough to play sports for physical exercise only; an athlete had to prove his masculinity by competing. A man's actions and results, not his beliefs nor his philosophical ruminations, were what characterized the new male identity in this era.[10] This new competitive environment on the baseball field emerged along with a more cutthroat industrial-capitalistic society in the United States after the Civil War. Ballplayers' attitudes toward their games changed as well, as baseball became the first sport to take advantage of the shifting perception toward games, going from fun and recreation to cutthroat competition.[11]

Though Chadwick was nervous about the changes occurring in baseball, changes that caused a shift away from its more genteel-like framework, one that had been more akin to cricket familial relationships, he began to embrace baseball's evolution from a genteel, gentleman's game to a more seriously competitive sport where winning and losing mattered. The very thing that had separated and made baseball different, more American, than cricket — its ruggedness, its fast pace, the very essence that Chadwick had picked up on in 1856 while watching the Eagle and Gotham baseball clubs in action — was also beginning to express itself more intensely in other areas around the game. On one hand, Chadwick embraced and encouraged this difference because he knew it was the very thing that had made baseball uniquely American. On the other hand, Chadwick dearly tried to keep baseball as much like cricket as possible. This was one of the great contradictions in Chadwick's approach to shaping baseball, one that would always emerge from time to time throughout his life.

As competition between clubs increased and the game moved away from its fraternal origins, clubs went beyond the norms for acquiring players. Just prior to the Civil War years, the Excelsiors hired a player in order to make a good squad more competitive. The club financially compensated nineteen-year-old James Creighton, a brilliant player known primarily for his pitching, to help them win games. Creighton, who played in the Silver Ball match, began his career in his early teens. His first club was a junior team called Young America. After disbanding in 1857, Creighton joined the Niagara club of Brooklyn, where he played second base. After making an impressive debut with his tricky delivery as a pitcher against the Star Club of Brooklyn, he was convinced to join the Star Club, where he continued to shine as a pitcher and hitter. The next season, however, with the chance to make money, Creighton joined the mighty Excelsiors, leading them to dominance over the next several years.[12]

Like many players of that era, Creighton played cricket, too. Chadwick greatly admired Creighton's talents and wrote how "not one player in five thousand has the capacity to fill all positions ably and to excel in each, the ability required being too great except for one like the admirable Creighton."[13]

Creighton's career was significant in many ways. His dominance as a pitcher was such that many believed his underhanded delivery was illegal.

Chadwick, in defense of Creighton, presented an analysis on the right-hander's style in an article published in the *Brooklyn Eagle*. Describing Creighton's mechanics, Chadwick, who was covering a match between the Excelsior club and the Putnam club, wrote:

> We have heard so much of late, in Base Ball circles, about the pitching of Creighton, of the Excelsior Club, and its fatal effect on the scores of those who bat against it, that we determined to judge of the matter for ourselves ... to ascertain whether he did pitch fairly or not, and whether his pitching was "jerk, an underhand throw," or a "fair square pitch," and the conclusion we arrived at was, that it was unquestionably the latter....[14]

Chadwick praised Creighton's ability to change speeds, and used Creighton's success as a pitcher when arguing that the "ideas of mere speed alone making a swiftly pitched ball a difficult one to hit" were "nonsense." Chadwick cited the Massachusetts game, which differed from baseball because it used overhand pitching rather than the underhand pitch. Chadwick wrote that in the Massachusetts game "the ball [is] *thrown* very swiftly to the bat and they are hit often enough by all." Chadwick added how "speed is not the difficulty." Chadwick, noting the efficacy of Creighton's pitching, wrote "that whenever [he] pitched his balls, [Creighton] delivered them from within a few inches of the ground, and they rose up above the batsman's hip, and when thus delivered, the result of hitting at the ball is either to miss it or send it high in the air."[15]

Creighton was the game's first professional player and truly its first superstar, though his career was short lived. Creighton died after collapsing during a game against the Union club from a wild swing that was suspected of rupturing his already-weak bladder, originally injured while playing cricket. Creighton was brought back to his father's residence on Henry Street in Brooklyn Heights, and died four days later, on October 18, 1862. The entire city of Brooklyn and those who played the game in and around New York mourned his death.[16]

In the October 25 edition of the *New York Clipper*, Chadwick paid homage to Creighton, writing:

> As a base ball player, Creighton had no equal. As a pitcher, he stood alone, and in his skill in batting and fielding, he never had a superior. In cricket too he excelled, taking rank as a first class batsman, and the swiftest bowler in the country. He was remarkably unassuming in his manners, and obliging and courteous in his demeanor, and was a favorite with all who knew him well.[17]

Because of his early demise, Creighton became an innovator in death. When he was buried, his teammates paid homage to their fellow club member by erecting an impressive baseball-themed monument over his grave in Green-Wood Cemetery. The monument was adorned with bats, bases and other related equipment etched onto the limestone surface and included a carved sphere that resembled a baseball on top. The design, weathered by time, still stands today, sans the ball. The monument served as "baseball's first off-the-field tourist destination and the game's first formal recognition of the greatness of one of its own."[18] It also served as a model for future monuments and plaques dedicated to those who made baseball great, later seen at Cooperstown, in the Baseball Hall of Fame, and even at Yankee Stadium's Monument Park.[19] It was to have an impact on Henry Chadwick, too, whose own monument at Green-Wood would be modeled to a large degree on that of the late great pitching ace.

Creighton's enormous talent was undeniable. Future athletes who were to dominate the game in the ensuing decades would try to emulate his greatness as a player, both as a hitter and pitcher. Despite his greatness, Creighton's lasting memory for baseball historians is his contribution as the game's first professional player. His employment showed the extent to which the Excelsiors — and most likely some other teams — were willing to go to win ball games. But it was only the beginning of the changes that were to come. Soon more clubs would begin to pay players as winning became tantamount to a team's fortunes. Some clubs would be more successful than others. Two of the more successful ball clubs were, of course, the Excelsiors and their rivals, the Atlantics. But it was the Excelsiors who were at this time the true innovators of the game. Aside from hiring the game's first player, they helped to popularize baseball outside of New York with a tour in the summer of 1860. Chadwick was prophetic when he boldly predicted, "it would add greatly to the advancement of the popularity of the game of base ball in every locality visited."[20] Henry Chadwick, in the *Eagle*, announced the itinerary:

> The plan is to arrange a series of matches with clubs in the interior, and play them in succession — starting from New York to Newburg, thence to Hudson, Poughkeepsie, and thence to Boston, Providence, New Haven, and, if circumstances permit, the excursion may be extended to Baltimore and Washington, stopping at Philadelphia on the way.[21]

Between their visit to New England and the South, the Excelsiors returned to Brooklyn to play the first of a best-of-three series with their archrival, the Atlantics, and won, 23–4. The Excelsiors took to the road

An 1865 woodcut celebrating the great Atlantic-Eckford match. One of the game's first stars, Jim Creighton (1841–1862), is memorialized at top. Chadwick is featured to the right and center (courtesy Rob Loeffler).

again and did in fact venture as far south as Baltimore, beating every hometown team along the way.

After they returned home to Brooklyn, the Excelsiors battled the Atlantics two more times. The Atlantics won the first game to even the series, but in the third and deciding game, played on the grounds of the Putnam club on Broadway and Greene Avenue in Brooklyn, with the Excelsiors leading the contest 8 to 6, their captain, Joseph Leggett, pulled his team from the field to protest the unruly Atlantic fans after several close calls. The games between these two clubs had become an intense rivalry attracting reportedly between 14,000 and 20,000 fans. Chadwick was clearly disturbed by the game being disrupted. He wrote that the rowdiness of the fans caused the game to end too quickly, and was "deeply regretted by the ball playing community, as it cannot but have an injurious effect on the best interests of the game."[22] Rather than comment further in the issue, which was first published in the September 1, 1860, issue of the *New York Clipper*, Chadwick waited until the following week. Remarking that many in the ball-playing community attributed these wild behaviors by the fans to betting, Chadwick added that while there was some merit to this point, the real reason behind the rowdiness was "the *spirit of faction*."[23] This was serious social commentary on the part of Chadwick, and very much in line with his upbringing and background. Chadwick continued on this point by adding:

> The factional spirit is the bane of every community wherein it is once allowed to obtain a foothold. It largely prevails in the politics of our country, giving rise to almost all the bitterness of party spirit and sectional strife. It is the great curse of our noble fire department, and is the sole cause of the evils that have let to the almost total abandonment of the self-sacrificing and manly volunteer force of the department ... its poisonous breath permeates through the lower strata of our heterogeneous population, with a pernicious effect that destroys every noble instinct of humanity, and imparts rapid growth to those human fungi knows as "Dead Rabbits" in New York, "Killers" in Philadelphia, and "Plug Uglies" in Baltimore, etc. It even invades the sanctuary of religion, imparting sectarian jealousies where peace and brotherly love should alone prevail.... Betting is a mere accessory evil — the chief conspirator is Faction.... The remedy of the evil lays in the *self control* of contending clubs and parties, *and in a strict adherence to the rules that guide the actions of a man of honor and a gentleman*, and those who cannot observe this line of conduct had better leave the manly recreation of Base Ball to others who can and will, or else the sooner the game becomes obsolete or better.[24]

What Chadwick was reacting to was the reality of political life in New York. This era was the period and heyday of Tammany Hall and Boss Tweed and political machines. In the spirit of reform, Chadwick wrote on its evils. Only several years earlier, a mayor imbued with the spirit of reform had been elected in New York. Fernando Wood, sworn in to the office on January 1, 1855, promised to clean up the city with frugality and establish public order. He promised to eliminate prostitution in lower Broadway and punish those who violated Sunday closing laws. Wood advocated among other things clean streets, sanitary police, and "metering of an expanded Croton water system, a new City Hall, a full size Central Park ... and creation of a great university and a free academy for young women."[25]

Despite all of his good intentions, the problem of factions still existed. The most glaring example of "*the spirit of faction*" that reflected Chadwick's concern were the draft riots of 1863. The U.S. Congress set off the draft riots with their passage of the National Conscription Act. The law, on the surface of it, was harmless. It gave government agents authority "to go house-to-house, enrolling all men aged twenty to thirty-five (and all unmarried men thirty-five to forty-five)." The twist, however, that ignited the riots was a kind of exemption that allowed those of means, certainly not working-class families, to buy there way out the draft. It gave citizens the right to purchase a substitute for $300. The riots, which occurred during the hot and humid days of summer, sparked passions as mostly poor, working-class white men, and in some cases women, ransacked the homes of the wealthy and turned their fury against blacks and others who held their ire. If it were not for the Union army, fresh from its victorious battle at Gettysburg, the riot would have continued.[26]

Therefore, the crowd behavior at the Atlantics-Excelsiors match was certainly in line with what was going on during that period, particularly the class struggles between rich and poor. Class was a factor at play during the important match between the two clubs, and certainly Chadwick was also commenting on the greater meaning of competition. Thus, not only did competition begin to have a greater connotation for the player, it also became of greater significance to the spectator. Oftentimes, fans reacted harshly if their local club lost, particularly if the contest involved two first-rate "nines."

Chadwick suggested that clubs set up an admission fee that would restrict attendance to middle-class spectators, admitting that a "twenty-five-cent charge for first-class contests [would not be] relished by the masses." He believed that hundreds of boys and roughs would be prohibited from attending the matches, "while the respectable patrons of the game are afforded better opportunities for enjoying a contest."[27] Though it did not eliminate fan interference, fights or crowd disturbances, charging admission to enclosed fields did improve accommodations for ladies, journalists, and the rest of the paying public.[28]

Chadwick's ideas on restricting ball game attendance were consistent with a general tendency in popular audiences for entertainment and his tendency for reform. During the 1860s and 1870s, like their baseball counterparts, theater owners attempted to attract a more respectable audience by enticing women to come to their shows. Theater owners ran matinees, periodically sponsored nights that allowed "ladies" to attend free, and offered household goods like flour, coal, and dress patterns as prizes in an effort to attract women and create a more respectable environment, free from violence and obscenity. The entrance of women into vaudeville and at ball games made these places a more suitable environment for the respectable public to enjoy its time.[29]

Chadwick noted the "great improvement" in the United States in the attendance of women at ballgames and attributed it to the "familiar intercourse with England, which has been brought about by the facilities afforded for transatlantic travel.... We now therefore see hundreds of ladies at base ball, cricket, and football matches during each season, and also at the best class of race courses, as in England."[30]

Gate receipts would help pay for new ballparks due to the building boom taking place within the cities. Chadwick also "urged clubs to acquire a permanent ground and to collect gate receipts on match days to defray the expenses of purchasing and maintaining the facility. This new system increased the chances that future contests would be played on a field clear of spectators, leading to fewer problems and crowd disturbances."[31]

Though no one emerged the victor in this first championship match, the Brooklyn Excelsiors had already established themselves as the preeminent club in baseball, that is "New York" baseball, and they along with the Atlantics and the Eckfords established Brooklyn, the home of Henry Chadwick, as the Mecca of the game. More importantly, the Excelsior tour was the first step toward making baseball a national, rather than a local, sport.[32] And before the Excelsiors toured various locales to show what New York "base ball" was all about, it was Henry Chadwick who paved the way as the leading baseball journalist writing about the "national game" in the publishing hub of the nation, New York City. Thus, it was the pioneering journalism of Henry Chadwick in this era that led to the development and growing popularity of baseball in the early decades, which were laying the seeds for the more competitive decades that followed.

Because of the journalism of Henry Chadwick in New York and Brooklyn and the Excelsior tour of the Northeast and Mid-Atlantic states, baseball teams began to pop up in other localities across the country. In late June 1866, *Wilkes' Spirit of the Times* reported on a ten-team tournament in Rockford, Illinois, the most important baseball tournament to take place outside of New York. The tournament included clubs from Milwaukee, Wisconsin; Chicago, Freeport, Forest City, Pecatonica and Rockford in Illinois; Detroit and Julian from Michigan; and Dubuque from Iowa. There were eleven prizes awarded, ranging from "the Norman Prize," a magnificent golden ball given to the winning club of the tournament, to the eleventh, "the worst beaten club," named the Chandler and Humphrey Prize, "a horn given to these contestants so that they may be enabled to blow their own trumpet and so they will be independent of outside praise."[33]

Another important aspect regarding these games, aside from the fact that they demonstrated the popularity of baseball, was the spotlight cast on a fifteen-year-old pitcher who demonstrated the dominance of a seasoned veteran. Little did those in attendance realize that this individual would come to dominate baseball as a player, manager, owner, sporting goods entrepreneur and spokesman over the next five decades. Young Albert Goodwill Spalding may have been in his mid-teens, but he led his Forest City nine of Rockford, Illinois, in a surprising upset.

The following year, on July 25, 1867, at Dexter Park in Chicago, Spalding, only sixteen, led the Rockford team to another upset victory over the touring Washington Nationals club that featured Harry Wright's brother, George, at shortstop. More importantly, it was at this match that Spalding met Henry Chadwick for the first time. Chadwick had been acting as official scorer and was at the game because he was accompanying the Nationals on tour. Chadwick joined the Nationals after being named an honorary member on September 24, 1866. Chadwick came away impressed with the young man and the two began a friendship that would prove to be vital to the development of baseball for over forty years.

The Chadwick and Spalding connection was one that would develop complications as the years passed, largely due to their differences in temperament. Over the next several years, as Spalding transformed himself from athlete, to manager, to sporting goods entrepreneur and baseball executive, and lastly to promoter of an inane, but effective, theory of baseball's ancestry, the friendship suffered strains and complications. Some of it had to do with differences in temperament, age and ideology; some of it had to do with Chadwick, who in some ways was a mentor to the young boy, switching roles when he later became an employee of Spalding's. Still, despite whatever problems existed between the two, both maintained a deep respect for each another and for what the other had done for the game. Chadwick certainly admired Spalding's many talents. Chadwick described Spalding as "a model professional pitcher," one "who is [one] of the most gentlemanly and intelligent players of his class." Spalding, Chadwick later wrote, was "of thorough integrity of character, quiet demeanor, and of marked executive ability, even outside of this special position he stands as a most credible exemplar of the national game."[34] Spalding, for his part, certainly had respect for Chadwick's contributions and was among the many who called Henry Chadwick the game's father. Spalding spoke fondly of Chadwick's integrity:

Mr. Chadwick always stood for the best in Base Ball, and his trenchant pen could always be depended upon to aid in raising the moral standard of the game, and [he] was utterly opposed to anything that would tend to drag it down.[35]

Spalding credited Chadwick with nursing the game in its infancy, and recognized how the dean of sports writers was there to help baseball grow as it emerged as the national game of America.

When Chadwick connected with the young, promising right-handed pitcher from Illinois, he was also taking part in an historical tour of the Washington Nationals club. This tour proved to be an extremely important factor in further popularizing the game and for laying the seeds for competition between east and west. Chadwick toured with the Nationals, the first club comprised of all-stars recruited for the purpose of winning ball games. Not only were the Nationals comprised of the likes of some of the game's best players, they had the benefit of being covered by the most prominent baseball journalist in the country. The Nationals wanted the best, not only for its play on the field, but also in its coverage of the game.

Chadwick's connection to the Nationals dated back to the previous year. It was through his relationship with the club and its leader, Senator Arthur P. Gorman, that Chadwick met President Andrew Johnson in late August 1865, only four months after the Tennessean ascended to the office. Already having been graced to be in the same theater as Johnson's more famous predecessor, Chadwick, who was journeying with the touring Brooklyn Atlantics, was brought into the audience chamber to be introduced. Chadwick was last in line as each Atlantic player was formally presented to Johnson by name, shaking his hand, "retiring in the same order."[36] After finally shaking President Johnson's hand, Chadwick remarked to the American leader that "the ball-players had hoped to have seen him present at the tournament." Johnson respectfully replied that "his time was in such constant demand that he could scarcely call a moment his own and he regretted not being able to witness the game." After the president admitted that the Atlantics had "whipped" the host team "pretty badly," Chadwick told the president that the Brooklyn Excelsiors would be visiting Washington in September and "expressed hope that the President would favor them with a visit, if but for a few minutes, as such countenance of the game would give a national stamp to it which would greatly promote its popularity." Johnson responded by promising, if schedule allowed, his presence at "the occasion." After these remarks, Johnson thanked Chadwick and the Atlantics "for the honor" of their visit, and the meeting ended.[37]

Chadwick and the Atlantics' historic visit with President Johnson helped to set the stage for the connection between baseball and the oval office. Chadwick's request, in and of itself, was an historic act. And while the president did not appear at the Excelsior game, he later attended a match between the New York Mutuals and the Washington Nationals in August 1867 and was named an honorary member of the New York nine and given a badge of membership.[38] Johnson, despite his political woes, was truly the first president to have an undisputable connection with the game.

Clearly, the city of Washington, D.C., thanks to the Nationals, had become the first city outside of New York to have a significant role in baseball. Years before their innovative tour, the Nationals had the distinction of being the first club formed south of New Jersey. The Nationals were founded in 1859 by federal government employees who had, like their counterparts in New York, Brooklyn and New Jersey, decided to form a team for the sake of "deserting taverns and the Willard and Ebbitt Hotel bars" for the invigorating exercise of baseball in the outdoors.[39] Modeling themselves on the baseball clubs of New York, the National club developed their rules which involved laws that required their members to be "exemplary and polite" in keeping with the morals and propriety that Chadwick had always advocated in his well-known writings on both cricket and baseball. Among the rules established to keep each member in line were such laws as a 10-cent fine for profanity and a quarter for disputing an umpire's call.[40] These laws were common among the clubs forming at the time and were in keeping with the Chadwickian philosophy of substituting the invigorating sport of baseball for the bar room and keeping the game clean and a gentleman's sport. Thus clubs were highly influenced by Chadwick's call for propriety.

One of the most important members of the organization was a 22-year-old messenger named Arthur Pue Gorman. Gorman later became an important political figure. He would eventually rise to become a United States Senator from Maryland, but equally important, he became a member of the most controversial committee put together in baseball history. Gorman became a member of the Mills Commission, established in the early 1900s by Spalding to determine baseball's origins.

During this era, however, Gorman was just beginning to establish himself in baseball, starting with his role with the Nationals. Originally elected as the team's secretary in 1859, Gorman during the 1860s rose to the club's presidency. His rise in political status within the club coincided with his political career outside the club, as he was appointed postmaster of the United States Senate. By 1867, Gorman became the president of the National Association of Base Ball Players, an important appointment signifying that the game was spreading not only north, but also south. Gorman's rise to the association's presidency showed how much respect the Northern clubs had for Gorman's ability as well as for his National club.[41]

Chadwick had great admiration for Gorman's organizational ability and wrote a glowing biographical portrait of Gorman in the July 11, 1867, edition of *The Ball Players' Chronicle*. Remarking on Gorman's rise to the presidency of the National Association, Chadwick wrote:

> A better man could not have been selected, or a more judicious choice made. An ardent admirer and most liberal supporter of the game; familiar from his years of service at the capital with parliamentary ruling, personally esteemed by all his acquaintances, and warmly regarded by his friends, no man occupied a more popular position or exercised more influence in the fraternity than Mr. Gorman.[42]

Chadwick's admiration of Gorman did not go unrequited. A letter signed by Gorman, who was serving as a member the Committee of Rules and Regulations of the National Association, heaped praise on Chadwick's contribution to the game. Only ten years after Chadwick's chance encounter with the game at Elysian Fields, Gorman, Dr. Joseph B. Jones, chairman of the committee, and several others sent Chadwick a public letter that read:

> NEW YORK, December 12, 1866
> *To the Base Ball Fraternity at Large:*
>
> We, the undersigned, members of the Committee on Rules and Regulations of the National Association of Base Ball Players, having known Mr. Henry Chadwick as an experienced and impartial reporter of the game for the past ten years and having been associated with him in the Committee of Rules, of which he has been a prominent member for several successive years, hereby indorse him as a competent authority on all questions appertaining to base ball and, especially, as an author of commentaries on the rules of the game; and we heartily commend his existing publications on base ball as standard works on the subject. We also especially recommend his last work, entitled "The Base Ball Player's Book of Reference," as a book that should be in the hands of every member of the fraternity.
> [Signed]

J.B. Jones, M.D., President of the Excelsior Club,
  Brooklyn, and Chairman of the Committee
Peter O'Brien, of the Atlantic Club,
D.W.C. Moore, President of the Eclectic Club, New York.
A.P. Gorman, President of the National Club, Washington.
Thomas G. Voorris, President of the Empire Club, New York.
Charles E. Thomas, of the Eureka Club, Newark.
Mortimer Rogers, of the Lowell Club, Boston.[43]

Clearly, Chadwick's place on the committee was unique. Unlike the others, Chadwick was not a baseball player. He kept a healthy distance from the game. This distance from the game is the root of Chadwick being the "father" of the game. Rather than being involved as an athlete, Chadwick chose the role of journalist and outside observer. The members of the rules committee absolutely had an appreciation for Chadwick's contributions and certainly understood his standing in the press. Chadwick was virtually the only man publishing baseball manuals, instructional handbooks and guides. His was clearly the voice of the game. Chadwick certainly had the ability to recognize the others strengths, particularly Gorman's. Gorman's rise to the National Association's presidency had much to do with his daring ability to arrange matches between his National club and its northeast opponents. Chadwick credited Gorman with assisting the National club to increase "in strength and influence."[44] Chadwick added that the 1866 tour of the East cast Gorman, his club and its players "in the most favorable light before the whole Northern fraternity."[45] The Nationals, Chadwick wrote, were dubbed the "Champion of the South," for the respect garnered by their tour of the Northeast. On that excursion the Nationals challenged and lost to the mighty Brooklyn Atlantics and Philadelphia Athletics. But their most notable loss was against the Excelsiors.

On Thursday, July 5, 1866, the Nationals would take on the Brooklyn Excelsiors, the club that had been led by James Creighton earlier in the decade. Billed as "one of the most recherché affairs of the kind ever gotten up on similar occasion," the date between the Nationals and the Excelsiors was not typical.[46] Chadwick took part in this special day and journeyed with the two clubs to Green-Wood cemetery in Brooklyn to visit Creighton's gravesite.

The day began early, "with the Reception Committee of the Excelsiors waited upon their guest [the Nationals] at the Astor House, and took them in charge. Some twenty barouches had been provided for the occasion," where the Excelsiors and Chadwick took the Nationals on a brief tour through "the City of Churches." The tour stopped at the graveyard, where "a silent tear was dropped to the memory of the lamented James Creighton, whose beautiful monument is a prominent feature of the city of the dead."[47] It was an extremely emotional moment for all involved. It must have been particularly sad for Chadwick, whose parents and two dead children were already buried at the cemetery. As mentioned earlier, the get-together came only one year after the Civil War, so what transpired at the graveyard added a touch of poignancy. After leaving the grounds, Chadwick, both ball clubs and other dignitaries visited some of the wealthier residents of Brooklyn, such as "Van Brunt Wycoff, where they were 'wined and dined.'" Chadwick and the rest of the entourage certainly were treated like foreign dignitaries, even though Chadwick was a local figure. His association with the Nationals as an honorary member of the club made him part of both the visiting and home audience. Although there were plenty of activities during the early part of the day, there was a game to be played. By 3:35 P.M., the match between the Excelsiors and Nationals commenced at the Capotiline grounds in Bedford, Brooklyn. A high-scoring affair, the Excelsiors defeated their guests, 46–33.

After the match, everyone was led "to the club-room of the Excelsiors," on Fulton Street, opposite Brooklyn's City Hall. They remained there until 9 P.M., when on foot or horse-drawn carriage, "they journeyed to the Mansion House where entertainment was furnished surpassing everything of a similar kind in the annals of Base Ball."[48] There was much singing and great revelry at the event. Several guests made speeches, one by the Reverend Matthew Hale Smith. Smith spoke, with Chadwick surely nodding in agreement, about how the church needed to support manly games, outdoor sports, particularly "base ball." He added that much work had to be done to unify a nation torn apart by the Civil War. The reverend added that the National Base Ball Convention could act as a "bond which would keep close together North, South, East and West, for in this game there could be no distinction."[49] Others spoke on a variety of different subjects before there came a toast to the press. As its most senior representative, Chadwick said:

> May the Athletic game of Base Ball by the *Keystone* in building up the physique of America; may *Excelsior* be the motto of our National Game, and may the fraternity be ever ready to defend the Union and uphold liberty from *Gotham* to the *Pacific*.[50]

There was certainly hope that baseball could be the very solution to all the sectional problems that remained only one year after the end of the Civil War. The country was still grieving over a murdered president, was still recovering from all the carnage from the deadly war that had killed or severely injured thousands of young men from both the North and South. By paying tribute to a fallen player, a twenty-one-year-old man who had died on the battlefield of baseball, the players were paying homage to their "soldier" who had helped to bring baseball to a higher level.

While the Nationals continued on their tour of the East, they were eventually able to avenge their defeat to the Excelsiors in October. The Nationals defeated the Brooklyn Excelsiors, 36–30, winning the highly acclaimed "trophy ball." It was between their defeat to the Excelsiors in July and their victory over the Excelsiors in October that the Nationals made Henry Chadwick an honorary member of the club.

> Washington D.C.
> Sept. 25th 1866
>
> Mr. Henry Chadwick
>
> Sir
>
> I take
>
> Great pleasure in informing you
> That at a special meeting of "National B.B. Club."
> Held last evening, you was unan-
> Imously elected an honorary member of Same.
> Trusting the above may
> Be acceptable to you I have the
> Honor to subscribe myself
> Very respectively yours
> Mr. A. Tappen
> Rec Secy[51]

Having Chadwick, a representative in the press, as an honorary member would be important because Chadwick would represent the club at association meetings. Rather than send a member from Washington up to New York, Chadwick would be their point man. Having Chadwick as an honorary member was also symbolic of the extent the Nationals would go to make their club as competitive as possible.

Those games with the eastern clubs served as preparation for the Nationals and showed them what they needed to do to build a winning nine. Hiring Chadwick was part of this program. Perhaps it was during these games with clubs from the East Coast that the Nationals came up with the idea of a new tour. Of course, the Brooklyn Excelsiors had helped popularize the game with their initial go-round of the Northeast. But this would be a new tour, one that would take the Nationals west, not north. In 1867 Gorman and Colonel Frank Jones, the former Union officer who had risen to become Washington's new club president, hatched a plan with the idea of touring the Midwest rather than rehashing another tour of the Northeast. The tour, however, would not be with the same players. The Nationals, led by Gorman and Jones, successfully recruited some of New York's finest to play with the team, among them Harry Wright's younger brother, twenty-year-old shortstop George Wright of the Bronx's Morrisania team, the Brooklyn Excelsiors' catcher Frank Norton, and his teammate, first baseman George Fletcher.

While other Brooklyn and New York players were brought aboard the team to bolster its reputation, another important figure in New York baseball circles was brought in to be the public relations voice of the tour. Henry Chadwick was baseball's premier journalist, and as discussed previously, was recruited to go along with the other great players of New York. His role in the tour of the West symbolized the extent the Nationals were taking to make an all-star team. If the Nationals were intent on recruiting the best players, why not recruit the game's premier writer to promote tour? After all, Chadwick was already an honorary member of the team; why not bring him along to spread the gospel of the National club tour? Chadwick by then had conceived his own publication, *The Ball Players' Chronicle*, which was used to promote the tour. Though the *Chronicle* only lasted for two years, changing its name after the first year to the *American Chronicle of Sports and Pastimes*, the paper played a pivotal role in giving life to the Nationals' excursion to the Midwest. The *Chronicle* was the first weekly publication dedicated to *"the Interests of the American Game of Base Ball and Kindred Sports of the Field,"* and it helped baseball, in a sense, receive a level of attention that it had not previously. Why it did not succeed in the long run may have had something to do with it being ahead of its time. While baseball and other sports were becoming part of American society, the game and sports in general had not become so engrained in the society to warrant a dedicated weekly journal. In the future, journals or magazines that specialized in sports would find tremendous followings and have great success in American culture. Today, there are numerous publications as well as many television and cable shows dedicated solely to sports. What Chadwick was doing with *The Ball Players' Chronicle* was decades and perhaps even a century ahead of its time.

In the *Chronicle*, Chadwick not only wrote about the tour, he provided the latest information "to other traveling journalists from the *New York Times, New York Mercury* and *New York Clipper*." Because of Chadwick, "the Nationals tour was to get press coverage that far exceeded anything ever done in sports before," eclipsing the coverage of previous baseball tours.[52]

Chadwick accompanied the Nationals for the entire trip and seemed to report every nook and cranny of the tour. Chadwick was clearly excited about traveling out west with the Nationals and was on the 4 P.M. train that departed for the West on July 11, 1867.[53] He described how he and the other "excursionists left the Washington train at the Relay House and took the express train from Baltimore for Cincinnati, having a car to themselves." Chadwick recorded that on their way through Columbus, Ohio, the train passed a number of sites "made historic by the [Civil War]." Chadwick's train trip took him past "Harper's Ferry, Martinsburg, Cheat Mountain, and Grafton." Chadwick remembered how he, along with the rest of the touring party, took breakfast at Grafton and by noon "they arrived at Belair, three miles [south of] Wheeling [West Virginia] where they crossed the river in a steamer and entered a special car provided for [us] on the Central Ohio Railroad." The trip out west, to Columbus, Ohio, was long and grueling, a journey of 550 miles that took twenty-four hours to complete. After the trip was over, Chadwick and the others went right to bed after "due ablutions and refreshment," though some of the players, Chadwick wrote, attended a Japanese-themed performance at the Opera House.[54]

The tour was so exciting and eventful that a song was written about it. Here is "The Song of the Washington National Nine: Westward Ho":

Come all ye jolly Nationals, and fill your glasses up.
Success to all who toss the ball be this our parting cup;
Our banner floats the breeze upon our comrades wait below,
Farewell awhile to Washington, we're going westward ho.

Chorus: We're going westward ho, we're going westward ho
Farewell awhile to Washington, we're going westward ho.

Amid the Valley of the west are brothers true and tried,
Who stretch a hand to welcome us across the prairies wide;
We'll play them all a friendly game, a tho' but short our stay
We hope to leave some friends behind and take some balls away.

Chorus: We're going westward ho,' we're going westward ho.
Success to all who toss the ball, we're going westward ho.

We know our catcher is all "Wright," our nine good fellows all
And if the umpire don't get tight we need not lose a ball;

Our Fox will gobble up their "fowls" and such their goose eggs too;
And if our "Eb" should miss a ball, why "Ed" will put it through.

Chorus

Our pitcher holds enough for all, he's hard to "crack," they'll find;
He never pitched the losing ball when "Johnnie" played behind
And when our bases all get full we will not care for that,
We know the boys will all "come home" when "Windmill" takes the bat.

Chorus

With "George the Third" the field to play, and "Pete" to lend a hand
Fresh balls and laurels every day will greet our little band
We'll take no heavy hearts along, no faces grave and blue
For while the Colonel's at the helm he's bound to put us thro'

Chorus

And when our battles all are fought, and all our games are mon
We'll turn our faces east again and make our last home run;
And tho' no more our flag will raise where western waters flow
We'll ne'er forget the jolly days when we went westward ho

Chorus: When we went westward ho, when we went westward ho;
We'll ne'er forget the jolly days when we went westward ho.[55]

The tour took the Nationals to many stops. Cincinnati, which within a few years would field the first all-professional team, taking its cue from the Nationals, in retrospect would be one of the most interesting opponents. The Cincinnati club, later called the Red Stockings, was easily handled by the Nationals, 53–10. Chadwick reported an exchange worthy of note during this match, a testament to his skills as a reporter for making light of a fascinating exchange between George Wright, the Nationals' second baseman, and his brother, Harry Wright, the pitcher of the Cincinnati club. Chadwick wrote that it was "amusing to see the pair face to face." There was even some testy dialogue between the two.

> "There you are, are you," said Harry. "I am here," replied George, knocking the home base with his bat, "and I don't want any of your nonsense; so just give us a ball, will yer?" Whereupon Harry sent him one, and away it was sent along the ground in cricket style, as Harry expected, and George secured his first.[56]

The Nationals continued their domination over the western clubs, demolishing their counterparts with lopsided numbers. One victory that demonstrated the Nationals' superior play against their western opponents was an overwhelming win over the Capitals club of Columbus by the score of 90–10. Of course, the Nationals' tour was an exceptional and highly influential event. Their many victories and their lone defeat (at the hands of Spalding's Rockford club) had a profound influence on baseball's popularity in its westward spread throughout the United States. However, not every game went according to plan. And perhaps that was a good thing, for it led to some animus between the eastern press, led by Chadwick, and the western press. The Rockford club's upset over the Nationals created quite a stir in the Chicago papers. The hometown press in Chicago had a lot to crow about; after all, no one expected the Nationals to lose a game, especially to a club such as the Rockford nine. The *Chicago Times* and the other papers had much to say on the subject. Chadwick was irate. Segments of the *Chicago Times* article were included by Chadwick in the August 8 edition of *The Ball Players' Chronicle*. The clip stated that:

> When the Nationals shall have lived among us a few days, imbibed pure water from the clear depths of Lake Michigan, breathed the brawny breezes from the Prairie and taken a few lessons in base ball playing, they will begin to realize how profitable has been their trip to the North![57]

Chadwick also pointed out how the other Chicago-based papers had their fun with the National loss, too. But Chadwick and the Nationals responded to their loss to the Rockford club with a rousing drubbing of the Chicago Excelsior club (not to be confused the Brooklyn-based team), the best team in the West at that time, by the lopsided score of 49–4, deflating the Chicago fans' hopes of defending their reign in the region. Chadwick reacted to all this "braggadocio style" of the Chicago press by saying that the arrogance on behalf of the Excelsiors had merely inspired the Nationals to play harder than they had before "to offset their loss with a victory so signal as to make it a surprise how they were ever defeated."[58]

Chadwick related how the Nationals' win came as a great relief to all those involved with the tour and served as quite a contrast to their emotions following the Forest City debacle, given the fact that "their friends in Washington, after their brilliant achievements in the previous games, had backed them heavily to win every game of the tourney."[59] The Nationals, newly crowned as the champions of the West, were "curious to see what the Chicago editors would now have to say after their premature braggadocio over the Forest City victory."[60] Chadwick described the attacks on his Nationals team after their loss to the Rockford club as "undignified, discourteous, and more like village newspapers than metropolitan journals." While Chadwick reported that the articles about the Excelsiors-

Nationals games by the Chicago press were fair and correct, the editorials, however, continued with their diatribe against the newly crowned western champions. Chadwick was clearly incensed. The editorials now accused the Nationals of being paid players and throwing the game against the clearly inferior Rockford club. Chadwick blamed the Chicago press of picking up the "rumor started by disappointed gamblers and blacklegs" when they accused the Nationals of throwing the game for the purpose of "winning heavy bets on the second match." Rather than giving the Nationals credit for their hard-earned victory, the Chicago press instead accused the Chicago Excelsiors of being "the greatest muffs in the country."[61]

A clearly rattled Chadwick accused the Chicago press of ignorance and not knowing or understanding the vagaries of baseball. He reminded the Chicago press "that the strongest clubs sometimes play the poorest games when least expected, and that the weakest nines sometimes do the very reverse."[62] Chadwick reported that after reading the accusations made in the paper, both Gorman and Colonel Jones, the ex-president and president of the Nationals nine, confronted the *Tribune* and *Republican* "to ask an explanation of the libelous charges made." The *Tribune*, after discovering that the charges against the Nationals were false, "wrote an *amende honorable*" the following Monday. The *Tribune* admitted that accusing the National club of throwing the game "was an entire mistake, and that the members of the Club are neither 'professional' players nor gamblers, but merely clerks in the Departments, and citizens of Washington, of exemplary character."[63]

The *Tribune* made an honest effort at apologizing, but were they incorrect in accusing the Nationals of being a professional team? Dating back to Creighton, it was common practice in baseball to hire players the way the Nationals did, giving each a position in Washington and paying them for their services while playing baseball for "free." George Wright was given the position of being a "clerk" in Washington on 238 Pennsylvania Avenue; Frank Norton was a "clerk" in the Treasury. With the exception of two who were law students, all the Washington players were hired as "clerks" when, in fact, the real reason they came to Washington was to play baseball. While the accusation of the Nationals throwing the game against the Rockford club may have been false, the accusation that they were professionals certainly was not.[64]

In the meantime, while the *Tribune* was making its apologies to the Nationals, the editor of the *Republican* newspaper denied hurting the reputations of the Nationals. In response, Colonel Jones and Henry Chadwick wrote letters defending the Washington nine. Jones, like Chadwick, had asserted the notion that the "boastful editorials in the Chicago papers ... had much to do with our victory ... as they proved a powerful incentive to extra exertions." As for the accusation that the Nationals were a team of paid professionals, Jones went so far as to list every occupation of each player in an effort to diffuse any notion that the Washington club was paying each one directly for his efforts. Chadwick chimed in as well.

Writing to the *Republican*, Chadwick wrote that his "object being to relieve the game from the stigma the editorials attach to it." For Chadwick, the man who throughout his days of covering baseball had fought the evils of hippodroming and gambling, this matter was of particular poignance. "The evil of gambling," he wrote, "is one I have battled with for years as the most potent evil the game has to contend with." Chadwick added:

> Under no circumstances would I countenance a club who either engaged in such a practice or whose object was to make base ball playing a business or a means of subsistence. Knowing the National Club to be governed by gentlemen who have the best interests of the game at heart, and being aware that one of their objects in taking this tour was to extend the popularity of the game westward, I accompanied the club to duly chronicle the games in the columns of the metropolitan journals with which I am connected; and throughout the tour I have yet to see the first action of any member of the club evidencing with any desire to make the contests [financially] advantageous to themselves or their club, or in any way to countenance the evil of heavy betting, which you very properly condemn.[65]

Chadwick made the additional point of emphasizing the ball playing skills of the Nationals had been admired and respected by all the editors and journals of the other cities they "visited until they reached Chicago; and here for the first time, [he] regretted to state, they first meet with boastful comments over a defeat sustained under peculiar circumstances, and lastly, are charged with fraudulent conduct when victory rewards them in an honorably fought battle."[66]

Chadwick's comments regarding the Nationals' defeat by the Rockford nine were even-handed. In the editorial to the *Republican*, Chadwick wrote that the Nationals' loss was as much due to their overconfidence and of "natural sequence" than it was to their poor play. Not wanting to portray the Nationals as being immoral or even unprepared, he credited the Rockford nine as being "not only stronger than ever, but played a better game than they ever did, while they had the advantage of everything to win and nothing to lose — an important aid to success in all contests."[67]

In his letter to the *Republican*, Chadwick also had high praise for the Excelsior club to counter the criticisms of the Chicago press, which had accused the Chicago nine of poor play. In his conclusion, Chadwick hoped that these "explanatory remarks, which I have been called upon to make in the interest of the game," would remove from doubt the "unjust impression created by the mistaken editorial comments on the play of the National Club."[68]

In response to Chadwick and Jones' letter, the *Republican* put forth an explanation. Commenting on Jones' letter, specifically with regard to the accusation that the Nationals were really a "professional" club, the paper held its ground. The *Republican* described Colonel Jones' letter as being written in an "excited style" and that his response merely was to provide a list of the occupations of the Nationals.

> It is not in any sense of the word a reply to our comments ... showing that they are nearly all engaged in some of the official Departments at Washington, and that they are not "professionals."[69]

In response to Chadwick's letter, the *Republican* was more flattering, writing that Chadwick's reaction was "more temperate in its tone, and better calculated to aid the cause it represents."[70]

With that, the tour of the "amateur" Washington Nationals was over. The three-week tour was a complete success and Chadwick was happy to be home, once again at his desk at 102 Nassau Street in Manhattan, the home of *The Ball Players' Chronicle*.[71] For Chadwick, it had been a great opportunity to expose himself first-hand to the talent and caliber of play of the western clubs. Rather than remain sheltered in his nest in the East, particularly with the New York and Brooklyn talents, he was able to journey west and see the sights of some of the western talent and competition, which must have made Chadwick feel especially proud. After all, what he was able to do in helping to promote the game was paying off. And even though he got involved in a small melee with the Chicago press, he was able to lay the foundation for a rivalry between east and west while laying the groundwork for all future frictions that proved helpful in making baseball popular and intriguing. Within the next few years, there would be a complete shift from eastern dominance to western dominance thanks to the groundwork made by the Nationals' tour. Now, the West had to figure out a way in which it could advance in the game.

Though it was increasingly clear with the greater competition that the players would, in fact, have to be paid for their work on the field, it was not until 1869 that the first openly all-professional team was formed. Under the leadership of former Knickerbocker Harry Wright, the Cincinnati Red Stockings became the first all-salaried baseball team, exemplifying the more competitive atmosphere emerging in the sport. Wright, like Chadwick, was British born and weaned on cricket. And like Chadwick, Wright was known for his great honesty and temperate habits: he did not swear, drink or smoke.[72] But William Henry Wright, who was born in Sheffield, England, on January 10, 1835, took a different path to baseball gentlemen than the dean of baseball writers.

While Chadwick's career in baseball came from writing, Wright was a player, an athlete who excelled at the outdoor games, namely the games of cricket and baseball. Before entering the sporting world of New York, Wright had left the New York City public school system at 14 to help support his parents and three brothers and sister by working as a jeweler, apprenticing at Tiffany's, the old bric-a-brac store that had become the premier jewelry store in town. The following year, like his father had in England, he began playing professional cricket. Harry joined the St. George Cricket Club of Staten Island in 1850, quickly developing a reputation as the best round-arm bowler — the position most similar to baseball's pitcher — in the United States. Eventually, Wright was drawn to baseball. He joined his first club, the innovators of the New York game, the famous Knickerbockers, in 1858. That year, Wright put his skills on display in the Fashion Course Games for the New York side, taking part in their two games-to-one victory over Brooklyn.

In the spring of 1866, Wright left New York for Cincinnati. He was to play with and instruct the Union cricket team, but soon realized baseball's popularity and immense profit-making potential. Wright claimed that the public would gladly pay "seventy-five cents to a dollar-fifty to go to the theatre, and [that] numbers prefer base ball to theatricals." In July 1866, Wright left the Unions to work for Aaron B. Champion's baseball club, becoming its captain and financial administrator. Wright may have gotten the idea of putting together the best players in the summer of 1867 when he saw his Red Stockings lose to the all-star laden Washington Nationals. The twist, however, was that Wright's team would be openly professional, hired for the purpose of winning, whereas the Nationals went under the guise of an amateur team that was indirectly paying its players for the purpose of being a successful team.

During the winter of 1867-1868, the Red Stockings, led by Wright and Champion, who endeavored to put western baseball on a par with eastern baseball, lured several players from the East with pay: pitcher/ outfielder Asa Brainard (the namesake for the term "Ace" pitcher), third baseman Fred Waterman and outfielder Johnny Hatfield. These acquisitions allowed the Red Stockings to dominate their cross-town rivals, the Buckeyes, and soon began their quest to become a great force in the baseball world by going on a tour of the East.[73]

The emergence of the Red Stockings as a professional team altered the balance of power in baseball from New York/Brooklyn and even Washington in the East to Cincinnati in the West. By 1869, due to Cincinnati's ability to "hire" the best players, the Red Stockings became the most dominant team in the country. It would be several decades before a team from the New York area would dominate the game the way the Brooklyn clubs had in the late fifties and early sixties.

Harry Wright, baseball's first strategist and businessman. Photograph circa 1870 (Baseball Hall of Fame Library, Cooperstown, New York).

Though Chadwick was initially apprehensive about the professionalization of the game, in hindsight he was able to recognize the contribution that professional baseball, and thus Harry Wright, made to the game. Chadwick later wrote that Wright's creation of professional baseball "elevated" the game. He noted that the "amateur class," because of its inability to devote time and effort to perfect its abilities, could not raise its level of play and make the necessary improvements the game needed during its development. Chadwick wrote how baseball "would have stood still and never advanced beyond the point of the amateur displays on the field of the early sixties but for the inauguration of the professional methods started by the Cincinnati Club under Harry Wright's management."[74]

Thanks to Harry Wright and Aaron B. Champion, baseball had reached the Midwest. If there was any doubt that "base ball" had become the National Pastime, they were laid to rest with the dominance and popularity of the Cincinnati club. The Red Stockings, who perhaps had modeled their tour on the Excelsiors, went undefeated for more than an entire year and amassed an eighty-seven-game winning streak. But there was something even more significant about what Wright had shown the baseball world; he proved that baseball could be managed as a successful business. Wright also demonstrated the growing rift in baseball between clubs that were playing simply for the sake of outdoor recreation versus clubs that were professional, those that were championship-oriented.

Though Henry Chadwick had some reservations about the more competitive game, it was the more competitive professional baseball that facilitated an increased role for him as an observer and an expert within the sport. With games becoming business oriented, clubs began to realize that the press played a significant role in promoting their sport and would facilitate the access of journalists as they journeyed with clubs on extensive tours, as in the case of the Washington Nationals' tour. Journalists like Chadwick and others would provide "play by play accounts of the games and details of the travel and social aspects of the trip."[75] As ball games took on more meaning, baseball would need now more than ever the likes of Henry Chadwick to report on the game. Because there was no television nor radio in existence, journalists like Chadwick became the voice of baseball. What is more important, however, they would need the likes of Chadwick to seriously enforce the rules.

According to legend, as written by Albert Spalding in his overly dramatic early history of the game, *Base Ball: America's National Game*, Chadwick played a decisive role in the outcome in one of the most controversial games in baseball's early history. The undefeated Red Stockings of Cincinnati, led by their great leader, Harry Wright, were in Brooklyn to battle the semi-professional Brooklyn Atlantics. The Atlantics, of course, had been one of the most successful clubs of the 1860s, one of three great teams that had dominated New York baseball. The game took place in June of 1870 at the Capitoline Grounds in Brooklyn in front of a packed and boisterous crowd. With the score tied at 5 to 5 after nine innings of play, the Atlantic team

JULY 3, 1869.]   HARPER'S WEEKLY.   421

THE PICKED NINE OF THE "RED STOCKING" BASE-BALL CLUB, CINCINNATI, OHIO.—PHOT. BY E. L. HUFF, 344 BROAD STREET, NEWARK, N.J.—[SEE PAGE 422.]

The mighty Cincinnati Red Stockings of 1869, baseball's first openly all-professional club, in *Harper's Weekly* (courtesy Rob Loeffler).

gathered up their bats, and the crowd, assuming that the game had ended with a draw, were preparing to leave the grounds, when Harry Wright, captain and manager of the Reds ... protested to the umpire that the game was not ended. He knew that the rules required a tie game, under such circumstances, to be continued.[76]

A brief argument followed between the Atlantic captain, Robert Ferguson, who was happy enough to have played the world champions to a tie, and Wright, who wanted desperately to win and to continue the streak. Both captains pleaded their case to the umpire. When the umpire and the two captains failed to reach a decision, they turned the question to Henry Chadwick, chairman of the Committee of Rules of the NABBP, who immediately agreed with Wright, and the game resumed.[77]

In the *Clipper*, Henry Chadwick, however, explained that the umpire had actually left the field thinking he had heard Wright consenting to the tie. Then Chadwick wrote:

On consulting the rules in reference to a similar case, it was found that if either captain refused to consent to a tie game at the close of the ninth inning being considered a drawn game, then the party refusing to continue to play loses the game by forfeit and by a score of 9 to 0. When it was found also, that the Red Stockings stuck to their posts and that if the Atlantics did not soon take their places the umpire would declare the game forfeited. [Robert] Ferguson [captain of the Atlantics] got out his men again and the game resumed.[78]

The game remained tied until the top of the eleventh inning when the Red Stockings took the lead with two runs. Cincinnati now led, 7–5. At this point it looked as though Wright's protests in the ninth would lead to yet another victory for the Red Stockings. But as Henry Chadwick had pointed out, "If there is one feature of our national game of ball more than any other which specially commends it to popularity, it is the fact of the glorious uncertainty attendant upon it."[79]

In a stunning rally, the Atlantics came back with the help of baseball's tenth man: the crowd. Brooklyn fans and New York fans have always been reputed as some of the rowdiest. As there were no enclosed stadiums with fences to prevent fans from running onto the field nor formal rules to deter fan interference, the Atlantics made Wright rue the day he returned to his home, the place where he began his baseball career. With the Atlantics trailing by two runs, and with exhaustion and pressure mounting on Cincinnati's ace, Asa Brainard, the Atlantics began a rally. Star third baseman Charley Smith led off the bottom of the eleventh inning with a sharp single past third. With a wild pitch to Joe Start at bat, Smith took two bases and ended up on third. Then Start, who waited patiently to get the pitch that he wanted, sent a high fly to right field and "as the ball came towards the crowd they gave way, and it fell upon the bank side almost dead." Cincinnati's right fielder, Cal McVey, was on the ball in a flash, but as he stooped down to grab the sphere, a spectator jumped on his back, allowing Smith to score easily, with Start ending up at third base. No penalty was assessed against the home team, as there was no fan interference rules back then. Actually, most in the crowd did not find favor with this act, and but for the police escorting the fellow off the field, he, according to Chadwick, would "have been roughly handled" by the cranks.

Next, switch-hitting Atlantic captain Robert Ferguson came to the plate batting left-handed, "the point to avoid George Wright [Harry's brother at shortstop] ... [and] drew that ball round from George's reach towards right short, and thereby secured his base on his hit and sent Start home." Now that the game was even, Brooklynites were in such a frenzy "that nothing could be heard for the yells and cheering which resounded from the crowd." After the noise settled down, Atlantics pitcher George "The Charmer" Zeitlein came up and hit a hot line drive to Cincinnati's first baseman, Charlie Gould, who merely stopped the ball and was unable to grab it cleanly. Meanwhile, Gould picked up the sphere and threw it to Charlie Sweasy at second base. As Ferguson raced to third, Sweasy badly muffed the ball, allowing Ferguson to speed home with the winning run. The Atlantic upset was complete as the mighty Red Stockings' eighty-seven-game winning streak was no more.[80]

There were several important things that made this game significant. Wright's defiance not only stood in stark contrast to the way "model" ball players of the earlier part of the decade were expected to behave, but also contrasted the way games were conducted. In the early 1860s, a match could have ended in a tie, and would not have resulted in an argument. The fact that the professional Red Stockings wanted the game to continue reveals how much emphasis they placed on winning and protecting their streak. This game also typified the way in which rules outlined by the National Association were not consistently adhered to and how the National Association was not an omnipotent, omnipresent organization the way we know the current professional game to be. In fact, if it were not for the presence of Chadwick, the game might have ended the way the Atlantics had originally intended. What is interesting is how Henry Chadwick allowed the match to continue, forcing the participants to observe the strictures of the NABBP rules. That fact reveals how he began to acknowledge, or perhaps embrace, the increasing competitiveness of the games. It also reveals what kind of power Chadwick wielded within the current system.

While the influences of industrial competition affected the culture of baseball, the game in its emerging popularity had a simultaneous effect on the practices of big business during the 1880s. Henry Chadwick, with his eloquent pen, was right in the middle of the action. In the late antebellum period and the early post–Civil War era, Chadwick implored the business world to use baseball as a means of creating better physical and mental health among factory workers.[81]

By allowing factory workers to play ball, Chadwick believed, companies would find that they had created a more effective worker, one whose productivity would increase company profits. From the 1850s to the early 1870s, however, most owners of businesses resisted the idea that baseball, or other ball games, could be included within the environment of work.

They believed that games reduced the workers' attention to their tasks, and would adversely affect the production of the company.[82] In 1871, Henry Chadwick noted how the corporate world:

> had [been engaging] in quite a crusade against the national game of the country on the absurd plea that it prevents their employe[e]s from attending to their business.... To attend to business is of course the first duty of an employe[e]; but ... recreation and excitement young men must and will have, and if they cannot get it healthily and morally on the ball and cricket field of an afternoon, they will seek it unhealthily and immorally at night, in the drinking saloons or at the gambling tables, and from these dissipations to those of a lower depth, the gradation is easy ... [but] it is far less costly to allow your clerk to have a few hours each week for afternoon exercise on the ball field than it is to drive him into the night dissipations, which young men are tempted to indulge in when deprived of afternoon opportunities for relaxation.[83]

It is obvious that Chadwick believed that sports was a substitute for gambling and drinking, but he may also have had something else in mind, namely sex. "Sport and sex were seen as polar opposite activities affecting the character of young men." Boys, or young men, who participated in sports, were believed to have mastery over their passions, while inactive and intellectual boys were believed to suffer from perverse thoughts.[84] Eventually businesses began to use baseball and other sports with the intent of creating a more productive worker along with greater peace between themselves and their workers.[85]

By giving laborers exposure to the fresh air and engaging them in a healthy and competitive environment through baseball, companies maximized efficiency, and thus their profits. Their interests coincided with those articulated by Chadwick.

Although Chadwick was initially apprehensive about the professionalization of baseball, he endorsed the professional system as long the players stayed away from immoral practices like betting and gambling.[86] After all, Chadwick asked, "If English cricket professionals had already proven their honesty ... why could not Americans do the same?"[87] Subsequently, tensions between clubs that protested the infusion of paid players and professional "nines" resulted in several teams, like the Knickerbockers and the Excelsiors (ironically the first club to have gone into the business of hiring players) breaking away to form an amateur league, while the remaining association teams elevated themselves to professional status.[88] In the 1869-1870 offseason, the professionals seized control of the National Association of Base Ball Players and eliminated the distinction between amateur and professional players that the association had adopted after the 1868 season (the 1868 convention, which followed the 1868 season, was a pivotal one because the association finally recognized professionalism).

When the 1869 season began, it was the Red Stockings of Cincinnati who fielded an openly all-professional nine, ending the supposed sham. Chadwick railed against the professionals seizing the association. He wrote that eliminating the distinction between professional and non-professional would be harmful because "not only are all clubs placed on the same level as regards (to) playing strength, but all that has been previously done to place professional ball playing upon a reputable footing has been nullified." Chadwick was truly worried how this would affect baseball's reputation. He believed that for the past two years, professional clubs had shown how inept they were at running their teams' finances and overall management (with the exception of the mighty Red Stockings of course) and this blundering tendency had transferred now to the decision-making process of the convention. Chadwick railed against this move and saw it as a way to eliminate the boundary that had been set up between professional and amateurs and as a danger to baseball's integrity. Chadwick, already the voice and perhaps the face of baseball as its leading journalist, was again establishing himself as the game's moral conscience. We know that Chadwick was by now dissatisfied with various aspects of the game and was ready to take on via the press whatever problems he felt were detrimental to the game's interests. He was willing to use his power as a journalist as well as his position as head of the rules committee to guide baseball through what he believed was going to hurt the game in the eyes of the public. Chadwick, using his pen like a mighty sword, wrote:

> The experience of the past two seasons has conclusively shown how badly many of our professional clubs have been managed, and now, to cap the climax, what must they do but carry out the same blundering management in the Convention. Not content with lowering the national game to the level of the hippodroming of the turf, they aim to get control of the National Association, and especially of its Committee Rules, the chairman of which they know to be the bitter opponent of all "ring" tactics and management, and in favor of amateur club rules in the Association, the object in view of course being to use both in the special interests of the professionals, if not of the worst phase of professional ball playing. The result of all this, it is thought, must necessarily be either the withdrawal of amateur clubs from the association or the dismissal of professional clubs.[89]

Chadwick brought up several key points. Aside from leveling criticism at the changes taking place between the professionals and amateurs, he pointed out several trends that were beginning to hurt baseball. One such problem was hippodroming — an act of collusion between two clubs, one strong, one weak, to build the gate receipts and increase revenue leading up to a series. Typically, when visiting a city, the stronger of the two clubs would throw the first game to the weaker home team to create a false sense of hope. In the second game, the stronger club would allow the weaker to take an early lead, once again, to create a false sense, only to have the stronger nine rally and emerge victorious. In the third game, the stronger team would show its superiority and win the rubber game decisively. All this was to take advantage of the fans, who wanted to see their home team succeed. Chadwick despised this type of deception and was not shy about airing his grievances in print. Was Chadwick helping or hurting baseball's reputation by writing about these facts? In Chadwick's mind, he simply wanted baseball in its purist form and was doing his best to shape the game like a father reminding his child to act with moral integrity.

If Chadwick were to have his way, if he were the baseball czar, he would see to it that the game was kept pure. But, alas, Chadwick had no overt power, aside from the power of the pen or his influential role on the rules committee.

In the late winter of 1868, the new National Association realized that its ban on hiring players had become impossible to enforce and subsequently "voted to officially recognize two classes, professionals and amateurs, with state associations governing their relations."[90] Over the next several years there would be an evolution of sorts as the thrust toward an all-professional league would soon shift and come about. Following the winter of 1868, the new issue of the *DeWitt's Base Ball Guide* had its editor, Henry Chadwick, also a member of the rules committee, explain the need for this separation. First, here is the rule:

SECTION 7. All players who play base-ball for money, or who shall at any time receive compensation for their services as players, shall be considered professional players; and all others shall be regarded as amateur players.

Chadwick wrote that the "above is the most important amendment made to the rules." He goes further to explain the reality that necessitated the new implementation was "apparent to all, and hence the Committee of Rules thought they would ... try the experiment for one year of recognizing professionals, to see how it would work."

A little over two years later, in response to the growing number of teams consisting of paid players that "were paying their players good round sums of money in devious ways," something needed to be done "to save the game from disrepute." In March of 1871, two separate associations were formed to divide the professionals from the amateurs. First, "By wise and effective legislation ... the two existing classes of baseball players [having] been placed on a distinct footing" were separated with the formation of an association. Chadwick was part of the Amateur Association official separation as a member of the Newark baseball club.[91] The meeting of the Amateur Association was called by the Excelsior Club of Brooklyn on Thursday, March 16, 1871, where a large number of delegates, which included Chadwick, assembled at the Excelsior Club Rooms on Fulton Street in Brooklyn. The very next day, a professional convention was held. On March 17, 1871, Saint Patrick's Day, a meeting was called at the Collier's Room, on the corner of Broadway and Thirteenth Street in Union Square, in New York City. The purpose of the gathering was to decide on a code, as none existed, on rules governing championship matches.[92] But the meeting turned out to be something quite different. Described as "by far the most intelligent and influential which the professional clubs have ever sent to a convention," the National Association of Professional Base Ball Clubs was formed and thereby began the process that would forever separate the amateur and professional.[93]

There were other causes unrelated to the supposed underhanded payments to players that accounted for the formation of the professional association. With the rise of the professional Cincinnati Red Stockings and other clubs of their ilk, there needed to be an official association that would consist of all professional teams, as those clubs dominated the amateur teams because of their clubs' ability to hire superior players. The establishment of the National Association of Professional Base Ball Players in 1871 completed a series of steps begun in the late 1860s.

The further commercialization and urban industrialization of American society only increased the competitiveness between teams from across the country. With the formation of the National Association in 1871, there was now a truer representation of a "national" organization, and it reflected the way in which other national organizations generally had redefined themselves in the post–Civil War era. During the antebellum and early post–Civil War period, national organizations did not actually include members from across the country. Instead, national organizations were national in name only, due to the lack of railroad transportation. When the original National Association of Base Ball Players was founded in 1858, it reflected the pre–Civil War definition of a "national" organization. Chadwick, for one, noted this discrepancy in 1858 when he wrote how the title of the "newly" formed league:

> was a misnomer, as the convention seems to be rather sectional and selfish in its proceedings.... National, indeed! Why the association is a mere local organization, bearing no *State* and existence even — to say nothing of a *National* one....[94]

Unlike the 1858 version, the new National Association incorporated clubs from various cities. With the advancement of railroad technologies and the construction of more railroad lines, the National Association had begun during the 1860s to include more teams from various cities outside the Northeast. The new association seemed much different from the heavily New York and Brooklyn-based league formed back in the late 1850s. The professional association of 1871 was now able to include more teams from cities around the country and were separated into two divisions: one in the East and one the West. The teams that comprised the National Association in its first year of existence were, in the East, the Troy Haymakers, Philadelphia Athletics, Boston Red Stockings and New York Mutuals, and in the West, the Chicago White Stockings, Cleveland Forest Citys, Fort Wayne Kekiongas, and Rockford Forest Citys.

Chadwick's contribution to the formation of the National Association put him several years ahead of those who organized groups under the modern definition of national organization, for it was not "until after 1876, with the nationalization of business, of transportation, and for that matter of education, sports, religion and so on — indeed, not until after the nationalization of the country itself," that the national association was discovered as an effective agent of control.[95]

In 1871, Chadwick also developed the concept of state associations so that the national conventions would "not be too cumbersome to handle expeditiously on account of too great a number of delegates.... [In] the sixties the number of clubs all over the country increased prodigiously." Chadwick reasoned that "to have each club send delegates to the national convention would have been detrimental to the best interests of the game: there would have been too many different opinions clashing."[96]

Despite the reorganization of baseball, there was still plenty of disorganization going on in the field. High-scoring games were the norm, with poor fielding being the greatest culprit. During the heyday of the

National Association, to curb the high scores, Chadwick advocated a plan, one that reflected his preference for low scoring and defense. Henry Chadwick believed that there was a correlation between teams that fielded well and winning. "An analysis of the play shows that sharp fielding in *preventing* runs has more to do with success of a club than skillful batting in obtaining them."[97]

Relating to his background in cricket, Chadwick also liked longer played games that involved low scoring and good pitching (which he described as the kind that put the ball in play for the fielders to do their work). Chadwick pointed to several games from the 1873 season that he felt demonstrated the best kind of baseball, the kind he believed would attract the most fans. Chadwick cited a fourteen-inning contest between the Atlantic and Philadelphia club nines that resulted in a 3 to 2 score. He declared that "[t]en thousand persons could be collected if it were possible to insure them so closely a contested match." He pointed to two other games with similar results — low scoring and nine-plus-inning contests.[98]

In an effort to create lower scoring games, Chadwick proposed in December 1873 that the games expand from nine innings to ten, and that a full squad increase from nine to ten. Known as the ten-man, ten-inning plan, Chadwick hoped to improve the scores — that is, make them lower — and lengthen the game. Regarding the tenth man on the field, Chadwick proposed several possible places where the extra fielder could play. One position Chadwick suggested would be between first and second base, but positioned further back, almost in the outfield, what Chadwick termed "right-short." With an extra player stationed thusly, Chadwick reasoned, the first and third basemen could move closer to foul territory, perhaps even playing in foul territory, to protect against the fair/foul hit. In the seventies, a ball was fair as long as it bounced once inside fair territory, even if the ball went foul before reaching the bag. This rule was established in 1864 to determine which balls were in play when hit and which were not. Rule 9 stated:

> If a ball from the stroke of the bat first touches the ground, the person of a player, or any other object behind the range of home and first base, or home and third base, it shall be termed foul. If the ball, however, first touches the ground either upon or in front of the range of those bases, it should be considered fair.[99]

Another place Chadwick believed the extra fielder could be placed would be behind the catcher to eliminate wild pitches, passed balls and missed foul tips. This positioning also would deal with fair/foul hits that were struck closer to home plate.

As far as expanding the game from nine innings to ten, Chadwick has less room to argue. Chadwick proposed that the extra inning would actually shorten the game. This defies logic, but Chadwick "reasoned" that with the tenth player on the field, the game would move faster, that it "may be said that runs will be so hard to get, that much of the interest will be developed by the very difficulty in obtaining runs, that the interest in getting there will be lost." For years the game was looking for a way to lower the scores, to make it more like what the game is today. But Chadwick wanted so little scoring because he felt that it was "the most attractive and exciting" type of baseball.[100]

In the winter of 1873–1874, Chadwick used the pages of the *New York Clipper* to espouse his proposal. He went as far as to call baseball clubs "tens" instead of "nines." One of the most glaring examples was in the January 1874 issue, when he referred to a team as the "Connecticut Ten."[101]

Though this proposal might on the surface seem preposterous to modern fans, who view the nine-man field, nine-inning game a tradition in baseball, this proposal was considered seriously on some level. In fact, there was even an exhibition game played on Christmas in 1873 that involved the two most important figures in professional baseball at that time, Albert Spalding and Harry Wright of the Boston Red Stockings. Perhaps to humor Chadwick, just out of curiosity, or even to show support to their friend, Spalding and Wright selected ten players each and played a ten-inning game. Taking place in Boston, Harry Wright's ten triumphed over Spalding's by the score of 18–16, with the two winning runs crossing the plate in the bottom of the tenth.[102] (See page 128.)

Chadwick may have been encouraged by what he perceived as Wright's and Spalding's enthusiasm for the new rule, as well as the participation of some of the game's finest names, like Harry Wright's brother George Wright, Arthur Soden and Bob Addy, who had hit .340 for the Red Stockings. He also may have been convinced of his omnipotence within the rules committee, and confidently presented his case in the *Clipper* every week. He believed that having a tenth man was so obvious that the "only surprise is that there should be the least objection to the change suggested."[104]

The convention was held in Boston at the headquarters of the Boston Base Ball Association on 591 Washington Street on Monday, March 2. Lightly attended because there were only seven teams to be represented

A TEN INNINGS GAME.

WRIGHT'S SIDE	R.	1b.	PO.	A	SPALDING'S SIDE	R.	1B.	PO.	A.
H. Wright, p	4	4	0	4	Spalding, p	1	0	1	7
Geo. Wright ss	2	3	4	7	Birdsall, c	3	2	4	3
S. Wright Jr, c	1	1	6	1	Soden, cf	2	0	1	0
Manning, 1st b	1	1	8	2	Ernst, 3d b	3	3	6	0
Dillon, lf	2	2	2	1	Matthews, rs	2	2	1	1
Sweasy, 2d b	4	3	8	2	Snow, ss	1	1	0	1
Addy, 3d b	1	2	0	1	Wagner, l.f.	1	0	0	2
McGlenen, r.f.	2	2	0	0	Putnam 2d b	2	2	5	0
Wilson, s.l.f.	1	1	0	0	Cone, 1st b	0	2	11	4
Stanley, cf	0	1	2	0	Mahn, rf	1	2	0	0
Totals	18	20	30	18	Totals	16	14	30	17

Spalding's side   5   3   0   1   3   1   0   2   1   0 — 16

H. Wright's side   6   0   2   2   4   0   1   0   1   2 — 18

Umpire — Dr. Pope of the Quickstep Club. Time — 1h. 50[103]

(Boston, Philadelphia, Hartford, New York, Chicago and Brooklyn), the convention attendees were to discuss two rule proposals. One was the ten-man and ten-inning proposal, while the other was a more popularly viewed amendment that would allow "a base to be run on a foul fly catch just the same as in the case of a fair fly catch." There was no question that the latter would be passed, but there were grave doubts about Chadwick's proposal. One unidentified newspaper from Philadelphia (found in Volume One of the Chadwick scrapbooks) argues on Chadwick's behalf, writing that "Mr. Chadwick" in 1873 "during the playing of important games in the professional arena ... made notes of the working of such of the rules as needed amendment, and in the new code he has endeavored to cover every point of play.... [H]e has looked only to improving the game so as to add to its attractions as a manly exercise for American youth."[105]

Despite Chadwick's confidence — some might say arrogance — that his proposal would be passed despite severe opposition to it, the convention rejected the proposal outright in 1874. Chadwick's loss signified not only his rejection of a particular plan, it was the first indication that Chadwick, who had been the most powerful voice in rule making, was beginning to fall by the wayside to some degree, that he was beginning to lose touch with the realities of the baseball world.

In most cities, there was much resistance to the plan. Only Alex Davidson of the New York Mutuals, out of the seven delegates, voted in favor of the proposal. Perhaps the feeling was that with ten men, the game would begin to resemble cricket, which featured eleven fielders. It was probably a factor in Chadwick's mind, consciously or unconsciously. There are many aspects of baseball that Chadwick liked or disliked that stemmed from his being influenced by cricket.

Despite his defeat, Chadwick held out hope that passage of the ten-man, ten-inning plan would eventually come to pass. He even compared the eventual adoption of the extra man and extra inning to the elimination of the one-bounce fly in 1864, believing it would be a positive step in the game's evolution.[106] What Chadwick may have failed to realize was that the game was beginning to establish some traditions, that nine innings and nine players had become one of those elements that began to cement itself into the fabric of the game. Perhaps many of the players felt that despite the high-scoring games due to poor fielding, the fans would maintain their interest in baseball compared to the slower-paced cricket.

An argument can be made that the new proposal did not get passed because Chadwick failed to make a logical case for the extra inning. Chadwick's argument that the ten-inning game would be faster than the nine-inning game with the extra fielder is senseless. Perhaps had he kept his proposal at ten players without the extra inning, his proposal would have stood a better chance.

There could have been other reasons why that the extra man/extra inning proposal was defeated. One of the reasons, as has been suggested, was to counter the fair/foul hit. However, the problem with the fair/foul hit was the difficulty in judging whether the ball was struck foul or fair when hit close to home plate. Even with an extra fielder, as Chadwick proposed, declaring the ball in play or not by the umpire was difficult simply because the laws of the game during the 1870s did not allow the arbiter to be on the playing field. Illustrations of the game during this era show the umpire was actually positioned in foul territory, "several feet to the side of home plate." Chadwick had mocked a proposal the previous year that would have dealt with the umpire's difficult call regarding the fair/foul hit. At the 1873 convention, a suggestion was made that any ball that hit the field between home plate and a line stretching from the pitcher's area to first base and third would be called foul. Furthermore, the foul-bound catch rule stated that a hitter would be called out should a fielder capture a foul ball after its first bounce. Chadwick criticized the proposal because it would, according to his estimations, triple the number of opportunities to retire the striker by a foul-bound catch.[107]

Also, unlike today's game where the bases are in fair territory, thereby giving the modern umpire an easier time in judging a fair or foul ball, the foul lines back then ran through the middle of the bases.[108] Obviously, Chadwick's suggestion of an extra man was to protect the fair/foul rule as it existed, and having an extra fielder would counter the excessive advantages that the batsman had in employing the strategy. Given his favoritism and bias toward the fair/foul hit, Chadwick's logic of adding another fielder to counteract the rule made sense.

Furthermore, the hitter in that era, especially one who had mastered the fair/foul hit, enjoyed many advantages over the pitcher. First, a foul ball in those days did not count as a strike. Therefore, a hitter could foul off any number of pitches until he got the one he preferred, and thereby prolong the at-bat. Another advantage that the batter had over the opposition was his ability to call for the pitch. A batsman could indicate whether he wanted a high throw or a low throw. Chadwick believed that a hitter needed a low pitch to successfully create the fair/foul hit. The success of the hit, he felt, was due to the batsman's ability to chop down on the ball, creating a spin that would cause the ball to veer sharply off into foul territory out of the reach of the fielders.[109]

The fair/foul hit was one of the most controversial rules during its existence, and was even up for debate years after the rules were modernized in 1876. Chadwick got involved in many of the discussions that centered on the fair/foul hit, particularly on whether the rules should be changed, voicing his objection to one proposal while supporting another.

Chadwick debated the merits of the fair/foul hit by defending it, adding that complaints against it were "absurd." It was perhaps his favorite kind of hit, as he deemed it the most "scientific" because it yielded "as its certain result the easy occupancy of first base without giving a fielder a chance to throw or catch the batsman out." Chadwick also believed the fair/foul hit was the most scientific hit because it was the most difficult to employ, claiming that the slightest miscalculation on the part of the hitter transformed the attempt into an easy out.[110]

There were other reasons too that Chadwick probably favored the fair/foul hit. For one to understand Chadwick's favoritism of this play, it is important to understand why he disliked the most famous type of hit associated with baseball: the home run. Though he was the first to calculate this statistic, Chadwick developed a disdain for the trip around the bases because he felt it was the least scientific hit, as it required the player to "expend too much energy." Chadwick felt there was too great "a cost" of hitting the ball over the heads of the outfielders since there were no fences to enclose a ball field as there are today in modern stadiums. Because players had to run at full speed even if they hit the ball a long distance, Chadwick reasoned that running around the bases at full speed would exhaust the player and not allow him to finish a contest at his best capacity. Chadwick also believed a home run took away from the one of the most "attractive" features of baseball — skillful fielding.[111] Given Chadwick's reasons, it is easy to see why he preferred the fair/foul hit, for it kept the ball close to home plate, did not require the player to run around the bases, and was able to advance runners from one base to another. It also kept the ball in play, causing the fielders to be involved.

Later, Chadwick's views on the home run would be mocked, particularly with the development of enclosed ballparks. Still, despite changes made in the game to make it easier on the hitter who hit the ball a great distance, he would continue to complain that the expenditure of energy also would be in the swinging of the bat as well as the traditional run around the bases. Chadwick's views, particularly as time inched closer to the twentieth century, seemed completely absurd to some observers, and rightly so. An 1890 editorial by H.I. Horton entitled "Chadwick Disagreed With," published by the *Sporting Life*, one of Chadwick's employers at the time, shows the lengths that some went to demonstrate some of Chadwick's archaic views. In the article, Horton charged that once again Chadwick "had another attack of home run fever." Chadwick had written once again in the previous week's edition his well-known views on the subject. Chadwick wrote:

> A home run is made at the cost to the batsman of a run of 120 yards at his topmost speed, which involves an expenditure of muscular power needing a half hour rest to recuperate from such a violent effort.... Now a single run made by a safe hit for one base, a good steal to second, and a couple of sacrifices, costs no violent expenditure of strength; gives the infielder ample facilities for an attractive display of skill, besides affording the spectators an opportunity to see some sharp base-running in stealing single bases.[112]

Chadwick's essay published in the *Sporting Life* is clearly indicative of his preferences for plays made in the infield and his love of "skillful hitting," which required a batter to advance runners from one base to another. It is also a reflection of his early love of the fair/foul play during the 1860s and 1870s that allowed players to keep the ball in play with a minimum amount of "muscular expenditure." Furthermore, his preferences for plays being made in the field were indicative of his background in cricket, which is a sport where the ball, after being struck by the batsman, is always in play. Moreover, if a batsman hits a ball out of the field of play, the batsman does not have to run from wicket to wicket. It is automatically counted as six runs, hence the term "six." But the very training that had made Chadwick such an important figure in early baseball had suddenly begun to hurt him, and would continue to do so later in his life in several different ways.

To the modern fan, one can only sympathize with Mr. Horton's sense of exasperation with Chadwick's views on the home run when he writes, "It is about time that a man of Mr. Chadwick's great knowledge of base ball ceased to make this misleading statement."[113] He then pointed to a game won by a home run in which the Boston player "'leisurely made the round of the bases.'" In showing the contradiction between Chadwick's previous statements, the writer asked:

> Was there any "topmost speed" about this home run, which was like the average home run, made on a hit over the fence, which allows the runner to take his time? If Mr. Chadwick's advice had been taken Bennett would have been content with a single and might have got around as far as third base before Long made the third out on a fly to [the] pitcher. Mr. Chadwick further says that "a home run yields just one run when no runners are on the bases." Mr. C. seems to be correct in this statement. A home run is one run. That is just what it is, and that happened to be all that was wanted at Boston yesterday.[114]

Horton added that Cincinnati's "Long" John Reilly's game-winning home run against Cleveland in the tenth inning was "only one run, but it won the game for [the Red Stockings]." To stress his point further Horton added:

> As Reilly's hit was over the right-fielder's head it is to be presumed that Mr. Reilly had to earn his salary by running 120 yards, but he had a chance for his "half-hour rest" after the game. Singles by [Malachi] Kittredge, [Walt] Wilmot and Cooney, and a sacrifice by Carroll won yesterday's game for Chicago, but at last accounts Mr. Reilly was in a good health as the four Chicago gentlemen named.[115]

It is understandable given Horton's frustration that his article would lead to sarcasm and a mockery of Chadwick's views, despite the "Father of Baseball's" long association within the game. Nonetheless, Chadwick's stance on the home run was, in fact, archaic, and was particularly so as baseball progressed and moved further away from Chadwick's guidance and steady hand. This is not to say there is anything wrong, naturally, with preferring a game with the ball in play. If anything, one could say that Chadwick was the game's first "purist" due to his views of effective batting. Chadwick never gave up on his position. Even as late as 1901, Chadwick still advocated hitting within the park. Oddly enough, this was during the heyday of the dead ball era when players were not hitting home runs at the rate at which modern fans have become accustomed. Perhaps the greatest exponent of the time period was "Wee Willie" Keeler of the Brooklyn Superbas. Chadwick elaborates of Willie Keeler's "treatise on batting." In an editorial to the *Brooklyn Eagle*, Chadwick mentioned that a number of letters had been sent to Keeler on whether he had written an official treatise on hitting. He replied in the affirmative, saying, "Keep your eye clear and hit 'em where they ain't; that's all." To Chadwick, "keeping your eye clear" meant that a "batsman must be temperate in his habits, so as to keep all his physical powers in perfect condition, thereby insuring clear sight and clear judgement." In other words, players should stay away from alcohol. In response to Keeler's "hit-'em-where-they-ain't" philosophy, Chadwick wrote, "Here is a chapter of suggestion in one line." It is advice that Keeler practically illustrates in every match game in which he plays, "for his constant endeavor is to hit the ball just where neither the infielders nor the center players can get hold of them in time to throw him out at base."[116] It is clear that Chadwick was a fan of Keeler's style of hitting. While elaborating on Keeler's philosophy, Chadwick took his dig at home run hitters.

> This advice of Keeler, to "Hit 'em where they ain't," is "never, or hardly ever," taken by the class of chance batsman known as "sluggers": fellows who go in for homers, as the *ne plus ultra* of batting skill, and are practically ignorant of the true science of batting, the main feature which is to bat so as to forward base runners, and that, too, regardless of sacrificing their individual records in the effort.[117]

It is remarkable that Chadwick essentially held the same views about hitting his entire life. Chadwick used Keeler, perhaps the best hitter of his era, the player who set a major league record for hitting in 44 straight games and was a lifetime .341 hitter, to espouse his philosophy. Given Chadwick's beliefs on the home run as well as his preference for keeping the ball in play, particularly within the infield, it was easy to see why Chadwick enjoyed the fair/foul hit and why he was reluctant to change the rule. He was so enamored with this play, Chadwick would later claim credit for the invention of the fair/foul hit. This took place around the time when there was a debate as to who was the first to employ it in a game. In the winter of 1894, Will Rankin, who had become the lead baseball writer of the *Clipper* after Chadwick's departure in 1888, led the investigation as to who invented the fair/foul hit.[118] Rankin believed, as did Chadwick, that Dickey Pearce of the Brooklyn Atlantics was the first to use the hit. Chadwick, unlike Rankin, actually claimed that he "pointed out to Pearce the advantage of hitting a ball so that it should become a fair-foul hit." Chadwick's point, as he claimed in his article, was that this type of hit was effective "especially when a runner was on base" because "even if the fielder got the ball to first in time — which was usually impossible — the runner would easily get to second safely."[119]

Regardless of the originator of the fair-foul hit, the play seemed to garner great controversy. The difficulty came determining whether the ball was in play or not, and it was up to the umpire who was usually blocked from making a clear judgment to decide. The 1873 convention of the National Association held in Baltimore attempted to come up with a solution. The delegates proposed that any ball that struck the ground between home plate and a line that reached from the pitcher's position to first and third base would be called foul. This proposal was never passed as law and was ridiculed by Chadwick. He wrote that if this proposal was made law, it would triple the amount of foul bound catches, outs that were made when a batter hit a ball that was captured by a fielder in foul territory after its first bounce.[120]

It was the following year when Chadwick came up with the idea of a tenth fielder to solve the problem of the fair/foul hit. But when Chadwick's proposal was rejected by delegates, he felt frustrated, even though the plan did not address the problem of the umpire not being able to see the ball unobstructed as soon as it came off the bat.

Although the concept of the tenth man never came to fruition, the idea of placing an infielder between first and second base eventually did. At that time only the shortstop played between the two bags, alternating between second and third, and second and first. Suggesting that another player ought to do the same may have been a precursor to move the second baseman, who at that time played on the base itself, to his left in order to play between the first and second bags.

Another aspect of this proposal was Chadwick's feeling that in order for baseball to be legitimized in the eyes of the public, it needed to improve the scores of the game. With no gloves on the players' hands to field a hard-hit grounder or catch a distant fly, it was very difficult to keep the scores of the game low. Eventually baseball would adopt a new ball, one described as "dead" because of its lack of carry and its inability to travel long distances, but until then, no one could figure out how to change the game. Still, there were teams that had skillful fielders, and even Chadwick went so far as to suggest that ties in the standings should be resolved by determining the number of low-scoring games that each team had played.[121]

While his suggestion of playing the first and third basemen in foul grounds was never incorporated — though it was assumed to have been part of the ten-man, ten-inning suggestion — the idea of moving the first and third basemen off their respective bags was, on some level, also years ahead of its time.

When the opening pitch was thrown in the National Association's inaugural season on May 4, 1871, by Fort Wayne's nineteen-year-old Bobby Matthews to the batter, Cleveland's James (Deacon) White, the establishment of professional baseball in the 1871 campaign was made official, and there seemed to be hope that the ills that plagued the game would vanish and a new era in baseball would begin. However, those hopes that were once held so high gradually were dashed as the National Pastime began to sour once again. Lax attendance due to gambling, boozing and overall instability damaged the game. Even with Chadwick's efforts, new leadership was still needed to shape baseball, for the future of the game was at stake. Though the National Association was an attempt to bring order and stability to the National Pastime, chaos had become synonymous with professional baseball. With a startling coup d'etat in early 1876 by the western owners, baseball underwent a major reconstruction, led by an ambitious Chicagoan who sought to consolidate the league under the aegis of the club owners, and, more importantly, to wrest control of the association from its "eastern influences." Chadwick was among those easterners targeted. For Chadwick, the establishment of the National League would forever alter and diminish his role as a key component in the development of the game. Henry Chadwick, the man who had done so much to establish the game in the minds and hearts of Americans, would no longer have the ability to shape the national game the way he had.

CHAPTER 5

Hulbert's Startling Coup d'État

The decade of the 1870s was a tumultuous time in American history. Though a popular Civil War general led the nation as president, Ulysses S. Grant had been challenged for the presidency in 1872 by the well-known editor of the *New York Tribune*, Horace Greeley, who had been credited with coining the phrase, "Go West Young Man." Though Greeley had the support of Democrats and liberal Republicans, Grant won reelection. Despite his reputation as a fierce war general, Grant refused the request of Mississippi's governor to use federal troops to stem violence against blacks. Grant's administration also was wracked with scandals as white Democrats gained a stranglehold on southern society. By 1876, Northerners were no longer interested in pursuing Reconstruction. The nation, though not by popular vote, had elected a new president, Rutherford B. Hayes. That year a pivotal Supreme Court case, *U.S. v. Reese,* had affirmed that Congress had no control over states wishing to disenfranchise black voters.

The year 1876 was also the date of Custer's last stand at the Battle of the Little Big Horn, where the Sioux, led by Sitting Bull and Crazy Horse, wiped out federal troops led by Colonel George A. Custer. The victory signified that the Native American population could still put up a fight and defeat the white man and that the conquering of America was not necessarily a *fait accompli*. It was also in 1876 when Thomas Alva Edison, along with his associates, moved into a wooden shed in Menlo Park, New

Jersey. Their goal was "to turn out an invention every ten days and a big thing every six months or so."

As America prepared to celebrate its Centennial on July 4, 1876, great changes had already taken place. Perhaps the most recognizable change was within the great American pastime. Baseball was indeed the national game. Henry Chadwick had helped it achieve that distinction. But a stunning coup in the early winter of 1876 changed baseball forever. For five years, the National Association was professional baseball. But like a rotten apple, once edible, the association had become impossible to digest.

One problem that plagued the association was a lack of competition. In four of the five years of the association's existence, the pennant flew over Boston's South End Grounds. Led by the venerable Harry Wright, the Red Stockings had once again won the pennant by dominating its nearest rival, the second-place Philadelphia Athletics, by 15 games in what would be, unbeknownst to most, the association's last season. For most of the 1875 season, the Red Stockings' dominance kept the excitement focused on the race between second and third place. On September 3, the one last hope for the Philadelphia Athletics to overtake the Red Stockings was extinguished when Boston obliterated them, 16–0, on the Athletics' grounds in Philadelphia, for a nine and one-half game lead.[1]

But it wasn't solely the lack of competition that damaged the association. The virus of "hippodroming" and the purposeful throwing of games by dishonest players had reared its ugly head again. The very reasons why the association had been created in the first place — to stem the evils that plagued baseball during the 1860s — had never really been effective. Though Chadwick may have been involved on some level in the creation of the professional National Association in 1871— and was certainly involved in the game's development leading up to those years — in an honest attempt at moral reform, the association's deficiencies in controlling its players and procuring a profit were quite evident to baseball experts by 1875. The problem of gambling stemmed from the players discovering that the salaries they earned paled in comparison to the riches received when dealing with gamblers. Traveling from town to town, "the players lived like princes, sporting diamonds, drinking champagne at dinner every night, and ostentatiously paying the tab by peeling off folding money from wads of the stuff that mysteriously reproduced themselves." To some extent the players simply could not be blamed, despite Chadwick's moral calls of impropriety. This was, after all, the era of the Robber Barons. And when compared to the huge business transactions taking place in the corporate world while President Ulysses S. Grant sat benignly in the White House, the activity of the players paled in comparison to the actions of the wealthy corporate heads.[2]

In fact, Chadwick may have hurt the cause of the association when, in the *Clipper*, he showed the difference in gate receipts between the 1875 suspect Philadelphia club, which had $16,000, to that of the well-respected and sober Harry Wright's Boston Red Stockings, with $37,000. At the conclusion of the 1875 season, because of suspicious play, "the drawing power of teams such as the Mutuals, Philadelphias and White Stockings was virtually nil."[3]

Then, of course, there was alcoholism. Boozing had always proved to be cumbersome to baseball's popularity in the eyes of some, even before the advent of the National Association. Chadwick naturally had always fought against this particular problem. He believed excessive drinking was against the principles of morality and especially contrary to character-building advantages of sport. Bill Lennon, captain of the Fort Wayne Kekiongas, was the biggest culprit. In June 1871, Lennon deserted the team mid-game against the non-league Brooklyn Atlantics. Then there was the case of Charley Hodes, catcher of the Chicago White Stockings. Hodes had a reputation of being an alcoholic, and was signed on the pledge that he would avoid drink. There were those who suspected that his untimely death in 1875 stemmed from complications related to alcohol.

Despite the mass of problems afflicting the association, there were many who still believed in baseball. Some even had a new vision for the game. It was during the association's heyday when a new man appeared unlike any other the association had ever seen. The Chicago White Stockings had lost their ball grounds during the Chicago Fire of 1871 and did not field a team for nearly two years. Norman T. Gassette resurrected baseball in Chicago, but a new stockholder came in to help. William Ambrose Hulbert, a proprietor of a grocery store and coal business, a man who loved Chicago so much he declared that he'd rather be a lamppost in Chicago than a millionaire in any other city, had a new vision for baseball. Born on October 30, 1832, in Burlington Flats, Otsego County, New York, Hulbert was brought to Chicago in 1834 by his parents.[4] Hulbert had a varied and successful business background that included fifteen-year membership in the Chicago Board of Trade. Hulbert was cut from different cloth than the other club executives who ruled the National Association because he had never played baseball, and viewed the "game as a way of making money rather than a source of recreation or civic pride."[5]

Hulbert believed that by centralizing the league around business principles, an owner-controlled league would be better able to enforce rules and create a paternal relationship, one that existed in other major businesses, between owner and laborer, which would, more importantly, create the necessary ingredients for a profit-making league. Hulbert believed that baseball possessed great profit potential, and appreciated the game's ability to stimulate local business. A new league, he believed, must be stable in organization, balanced enough to appeal to fans, and, most importantly, be profitable to investors, in contrast to the old system that had only profited the players.[6] Given Hulbert's extensive business background, it was not surprising that he held such notions.

In October 1875, the *Chicago Tribune*, under the sports editorship of Lewis Meacham (who has been credited with devising the organizational plan of the National League), published a detailed article scrutinizing baseball's problems under the association and offered a remedy. The *Tribune* called upon the association to institute reforms, lest it lose its leading clubs to a newly formed organization, one of their own creation, adding that it would be "a closed corporation, too."

The *Chicago Tribune* was the mouthpiece of Hulbert's vision, and Meacham was one of the key players in Hulbert's plan to establish a new association. Hulbert utilized the press to articulate his views to the public and the world of baseball. The newspaper was also a tool for Hulbert as well as Meacham to express their disdain for easterners. The biggest culprit of them all, in their eyes, was the dean of all baseball writers, Henry Chadwick. While some westerners resented Chadwick's criticisms, others resented Chadwick's perceived "dictatorial control over the rules committee, an influence that led to the unpopular and widely ridiculed ten-man plan." The midwestern owners wanted a rules committee that would be freed from Chadwick, whom they likened to a czar.

The February 4 edition of the *Chicago Tribune*, the issue that announced the formation of the National League in New York, expressed a similar sentiment when it announced the election of Chadwick's old friend, Nick E. Young, as secretary of the new league. The newspaper continued by saying that they had finally "gotten rid of the Old Man of the Sea," a reference to Chadwick, "who has for some years been a dead weight on the neck of the game."[7]

While Meacham worked closely with Hulbert in promoting the concept of a new association in the press (not to mention the joint duty of disparaging Chadwick), it was also Hulbert's relationship with another key figure that helped him establish the new league. Albert Goodwill Spalding was the best pitcher in baseball and considered the smartest player in the game. A close friend of Henry Chadwick, Spalding, who had joined the Boston Red Stockings in 1871, helped the team dominate the National Association. Already respected for his brilliance, Spalding was drafted by Hulbert to reorganize baseball, revise the association's old constitution, rewrite the rules, and develop a "corruption-free league."[8] Though it would seem surprising on the surface that a player would actually turn against his own, Spalding learned from his boss, Harry Wright, the business aspects of running a successful team both on and off the field, and noted the various weaknesses of the professional National Association. Spalding would play a greater role than simply being a star player; he was also lured to manage the club.

What also may have impressed Hulbert was the fact that Spalding

had led Boston and the Philadelphia Athletics on a tour of England in 1874. As Chadwick wrote in his brief biography of Spalding, "His able management of the affairs of the team was noteworthy."[9] In fact, Spalding's wooing to Chicago may have been the key all along to the success of the new league and may explain why both Hulbert and Meacham treated Chadwick so harshly.

When Hulbert negotiated with Spalding in the summer of 1875, he was in violation of the National Association rules. The rules forbade an owner to negotiate with a player during the course of a season. To his fellow shareholders, Hulbert made known his negotiating activities with Spalding in order to get their complicity.

William Hulbert (shown here in the 1870s), founder of the National League, excluded Chadwick from the planning for the new circuit. Hulbert never forgave Chadwick for siding with Philadelphia over the Force case (Baseball Hall of Fame Library, Cooperstown, New York).

Chadwick and Albert Spalding, shown here as a member of the Boston Red Stock-ings in the early 1870s, were friends, though the two would famously clash over baseball's origins (National Baseball Hall of Fame Library, Cooperstown, New York).

Mr. Hulbert then read a letter from A.G. Spalding of the Boston (Mass.) Base Ball Club offering his services as "Management" of our club for 1876—After consideration and discussion Mr. Hulbert was instructed to visit Boston, and confirm the best arrangement possible with Mr. Spalding, and also to engage such players for the season of 1876 as he and Mr. Spalding should decide upon ... [Hulbert] had visited Boston, New York & Philadelphia. That he had a long and full conference with Mr. A.G. Spalding and that he had finally entered into an arrangement with Mr. Spalding—and that preliminary Articles of Agreement were duly drawn and signed by Spalding & Hulbert.[10]

By telling the co-owners he was negotiating with Spalding, Hulbert shielded himself from any claims by the club's owners should they say they did not know he was violating an act if the team were expelled. Hulbert also knew that if Chadwick learned of his activities with Spalding and his attempts to scuttle the National Association and form the National League, Chadwick could have exposed him and caused Hulbert a great number of problems, if not outright ruin him. Chadwick had the power within the National Association bylaws to expel the Chicago White Stockings franchise. Therefore, Hulbert, through Meacham, schemed to discredit Chadwick as a way of fending off any exposure from Chadwick should he get wind of Hulbert's plans.

After bringing in the most important player in professional baseball, Hulbert's next focus was to include one of the other great minds in baseball, the man who schooled Spalding, the legendary Harry Wright. Considering Wright's business acumen, it was not surprising that he too would fall into the owners' camp. As head of the Cincinnati Red Stockings and then the Boston nine of the same name, Wright had shown how proper management, both on and off the field, could lead to a financially profitable club. Wright was known for demanding a third of the gate receipts when his Red Stockings visited another city because Wright was cognizant of his team's popularity across the country, and wisely preferred to play only clubs that had strong drawing power. Although he shrewdly looked out for himself and his team, Wright "nevertheless cast his lot with the rebels [who sought] to build a better [league structure]. He entered the conspiracy because he believed the Association to be a disciplinary failure."[11] Wright, like Spalding and Hulbert, understood that the association's failure centered on its inability to keep its members, punish its players and directors, and garner profits.[12]

Though Wright's support was important to the formation of the new league, it was Spalding who played the greater role in the actual *coup d'etat*. Besides, Spalding had value to Hulbert beyond the formation of a new association. While Hulbert schemed at devising a new league to bring about reform, he also wanted to bring championship baseball to Chicago. Hulbert successfully lured Spalding to Chicago to play for the White Stockings. Secretly, Spalding agreed to move from Boston to Chicago prior to the 1876 season after Hulbert promised him the captaincy, the manager's job, the highest pay in the league with a $2,500 base salary, a percentage of the profits, and "even freedom of action in managing." Then Hulbert, with Spalding's help, signed three of Boston's other stars: James "Deacon" White, Cal McVey and Ross Barnes. Although Hulbert was just as concerned about morality and the detrimental effects of gambling and alcoholism as Chadwick, Hulbert really was driven by self-interest. In fact, the incident that drove Hulbert to create the National League and fostered his hatred toward Chadwick stemmed from the Davy Force case.[13]

Hulbert was secretly appalled over the eastern control of the National Association and how it handled the Force case. Davy Force, a talented third baseman for the White Stockings in 1874, had signed with both the White Stockings and the Philadelphia Athletics, a common, though unfortunate, practice among players in the association and yet another disease that plagued professional baseball. A judiciary committee was established to determine which team Force would play for in 1875. When Philadelphia president Charles Sperring cleverly placed himself at the head of the committee, making him the third Philadelphian on the board, he naturally decided in favor of his club.[14] Hulbert, already enraged by losing Force in such fashion, was infuriated when Chadwick supported the decision favoring Philadelphia over Chicago. It was an uncharacteristic move for Chadwick. With Chadwick's great moral reputation, it would seem strange that he would overlook an action such as committee-packing and side with the Athletics. He even compared it to the Addy case of the previous year, even though the two cases were completely different.[15] However, Chadwick may have been reacting to something else. Though Chadwick may have been wrong to side with Philadelphia, he may have been reacting to Chicago's history of aggressive pursuit of players under contract.

The White Stockings had the reputation as one of the richer clubs in the association, helped by an incredibly strong fan base. In 1871, the first year of the National Association, Chicago consistently outdrew its opponents, and for its most important games had upwards of 10,000 spectators in attendance. Because of such great support, Chicago, like the present-day New York Yankees, had great financial leverage over its competitors in the association. Chicago had the reputation of buying players to win championships "no matter what the price is." Going as far back as 1870, a year before the professional association was established, Chicago would openly buy players from the Atlantic clubs, paying twice the salary offered by eastern clubs. Acting like a twentieth century franchise, Chicago scouted and recruited talent from other association teams.[16] After it returned to the association in 1874, Chicago resumed its aggressiveness, and perhaps that is why Chadwick, given his eastern bias and his old-fashioned views, sided with Philadelphia. Chadwick had certainly railed against high salaries in the past. And given Chicago's willingness to buy players at whatever cost, it certainly put Chadwick in a position to prefer Philadelphia. But Chadwick had no idea of the ultimate damage he was doing to his career when he sided with the Athletics. One wonders what went though his mind when he received a letter from Hulbert after he chose to back Philadelphia in the Force case. In a letter to Chadwick in February 1875, Hulbert defiantly confronted Chadwick on his position.

> Dear Sir,
>   I noticed in a late "Clipper" that you assigned Mr. D.W. Force be S.S. for the Athletics for the coming season.... I am led to understand by a correspondent — by the rumor, current in the East that we have relinquished all claim to Mr. Force's services. Now this is to inform you that we have *two* contracts with Mr. Force. One, and the one under which he is now service and drawing pay — terminating March 15, 1875. The other entered into on the 18th of Sept. 1874 terminates March 1st 1876.... Under *No* circumstances will Mr. Force be released by me from these contracts. There are *No* circumstances connected with these contracts that would in the least degree justify Mr. Force in attempting to break them.
>
> I am sir very respfy, yrs.
> W.A. Hulbert, Scty CBBA[17]

Regardless of Hulbert's ire toward the committee and Chadwick, Hulbert had to comply with the decision. But it did not stop Hulbert from infuriating others in the East, namely Boston's Harry Wright, when Chicago officers tried to get the New York Mutuals' premier second baseman, Jack Burdock, to break his contract. Wright warned Hulbert of the ramifications of such actions by reminding him that he could not "blame the players for not respecting the rules when the club managers do not."[18] But the association's ruling on the Force decision only spurred Hulbert to move forward with a new organization, thus setting in motion his plans for creating a new league the following year.

Finally, on February 2, 1876, the financial backers of the National Association, led by the burly and mustached Hulbert, who had become president of the Chicago Base Ball club, wrested control of the association from the players. The National Association of Professional Base Ball Players became the National *League* of Professional Base Ball Clubs. Legend has it that on that day, despite swirling seventy-mile-per-hour winds, perhaps symbolizing the power that the blustery president of the Windy City club put on display at the Central Hotel in Manhattan, Hulbert gathered all six delegates representing each eastern club and locked the door behind them, dropping the key into his pocket.[19]

While Hulbert may have locked in the league delegates, he made sure that Henry Chadwick, the great voice of the rules committee and the leading crusader against gambling, was locked out. Though the delegates of the rules committee rejected the ten-men, ten-inning plan two years earlier, Chadwick was still seen as an important voice on the committee and was still a respected, influential journalist. But given Hulbert's grudge, he was kept out of a closed-door meeting designed to "restructure" the National Association.

It took Chadwick several weeks to respond to the announcement in the press. Finally, in the *Clipper*, his delay perhaps showing his disdain, Chadwick responded with a mixture of anger and confusion. "What," he asked, "was the work of reform the clubs in question had to do? It was to put a stop to fraudulent play among professional players and to punish the clubs and their officials who countenanced it." Chadwick had no issue with these points actually. But "why," he questioned, "this secret meeting, with closed doors and a star-chambered method of attaining the ostensible objects in view." Chadwick believed that the National Association had the ability to enforce laws designed to curb dishonest play. But Chadwick was not being realistic when he pointed out that even though the association had been suffering due to its dishonest reputation, "the honest clubs of the professional class are in a large majority, and possess the power to carry out the needed reformation."[20]

In the *Clipper*, Chadwick expressed bewilderment and frustration; privately, Chadwick showed anger. In a letter written to Nick Young, one of the men who had been directly responsible for the creation of the now-defunct association, Chadwick unleashed his venom. Chadwick called the conspirators, which included Young, Spalding and Wright, "an ungrateful lot," expressing his frustration at being shut out while the association underwent its transformation. Hulbert characterized the letter as "foolish," noting that Chadwick in the very same letter asked "Young for the copy of the playing rules *for use in his forthcoming book.*" Hulbert, in the glow of having successfully completed the coup, demanded that Chadwick not receive anything.

> Don't grant this Mr. Director! The press everywhere so far as I have observed — and I have seen a great many articles applauding our [move].... It would hurt us badly should we [work] with Chadwick. We must *not*— let our book contain our own matter and nothing else. Next year Young will have a lot of suitable statistics. And matter of that sort that may properly be inserted in *our* book [emphasis added].[21]

Chadwick's reaction to the closed-door meeting was understandable. The NAPBBP was Chadwick's most coveted treasure. It was a body where he was able to exert his influence, one he helped to shape. He also believed that the association was strong enough to deal with its problems. To replace it without his consultation or contribution was doubtlessly upsetting to him. And because the meeting took place in a clandestine manner, Chadwick had accurately suspected that gambling was not the only thing the participants had in mind.

Interestingly, the conspirators had, earlier in the convention, consulted with Chadwick on specific weaknesses within the playing rules and club management, though he had no idea why his advice was being sought. Despite their consultation with Chadwick, Hulbert and the other midwesterners who were wresting control of the association away from the East Coast influences were also resentful of Chadwick's persistent charges in the press regarding gambling and corruption. Even though they agreed that gambling and corruption were evils, Hulbert believed that Chadwick's constant criticisms hurt the game's popularity.[22]

Chadwick's good friend, Harry Wright, the legendary manager of the Boston Red Stockings, acknowledged that Chadwick might have inadvertently hurt the association with his criticisms in the press. Wright, who had been exchanging numerous letters throughout late 1875 and early 1876 with Hulbert, was well aware of how the westerners were pitching "into [Chadwick] unmercifully." In a letter to Hulbert, in late December 1875, Wright asked, "Now what has he done to deserve it all? Does he not and has he not always supported honesty and honorable playing?" Philosophically, Wright agreed with Hulbert:

In fact it would have been better at times — looking at it from a distance — had he said less about "questionable games," and "suspicious play," and "crooked playing" for it only served to disgust the public and cause them to regard all games with suspicion without in the least abating the evils that he intended it should. *I have been provoked time and again when reading his notices of certain games, and I can imagine and I know they would affect others who were all luke-warm in their support of the game*; they would without a doubt ignore professional ball playing [emphasis added].[23]

Wright was indeed worried about baseball's reputation. Ultimately, he agreed with Hulbert and believed the players should relinquish to businessmen the job of "conducting the details of managing men, administering discipline, arranging schedules and finding ways and means of financing a team."[24]

Whether or not it was true that much of the public would have been turned off to baseball as a consequence of Chadwick's harping on fraudulent·play in the *Clipper* and the other papers, the perception certainly existed that Chadwick had done some damage. Despite all his great contributions — the statistics, the publicity in the press, not to mention all the fatherly nurturing he had given to baseball — some, indeed, had come to resent Chadwick. Chadwick's style and approach had begun to grow sour in the eyes of those seeking to shift the power of baseball away from the East and to the West. Perhaps, inadvertently, he had in fact hurt the game. Wright and many of the others who had helped the game grow in those early years understood the significance of Chadwick's contributions, but they, like the newer faces in the game, were frustrated with the whole system and Chadwick was an easy target. There was no question that Hulbert's grudge manifested itself in Wright and Spalding distancing themselves from Chadwick for the time being. Hulbert truly blamed Chadwick "for the present bad condition of affairs." While Hulbert understood that "the National Game needs the support of the press," he looked at the *Clipper* with contempt. He felt it was not up to par with other newspapers that reported on baseball.[25]

Hulbert made no secret of his intentions regarding Chadwick's role. Hulbert intended to prevent Chadwick from becoming an honorary member of the league. In a letter to Harry Wright, Hulbert acknowledged that he and the conspirators "don't like Chadwick." While Hulbert admitted that he and his followers couldn't prevent Chadwick "from saying anything it suits him to say," they did intend "to strip him of the official character he has assumed, [for] personally I so dislike Mr. Chadwick, I reject all he says, good, bad and indifferent."[26] Hulbert's disdain for Chadwick was obvious. He even resented Chadwick's "manner," the way in which he wrote. Hulbert explained that:

> A good plan to adopt is for a man to try to put himself in the shoes of the man he is about to censure. It seems to me, I never saw a trace of examination of this sort in any of Chadwick's writing. There is a want of *fairness* running through everything he writes on matters where his pristine theories are involved, or where an *admission* on his part runs counter to anything he has previously said.... I am sick and tired to death of this. We must throw this man off [emphasis added].[27]

Clearly Hulbert loathed Chadwick. But was Chadwick really to blame for the association's failures? It certainly wasn't his fault that players were gambling. As a journalist he was simply carrying out his function by both reporting what he saw in and around the playing field and expressing his feelings on the matter. Chadwick for years had tried to remedy the problem with his journalism. It seemed that Hulbert, who like Chadwick wanted to rid the sport of this pernicious evil, was looking for a scapegoat, and because Chadwick had sided with Philadelphia in the Force case, Chadwick became an easy target. Chadwick, who had helped the game in so many ways, the man who literally put baseball on the map, who gave his adopted country its athletic conscience, was, quite unfortunately, shut out of the planning for a new league.

After the National League's formation in February 1876, the attacks on Chadwick, the man, and his contribution to the National Pastime did not cease. In early April 1876, Meacham called Chadwick "a cynical, carping old man," saying that Chadwick had "outgrown his usefulness." Meacham went on to deny Chadwick's contribution to baseball by saying that because the *Clipper* had been considered "an authority in base ball, he came to believe that he made base ball, instead of contenting himself with the truth, that base ball made him."[28] This, Meacham wrote, led Chadwick to entitle himself the "Father of the Game."

But Meacham believed Chadwick hurt the game by keeping "the East under his thumb." Meacham likened baseball to an unruly child, rebellious against the weight of a dictatorial father. To say that Chadwick was an important and influential voice is one thing; to write that he controlled the East and that it was under his thumb was an exaggeration. If Chadwick had the East under his thumb, the ten-man, ten-inning proposal would have gone into effect. Meacham's most ludicrous point came when he accused Chadwick of "having made a handsome sum yearly by editing a book of rules with one hand and then puffing it into prominence and sale with the other." Then Meacham summed up his, and without a doubt, Hulbert's opinion of the dean of baseball writers thusly:

> Without spending more words with the man who styles himself "the Father of the Game," it is enough to say of him that he was always a fraud in the business; that he always depended on other brains than his own for his ideas; that he is played-out and passed-by man who never cared for the National Game further than as he could draw money out of it: and, finally, that members of the League will do themselves an injustice if they allow his efforts to break up the organization to influence them in any way.[29]

Meacham's attack was simply untrue. Chadwick had not assumed this title, as others — especially Wright and Spalding — had gladly granted Chadwick the moniker for all his great innovations and writings in championing the game when virtually no one else would in the 1850s. Meacham's attack on Chadwick's role — the statistical contributions, the development of the box score, the in-game scoring system, along with positive coverage of the game in its early years — were things conveniently ignored by the Chicago writer. Meacham portrayed Chadwick as if he had done nothing, as if Chadwick hadn't an original thought in his body. Meacham even wrote that Chadwick had stolen many of Wright's ideas and claimed them as his own. What these ideas were, Meacham failed to cite; nonetheless, he attempted to reduce Chadwick to a mere footnote in the game's development when Meacham knew for sure what Chadwick had done for the national game. If it were not for Chadwick's writings, his promotion of the sport, there would be no Lewis Meacham, baseball journalist. With the National League's formation, Chadwick was a defeated but not yet a conquered victim of Hulbert's and Meacham's plan to diminish his role in the game.

While Chadwick was left chafing and upset about the new changes taking place in the game, Albert Spalding attempted to reach out to his friend to calm Chadwick's nerves. Several weeks after the coup, Spalding wrote a letter to assuage Chadwick.

> Friend Chadwick:
> I have read your comments on the new National League and note what you have said in regard to it. As I had a hand in preparing the Constitution and Playing Rules as adopted by the League, I do not feel that I am in a position to argue on its merits. I fully believe the principles of the League to be right and shall do all I can to make it a success, for in my judgment on the success of this movement depends the future of reputable

professional Base Ball playing. Perhaps some of the rules and regulation therein contained may be too drastic, and upon application prove unfeasible, but of course experience will cause future legislation to change whatever crudities may now exist. The fact that of the eight leading clubs of the country ... have signed and agree to abide by the new League Constitution is sufficient guarantee to me that the thing is sound and bound to succeed.

    If I can be of any assistance to you in any way, command me.

Yours in haste,

A.G. Spalding[30]

    Despite the fact that Chadwick had been shut out of a new league and that his two friends, Albert Spalding and Harry Wright, had publicly distanced themselves, Chadwick remained active in the baseball world. In fact, just before the season began for the new league, Jack Chapman of the Louisville Grays paid a visit to Chadwick's "cottage residence" on Grove Street in Brooklyn to get the fifty-one-year-old man's opinion of his club. Chapman went to visit Chadwick out of respect, and to "give particulars about his nine," which Chadwick had requested. It must have been soothing for Chadwick to still garner the respect of a baseball manager and have Chapman visit him after having been jolted with the formation of the National League. Whatever Chapman's reasons were, he visited "the father of the game" to ask him what he though of his team's chances.[31]

    When Chapman entered Chadwick's home, he immediately realized he was in the home of an admirer of the National Pastime. Chapman observed "pictures of club nines, and a couple of bronze statues representing a pitcher and catcher." Chadwick walked down the stairs from his library, where he was preparing a revised code of rules for adoption by the convention. He was also engaged in revising his baseball book and intended to publish a centennial edition of all three of his latest guides: two on baseball, *DeWitt's Base Ball Manual* and *Beadle's Dime Base Ball Manual*, along with an umpire's manual. Point blank, Chapman asked, "Mr. Chadwick, what do you think of our team for 1876 as a whole?"[32]

    Chadwick said, "Well, John, I think you have some excellent material there, beyond question; but it remains to be seen how you will succeed in amalgamating it up to the point of first-class working order. A number of clubs have entered the arena with excellent players in their nines, and yet have failed to reach the goal of their base-ball ambition, you know. I know all but one of your men, viz: Carline, and they are all reliable players, and that is one strong point, to begin with. The object will be to get them well in hand in running in harness together. Engaging first-class players, who can not play in harmony together, is like putting two fast trotting horses to double harness who are unfitted to run together; their very mettle and speed are obstacles to their success, you know in a race."[33]

"Yes, I know that," Chapman responded, "and I think our boys will work well together ... and our men are determined, one and all, to do their best to win the pennant for Louisville."[34]

Chadwick cautioned Chapman on being too focused on a championship, and advised the Louisville manager to take one step at a time, to "keep that championship notion out of their heads, for it is an obstacle to success.... Let them go into the contest to win second, or even third place creditably, and then any disappointment in gaining first position will not be so demoralizing.... Remember, John, that no club can win every game in the championship arena, especially when the contesting nines are so evenly matched as they will be this coming season."[35]

Then Chapman asked Chadwick the magic question: "How would you place the team, Mr. Chadwick?"

"Well, about the same as you intended to do, I think. [Charles 'Pop'] Snyder is a very excellent catcher. He is plucky, keen-sighted, has brains, and knows how to use them in the game. [Jim] Devlin I have not seen him a great deal, but what little I have seen him do he has done well." Chadwick then critiqued some of the other players on the Louisville squad, like "Move Up" Joe Gerhardt and Johnny Ryan, and their newest acquisition, Chick Fulmer, whom Chadwick termed "a tip top man."[36]

Chadwick emphasized base running as an important part of the game and advised that Chapman follow the "Boston plan," or, in other words, Boston Red Stockings manager Harry Wright's mode of training players using baseball-related skills. Chadwick then complimented Chapman on his own abilities and reminded him that he had "the advantage in being under the control of such a gentlemanly organization." Then Chadwick answered a question posed by Chapman regarding Spalding's belief that the western clubs would have the four strongest teams in the league. Chadwick disagreed with Spalding's notion, saying that "while [Spalding was] right about the West possessing strong nines for 1876, that section will not have the *four* strongest teams by any means." Though, Chadwick added, that if "Captain or rather Manager Spalding runs his team as well as I expect he will ... I think the pennant will 'go West' next year."[37]

Chadwick gave Chapman a hint that he was finished speaking by offering the Louisville manager an opportunity to visit him again about Chapman's proposed visit to the South with the White Stockings. Chadwick remarked that it was a "good idea, and it would pay you well in the preliminary training and practice it would yield." Chapman closed his letter writing how Chadwick had positively refused a position in the "management of any base ball organization, for the simple reason that he has his hands full in his journalistic labors."[38]

Chadwick clearly preferred the life of journalism. Though the career he had did not pay much money, he had a passion for writing and being an outside observer. Perhaps had he gone into management, he might have been in a better position and avoided being shut out of the National League's development. But that obviously is not what interested Chadwick on any level. In earlier years he accepted honorary positions on ball clubs, but Chadwick was not a management-type person. Chadwick knew his limitations best. Unfortunately, he was not a soothsayer; otherwise, he would have been able to warn Chapman about the dangers that were to lurk around his ball club regarding gambling in the following season. Little did Chadwick realize that within two years, the Louisville club would be infested with charges of corruption and would cease to exist as a franchise.

The National League was established to deter gambling in a way the National Association could not. Though Chadwick remained an admirer of the amateur association because of its reputation "of honest, legitimate ball playing," and despite his initial apprehension of the new league and his disgruntlement over its shift in control from the players to the owners, Chadwick eventually recognized that baseball's centralization, its move away from the players to the owners, was for the betterment of the game.[39] He came around, just as he did when he initially protested the professional game in the 1860s and the new competitive atmosphere that had engulfed the game. Chadwick again came to accept the new order in baseball. He even wrote that it made the game a superior sport to the English national game of cricket. Ever the promoter of baseball, Chadwick wrote that the improvement of the English games into American pastimes derived from:

> ... our method of governing games by National Association Laws, instead of by single clubs as in England. While England's national game of cricket is subject to the arbitrary rules of the old Marylebone Club of London, our national game is controlled by leagues and associations, the college rules governing the amateur class and the National League the professionals.[40]

Chadwick had no choice but to accept the inevitable. He began to realize that new structure was what was needed to restore the integrity of the game. This was only the beginning for Chadwick's transformation from a man who was a voice for the players, an advocate for them both as a journalist and as a member of the rules committee, to a man who became a voice of the owners. It was a slow process. For example, the National League moved swiftly to display its strength over the players in 1877 when it expelled four players of the Louisville Grays — the team Chadwick had spoken so highly of, the club whose manager paid Chadwick a visit prior to the 1876 season — for throwing a championship series against Boston. Louisville was enjoying an excellent season that year. Up until August 13, the Grays had dominated the league with a 27–13 record, only needing to win half of their remaining 15 contests to clinch the pennant. Instead, Louisville dropped "eight in a row and lost to Boston by seven games."[41] Things began to go badly for the Grays when third baseman Bill Hague went down with an injury, a "boil under his throwing arm." Al Nichols, who had allegedly been involved with prominent gamblers in New York City, was signed by the Grays to replace Hague at the suggestion of George Hall.[42] Hall, Nichols, pitcher James Devlin, and Bill Craver, a shortstop and catcher, played suspiciously down the stretch, making costly errors during crucial games. Devlin, who had won over thirty games that year as well as in 1876, pitched badly, though the poor performances were only in exhibition matches. Nonetheless, all four players were tossed from the league once Chase and Devlin admitted their guilt to owner Charles Chase, who confronted the players.[43] According to Spalding, "The evidence of their guilt was so strong, that when confronted with it, Hall and Devlin confessed."[44] Devlin desperately pleaded for reinstatement. Out of sympathy, Hulbert whipped out a $50 bill and put it in Devlin's hand but said: "Devlin, that is what I think of you personally; but damn you, you have sold a game, and I can't trust you. Now go and let me never see your face again; for your act will never be condoned as long as I live."[45]

Chadwick had his own reaction to the players being booted from the game. Chadwick was the man who set the moral tone for the game in its earliest days and was pleased to see the league take such forceful action.

Not since the days of the noted Wansley case in 1865, has there been such excitement created by a charge of fraudulent play in a professional club team, as by the statement of criminality of Hall, Devlin, Craver and Nichols of the Louisville team of 1877 and their prompt expulsion from the Louisville club.[46]

When Chadwick spoke of the "Wansley case," he was referring to William Wansley, the catcher of the New York Mutuals, one of three players thrown out the game in 1865 for purposely throwing a game. Third baseman Ed Duffy and shortstop Tom Devyr were bribed into throwing a game against the Brooklyn Eckfords. Wansley's play on that day, September 28, 1865, was particularly atrocious: he had to be moved to right field after committing six passed balls. The three players were kicked out of the game after having confessed, but were allowed reentry, including Wansley at the 1870 convention.[47] Given that it was twelve years between these two cases, it is understandable why Chadwick termed this particular case of Devlin, Hall, Craver and Nichols as having "excitement." Clearly, Chadwick was pleased to see the league act so swiftly and efficiently by punishing the guilty parties, and believed that this act would clean up the game.

In his article on the banishment, Chadwick has his say regarding the punished ball players. First, Chadwick tackled Bill Craver. "Craver," Chadwick accused, "has been a ball player for years past and he has been through the mill and is versed in all the ways peculiar to the professional ball tosser who is well known by the habitués of the pool rooms."[48] Next up was Devlin. Chadwick wrote that he "too ... has a record not quite as pure as it should be," though Chadwick admitted, "nothing decidedly fraudulent has ever be brought home to him."[49] Chadwick seemed most surprised by George Hall. Chadwick noted Hall's good upbringing and questioned how someone like Hall:

> whose parents are in respectable society, whose home surroundings have been of a character to inculcate honor and morality, who has the advantage of education to enable him to resist vicious habits or dishonest conduct, the case stands an exceptional one.[50]

Regarding Hall, and even Johnny Nichols, Chadwick wrote that both:

> have hitherto been above suspicion even, and it is with painful surprise that we have read of the proof that has been offered of their direct complicity in the matter of selling games played by the Louisville Club during the past season.[51]

Chadwick was at the center of his moral universe when indicting the players for their actions; Chadwick was never one for taking the side of the players who felt cheated by management. Louisville had developed a reputation for not regularly paying its players on time. Chadwick, despite his reputation for fairness, never took into account the players' perspective. Chadwick could have written about Louisville's reputation for not paying its players on time, but chose not to.

Chadwick, in his 1878 edition of *DeWitt's Base-Ball Guide*, pointed out that the problem with "the gigantic evil of pool selling in connection with popular sports" lay in the Midwest. Chadwick noted that pool selling "was driven out of New York State by legislation in 1877, but its poisonous influence permeated nearly every other State in the Union." Then Chadwick accused the western baseball press of supporting the "pool-selling curse." Chadwick warned that the hope of reforming players, even by expulsion, the way the league had punished the Louisville four, "was illusory if reporters, like the ones in the West, club directors and managers countenance pool selling...." Chadwick's accusation regarding the western press along with the club directors and managers was a serious one.

Although Louisville's management, which regularly failed to pay its players, was partially to blame on some level for the players' actions, the league never granted clemency to its banished players. The league clearly wanted to make the Louisville four an example to the rest of the professional baseball playing fraternity. Despite his reputation as a hard-liner against gambling, Chadwick courageously railed against the extreme punishment leveled on the part of the National League's directors.[52] Though he sanctioned the decision of the N.L. to expel the players, "Chadwick warned of the dangers of unfair purges."[53] Chadwick wrote:

> During 1878 honest play in the professional area was the rule, and not the exception. There was no just cause for any action in expelling "crooked" players from league nines, as there was in 1877; and, though there were several club expulsions during the season, they were entirely for the comparatively venial offenses of inebriety and violation of contract service. And just here we beg to enter our protest against the injustice of applying the same penalty for minor offenses that is inflicted for that worst of all evils of professional play — "crooked" work.[54]

The 1870s proved to be an unprecedented decade for baseball's growth as a professional game and as a truly national sport. Influenced by the economic, industrial, and intellectual changes taking place within the country, baseball became more centralized, profit-oriented, competitive, and structured. Although baseball had many men, such as Wright, Hulbert and Spalding, to credit for its philosophical and economic revolution, it was Chadwick's initiative in 1871 that prompted the formation of the first professional association, an association that incorporated teams from outside the New York City and Brooklyn areas. Chadwick's contribution in the

development of the NAPBBP was the necessary step taken to pave the way
for the formation of the National League. By formulating the concept of
a centralized organization that would oversee the actions of the ballplayers on and off the field, Chadwick helped baseball become a more modern enterprise, ensuring its survival through the next century and beyond.
If Chadwick failed, it was because he lacked the entrepreneurial and business acumen that made Wright and Spalding successful. Chadwick was
many things: a musician, poet, composer and even an amateur scientist
and athlete, in some ways Jeffersonian in his well-rounded intellect. He
loved to play games, chess, checkers and various card games (not for money,
of course). But above all he was a journalist and intellectual who did not
have the background or perhaps even the talent of a businessman.

Chadwick's promotion of baseball as a successful journalist also
opened the doors for others to follow. If Chadwick was not the game's
father, he was certainly the father of the baseball writing profession. Chadwick possessed a list of writers he favored, Carl Joy of the *New York
Tribune*, David McAuslan of the *Brooklyn Times*, Abe Yager of the *Brooklyn Daily Eagle* and Al Wright of the *Philadelphia Sunday Mercury*.[55] Perhaps the writer that Chadwick had the most respect for was Oliver Perry
Caylor, his friend of many years, whose reputation as an authority on the
game was second only to Chadwick's.[56] O.P. Caylor, who was twenty-
five years younger than Chadwick, came from Ohio and earned his living as a lawyer before moving to sports journalism. Though much smaller
than New York, Cincinnati was a great baseball town with a fine tradition of baseball writing that included, along with Caylor, experts like
Harry Weldon and Byron Bancroft "Ban" Johnson. Caylor was part of a
wave of writers who hailed from the Midwest who were noted for a different style of writing. One style, particularly prevalent in Chicago, was
distinguished by breezy slang and grotesque humor, prose featured by
such writers as Leonard Washburne, Charles Seymour, and Finley Peter
Dunne.

But Caylor was not an ordinary writer. His ambition and passion for
the National Pastime led him to leave Cincinnati in early 1887 to go to
New York to begin his own paper, called the *Daily Base Ball Gazette*.[57]
Chadwick wrote a column for the *Gazette*, a series of articles that were
"reminiscences of old ball playing days."[58] Unfortunately, the paper did
not last and was "a considerable loss to its investors, John P. Day of the
New York Giants and Erastus Wimon of the New York Metropolitans."[59]
When Caylor's paper "died," in May of 1887, Chadwick, like a good friend,

"dropped in at Caylor's Gazette office ... to sympathize with the bereaved young editor." Chadwick "found him bearing his misfortune very philosophically." Joining Chadwick and Caylor was A.G. Mills, the former president of the National League. Together the men "adjourned to the Astor House for lunch, and," as Chadwick put it, "we participated in a rather melancholy valedictory feast." Chadwick explained that he, Mills and Caylor:

> Mutually lamented the non-appreciation of a good daily base ball paper by the metropolitan baseball world, who seemed to regard the Gazette in the same light as the boarder did his coffee. "It was very good," he said, "what there was of it." I told Caylor that New Yorkers, as a mass, preferred quantity to quality. "You will see wealthy people of our city," I said, "crowding the cheap store of the great avenues, and jostling each other around the 'bargain counter,' while the best materials for sale are but little in demand."[60]

Chadwick credited the *Gazette*, despite its short run, for forcing the New York dailies to give more attention to the National Game, writing that the *New York Herald* was "especially strong in this respect."[61]

The reason for the growth of this type of writing was its appeal to working-class people. During the 1880s, the game continued its growth, and it now became an even greater part of working-class culture. Baseball was once characterized as only a gentleman's sport during the 1850s and 1860s, but it slowly began to become a pastime for the working-class masses as the Industrial Revolution created a larger working-class culture. With less expensive ways to publish newspapers, working-class men could easily buy newspapers and read them.

Taking its cue from the formation of the National League six years earlier and its cue from the popularity of the same among the masses, a new professional league was formed to compete against the National League. The creation of the American Association reflected the greater popularity of the game as it attempted to market to the average working class. It proposed:

> an admission fee of twenty-five cents to all games, instead of fifty cents, as charged by League clubs. It was claimed by promoters of the new association that [National] League magnates were coining wealth [and] that the ... League was making Base ball a rich man's game; that none but nabobs could see a game of professional ball anymore.[62]

Although Chadwick was an ardent supporter of the National League, he realized the usefulness of the orientation of the American Association to the new working class. He recognized that the new baseball association "was brought into existence owing to the League's narrowing its sphere of usefulness by its tendency to become too close a corporation."[63] Still, he advised it to stay clear of the same pitfalls that other failed leagues encountered when they did not regulate gambling and other crooked elements affecting the game.[64]

Despite being upset at the formation of the National League back in 1876, Chadwick became an editor of the official league guide sometime after the death of Lewis Meacham, who succumbed to heart disease in October 1878. According to the Chadwick scrapbooks, Chadwick began editing the *Spalding's Official Base Ball Guide* in 1882 after leaving in 1881 his editing position at *DeWitt's Base Ball Guide*, a publication he began working for twelve years earlier. However, it is possible that he began earlier, since for many years Chadwick had edited the *Beadle Base Ball Guides* and the *DeWitt Baseball Guides* simultaneously.[65] Whether Chadwick's hiring was earlier than 1881 or not, his mere presence at the *Spalding's Official Base Ball Guide* was significant because it symbolized that he was back in the good graces of the powers-that-be in the game. As the eventual (though perhaps not immediate) replacement for Meacham, the man who had been so critical of Chadwick during the 1870s, was also symbolic. Meacham had claimed that the game had "finally gotten rid of the old man of the sea" in 1876, and now Meacham's own death led finally to Chadwick's editing the most important baseball guide in the professional game. Chadwick's appointment also may have been connected with a decline in William Hulbert's health. Hulbert fell ill in October of 1881 and was so sick that he relinquished his day-to-day duties as head of the National League to Boston president Arthur Soden. Then, on April 10, 1882, Hulbert died of a heart attack. With Hulbert's death in 1882 and Meacham's own demise three years earlier, the two men most responsible for neutralizing Chadwick's power were now out of the way, and the old sage of baseball journalism was able to resume his role as an influential voice of baseball.

Chadwick, in tribute to his old enemy, actually wrote a memorial piece for the *Spalding's Official Base Ball Guide* for the 1883 issue. Chadwick wrote that William Hulbert "was a man to command attention in any undertaking in which he might participate." He added that Hulbert "was a leader among men ... guided ... by a clear judgement and strict impartiality." Chadwick credited Hulbert with "elevating" the "moral tone" of the game "and in extirpating the evils which at one time threatened to ruin it."[66]

Chadwick had certainly changed his tune regarding the National League. Unfortunately, there are no letters or other forms of correspondence that revealed how Chadwick really felt toward Hulbert, particularly around the time that Chadwick got wind of the National Association's demise. But Chadwick was pragmatic. There was no reason to be bitter; after all, he had approved of the way the National League had attended business, particularly in its goal at cleaning up the game. Despite being cut out of the planning for a new league, despite Hulbert's disdain for the dean of all baseball writers, there was no reason at this juncture for Chadwick to express his bitterness. Hulbert had succeeded in making the National League a viable entity, whereas the National Association and its leaders had not.

But Chadwick's rise to editorship of the league guide was bittersweet. Though he had many of the same goals that the leadership of the National League had — the elimination of gambling, the rooting out of drunkenness and the moral uplifting the game's players — Chadwick had been reduced to a mere journalist. Rather than being an important cog in the machine of baseball, he was now a pawn, and this new allegiance would cost Chadwick. Though Chadwick was now editor the official league guide, he was no longer the force he had been during the heyday of the National Association. He was now at least on the inside and would use his pen in some cases like a sword and remain a voice in the game he had devoted his life to by promoting and nurturing.

As editor of the official league guide, Chadwick went to work. In 1881 he eliminated the "dry details of the League constitution and by-laws" frequently published in the journal and added in its place "valuable and instructive chapters on important points of the game derived from competent authority and experienced sources."[67] This edition of the *Guide* was significant because of its intent "to present a work exclusively for the instruction and use of experts in the game, whether of the amateur or professional class, as the game of base ball is too familiar in the land to require pages of elementary instruction in a work of this kind."[68] No longer did Chadwick have to explain the rules of the game, for there was now only one kind of baseball game played in the United States — the New York version — and baseball was no longer competing with cricket for preeminence. By 1882 the sport was clearly America's national pastime. It had become ingrained in the American psyche. Ironically, Chadwick's friend, O.P. Caylor, moved on to the *Spalding Guide*'s competitor. After working for the *Enquirer* of Cincinnati, Caylor transferred to editing *Reach's Official Base*

Ball Guide in 1882. Caylor's publication was second only in reputation to the Chadwick-edited *Spalding Guide*s, and it tended to focus on the National League's competitor, the American Association, a league that Caylor helped to develop and was responsible for the new Cincinnati franchise, nicknamed the "Reds."[69]

In the 1882 edition of *Spalding's Official Base Ball Guide*, Chadwick attempted to address the phenomenon of low scoring games that had become prevalent throughout baseball. He noted the improved defensive play of the game, writing, "It is a generally conceded fact among close observers of base ball that batting has not improved in the same ratio during the past few years as fielding, base-running, or other departments of the game."[70] The main reason for this low-scoring phenomenon was the new type of ball. According to Spalding, the use of a "lively" ball, the one used in previous seasons, "containing so much rubber as to cause the sphere to bound inordinately, was prejudicial to the best presentation of the game."[71] As a result, the league changed to a "dead" ball "which contained no elasticity whatever," resulting in few runs being scored on either side.[72]

The new "dead" ball was introduced to help the speed of the game, to prevent the postponement because of darkness, and to provide a greater balance between offense and defense. At first, however, it resulted in too few runs. In 1881 the league converted to a ball that did not have the elasticity of the one used in the "lively" ball era, but had more elasticity than the one in the dead-ball era. Despite the additional change "in placing the pitcher's position back to fifty feet," the new ball did not increase the offense to the level of the defense. Chadwick added that "flat bats [had] been suggested," but were deemed "too impractical."[73] Chadwick proposed that another problem with batting lay with the hitting instruction, "for the reason that no two batters bat exactly alike, and the theorists cannot agree as to which particular style is the best."[74]

By contrast, the defense showed remarkable proficiency, particularly the "out-field play." Chadwick added that it presented:

> a striking contrast to the old style of play in that part of the field which prevailed some fifteen years ago. In the olden times an out-fielder, as a general rule, never troubled himself to look after balls which did not come almost direct to his position. Now an out-fielder who, while standing in one part of the field, does not look after balls which go anywhere near his position, whether out of reach or not, is a very poor player....[75]

In 1882, there was discussion about playing professional games on Sundays for business reasons. The idea horrified Chadwick. Though he was imbued with secular humanism, Henry Chadwick was still connected to Christianity. Chadwick's traditionalism prevented him from accepting so grave a concept, at least initially. In some respects it would seem odd that Chadwick would oppose Sunday professional games, as he seemed to be the type of individual who would espouse new ideas. One of the supporters of Sunday games was Al Spink, sports writer and future founder of the *Sporting News,* who proposed the idea to Chadwick in his attempt to put the American Association on a paying basis with the aid of Sunday games. Despite Chadwick's initial hatred of the idea, Spink wrote how Chadwick, ever the pragmatist, would change his perspective:

> Ten years later I met Mr. Chadwick one Sunday on the old Ridgewood grounds at Brooklyn. He had come out with others to see the game. I said nothing, but marveled at the appearance of the old gentleman at such a time and place and wondered what had brought about his change in heart. Perhaps, like me, he had bowed to necessity.

The 1884 season witnessed another revolution in play, this time in the method of delivering the ball. Pitchers were no longer restricted to pitching underhand. As a result, any pitch sent from above the shoulder would be considered an acceptable delivery. This rule had been adapted from cricket and the Massachusetts version of baseball, known as "town ball." The league combined this change with the use of a cork-centered ball to help the batter.

Adjustments in the rules governing the offense and the defense had continued, but in the nineteenth century, baseball was constantly changing some of the most basic rules of the game, rules if changed today would cause a great outcry among baseball fans. For instance, in 1886, the league allowed a maximum of six balls and three strikes to a batter (as opposed to the four balls and three strikes allotted to the hitter in today's game), but the league abandoned it the following year. It seemed that after every baseball season, the league changed some rule. Chadwick discussed the proposed rule changes in the late 1880s and 1890s.

> [A] proposed ... return to three strikes, six balls, and the old underhand delivery ... would give the pitchers the same undue advantage they possessed in 1886, and the latter is simply an impossibility, as no rule limiting the delivery to an underhand pitch could be enforced. The new rules are favorable to strategic skill in delivery, by reducing the wild speed previously in vogue, and obliging pitchers to learn to control the ball in delivery more than they did. Four strikes and five balls is the best rule that has yet been in vogue, and batsman will find it so before the season ends.[76]

Chadwick regularly changed his views in this period to suit the needs of the baseball audience as well as its participants, for these adjustments reinforced baseball's ties to the American public.

In 1887, with George Munson elected as president, Chadwick became vice president of the Reporters National Association. The association was formed in order to promote the welfare of the national game by "improving the official scoring of games and the collection of playing statistics." Two years after the formation of the Reporters National Association, a scorer's league was formed for reporters "who served as official scorers of major league games."[77] The formation of the scorer's league served to create uniformity in its procedure, though "the practice of using local reporters as official scorers was a tradition." Also, with developments in communications technology came the trend for uniformity in reporting games. Invented in 1890, the Orr-Edwards Code created greater uniformity in reporting games via telegraph. In using the Orr-Edwards Code, the "reporter [would begin] by giving symbols for weather and attendance reports." After this came a line score, summary, and the record of each player.[78]

These inventions, the new technology, were all were positive factors in baseball's continued growth. Baseball's development can certainly be connected with the advancement in communications. The country was in the midst of its greatest economic growth and rapidly catching up to the rest of world. The Gilded Age transformed America. In a thirty-year period between 1870 and 1900, the annual production climbed from just under $2 billion to $13 billion, and the number of industrial workers increased from 1,300,000 to 5,300,000. Another interesting statistic regarding the Gilded Age was the production of steel that grew from 68,700 tons in 1870 to more than 4 million tons twenty years later. One more fact related to the development of steel was the total mileage of railroad track that increased from 30,000 in 1860 to 193,000 miles in 1900.[79]

All of these developments solved many problems the country faced as it was on its way to being a superpower. It doubtlessly helped baseball grow as the national game, but what it could not solve, however, were the growing tensions between the players and the owners of professional baseball. With strict rules that limited the economic means of these athletes, combined with strict rules of conduct, it was inevitable that there would be strife. Where would Henry Chadwick stand in these matters? He was respected among many players for his statistical contributions and his untiring efforts to promote baseball. Chadwick, however, would have to choose sides and perhaps sever his connection to the ballplayers who held him in such high regard. After many years of being independent in his opinions and views, Chadwick, the voice of baseball, would become more restricted in his outlook.

CHAPTER 6

Chadwick and the Players' Revolt

While the first half of Chadwick's career saw the dean of baseball writers help the game become established through his journalism, his statistical innovations, and his role as a rule maker, the second half of Chadwick's career had him in an important but diminished role as elder statesman. By the 1880s, Chadwick was getting older and, incredibly, more conservative in his opinions. His growing conservatism was a reflection of many things, but most important was his reliance on an institution that he initially fought against, the National League. He would be rewarded by and recognized by the same institution that he questioned at its birth back in 1876. As the game became increasingly cemented in its practices and grew in its independence from the likes of Chadwick, who had helped it grow in the early days, and more reliant on millionaire owners, Chadwick too would be affected by this change. This shift was felt in many ways, but it was first experienced by the players' revolt of 1889 and 1890.

By the mid–1880s, players from both leagues were seriously dissatisfied with the increasing control of management. The decade of the 1880s was one of growing tensions between labor and management in general, one that was also felt in professional baseball. Given the period, it is not surprising that baseball began to have its own conflicts between its laborers and management. Like other employees, before the late 1870s and early 1880s, baseball players enjoyed greater freedom in the work market. Other laborers belonging to unions, like those of the iron molders, typographers or even machinists and blacksmiths, could force concessions on wages and hours out of employers with a modicum of success. By the 1880s, baseball players as well as other workers were placed under with severe restrictions that reduced their ability to negotiate better wages.

Though players' salaries had always eclipsed those of craftsmen and laborers, players' choices had become increasingly limited under the ever-tightening grip of the owners. Luckily, the players had great leadership on their side in John Montgomery Ward. Ward was the rare combination of athlete and intellectual. As one of the top players in the game, he dominated baseball first as a pitcher, compiling an impressive 47–19 won–lost record for the Providence Grays in 1879, and later as a shortstop, after his pitching prowess had faded, leading the New York Giants to a world's championship over the St. Louis Browns in 1888. As he made the successful switch from pitcher to everyday player during the 1880s, Ward fed his intellectual abilities by earning a law degree from Columbia University in 1885. The unusual combination of athlete and scholar allowed Ward to easily rise to the leadership of the players' movement. As both a professional baseball player and an attorney, Ward clearly understood the plight of the professional baseball athlete who sought to escape from what they perceived were slave-like conditions. While Ward and Chadwick would tangle later over the origins of baseball, they would be on opposite sides regarding the players' break with the owners and the formation of their own league. Even though Chadwick had protested the "senseless" formation of the National League, he had become one of its great advocates and could not comprehend the players' rebellious position.

Ward pointed to baseball's peculiar labor-management relationship in several essays published in the mid-to-late-1880s.[1] He believed that the reserve rule, along with the buying, selling, and trading of players, constituted a devious plot by the owners to take money rightfully belonging to the players.[2] Ward wrote:

> [The owners] declared that players were demanding extortionate salaries, and that the real trouble lay in the extravagant and unbusiness-like methods of certain managers and in the lack of good faith between the clubs themselves.... The rule itself was an inherent wrong, for by it one set of men seized absolute control over the labor of another.... Clubs have seemed to think that players had no rights, and the black list was waiting for the man who dared assert the contrary.

In 1885, in order to break free of the owners' stranglehold, a handful of ball players formed the Brotherhood of Professional Ball Players as a secret society to provide economic help to their sick and impoverished brothers. The Brotherhood eventually became a conventional labor union.[3] Ward became its leader, and led the players into a full-scale rebellion against the club owners.

The players' dissatisfaction over their economic conditions centered mainly on the owners' manipulation of the reserve rule to contain salaries. As a result, the National League and American Association magnates began reserving "virtually their entire teams" as a way of cutting costs and increasing profits. The final and fatal blow that led to the revolt came with the publicized sale of Michael "King" Kelly of Chicago to Boston for $10,000 in 1889. Kelly, who was one of the best players in the game, was moved in the eyes of the players like a piece of chattel. This transaction symbolized the players' complete lack of power in the sale of their contracts to other clubs, in leverage in negotiations between themselves and management about rules, and in sharing baseball's increasing profits.[4]

As a result of Kelly's sale to Boston, the players, behind Ward's leadership, staged a revolt. Though the initial negotiation between the owners, who were represented by Spalding, and the players, led by Ward, went smoothly, and it seemed that a deal could be reached, their subsequent interactions failed to produce a breakthrough. The inability to reach an accord led the players to break off from the National League and American Association to form the Players' League. The new league began play in 1890, as it successfully established its own franchises in seven National League cities, luring away most of the league's veteran players.

In the May edition of *Spalding's Official Base Ball Guide* of 1890, Chadwick expressed his hope of luring the players "back to sorrowing and forgiving masters." He portrayed the National League as having strong managerial experience that looked out for the interests of the paying public. Chadwick's writing typified his attempts at easing the public's discomfort during a period of great changes in American society. Chadwick sought to portray these owners as being conscientious men who held the public's interest at heart. Whether his beliefs reflected his naiveté or whether they reflected his part in a conspiracy is not entirely clear. As time wore on, as it seemed that a resolution could not be reached, Chadwick's stance on the players' revolt became more conservative and pro-owner.

It is doubtful, given Chadwick's personality, that he would take part in any overt effort to kill off the players' union, though as a journalist, he played a significant role in espousing the views of management. His attitude reflected the common belief advocated by many writers in this era that men of wealth, like Rockefeller and Carnegie, who owned a large, hugely profitable enterprise, held the public's as well as the workers' (in this case the players') best interest at heart. Those laborers, men who toiled in a factory or athletes working for pay on the baseball diamond, were doing so against the public's best interest. Whatever factors may have influenced Chadwick's mind, there was no doubt that he would not support the players' rebellion and the union that backed it.

Although he had chastised the framers of the National League in 1876 as well as the league's formation in this struggle, Chadwick sided with the capitalists. By 1890, Chadwick had more allies and friends among the owners than the players, as he had remained friends with the likes of Spalding and Wright, men he had known since their playing days. Chadwick criticized the conduct of the Players' League, blaming them for not "effecting a compromise."

> The players should remember that they have had their innings this season and it has been a profitable one to nearly all of them, but only at the cost to the capitalists on both sides [the National League and the American Association]. The latter propose to have their innings in 1891, and if it happens to touch the players' pockets rather harshly the latter will only have themselves to blame.[5]

Because Chadwick edited the official owners' baseball annual, the *Spalding Guide*, it is obvious that he came under the influence of the owners' side. In fact, Chadwick stretched the truth when he reported that the Players' League made money, when in fact only one of its franchises, the Boston Reds, made a profit. That was better than the National League, which did not have a single profitable franchise that year. During the 1890 baseball season, "the players' [league] secretary admitted that since most franchises had cost too much, the poor gate receipts and bad managerial methods were [financially] killing the [players'] circuit." Chadwick stretched the truth even further by portraying the National League and American Association as victims of greedy ball players, just when discussions of a compromise were about to take place.

> The National and Players' League magnates have met in friendly converse and discussed the question relating to the existing condition of affairs in the professional base ball world, and upon one subject, both sides were found to be in full accord, and that was that the past season's campaign had been ruinously costly to the capitalists of both organizations, **each had been milked** [emphasis added], as it were, by their respective players, who alone had derived any pecuniary profit from the professional season of 1890.[6]

While there was a strong financial impact on both of the established professional leagues, the Players' League did not "milk" the National League and the American Association any more or any less than those two leagues "milked" the Players' League. In fact, the National League, throughout the 1890 campaign, increased the pressure on the players' financial backers by adopting a strategy to scare away reluctant investors.

The National League's schemed to divide the Players' League and their financiers because the league knew that the financial supporters of the Players' League had invested $50,000.[7] While the plan achieved a modicum of success, it was Spalding's next tactical maneuver that changed the direction of the negotiations. Spalding arranged a "peace" meeting between himself and the players at his suite at the Fifth Avenue Hotel in New York in October.[8] In the meeting Spalding stipulated that the owners of the National League and the American Association only wanted to deal with the player-capitalists — those who financed the Players' League. Spalding made it clear that he had no intention of dealing with the rebellious players and, as a result, the league and the association owners drove a wedge between the athletes and their financial backers.[9] Chadwick never reported the hard-line tactics of the National League and American Association owners in the press. Given Chadwick's sense of morality and fairness, and how he had always espoused morality within the game, it is somewhat surprising that he overlooked the players' position and failed to hold the owners accountable for their actions. As an intelligent man, Chadwick must have certainly understood the players' position, but he never seemed to understand or, at least articulate, the players' side in the press, choosing instead to appeal to emotion rather than logic.

Given his background and aside from his bias, Chadwick's criticism of the players for being greedy is believable. Chadwick thought that the players derived physical benefits of playing the game and that these benefits along with the salaries the ball players were already receiving, should suffice.

But why didn't Chadwick call out the owners for their own greed and unfairness? Chadwick's contradiction may seem shocking when we consider, once again, Chadwick's family and background. What would the great Andrew Chadwick have thought of Henry's opinion? Andrew was a great humanist, who because of his Methodist beliefs sacrificed financial security by not investing in real estate on the backs of the poor. He was a man with great religious and moral values, all of which may have made him equally astonished at his grandson siding with greedy owners. After all, had not John Wesley taught his followers — the poor, the needy, the working class — that their souls were just as worthy as their oppressors: the wealthy and the landed gentry? Moreover, what would Henry's father, James Chadwick, the great radical journalist who supported the French Revolution and the overthrow of the wealthy French monarchy, have thought about his son siding with greedy capitalists? After all, James Chadwick was a man who may have left Great Britain for the United States for the democratic principals that its Constitution espoused. There were mitigating factors that shaped Henry Chadwick's views, despite his background.

Chadwick's remarks about the weakened National League and American Association really showed Spalding's influence. Spalding was a multi-millionaire and used his economic might to influence the *Sporting Life*, Chadwick's employer, which sided with management.[10] Perhaps Chadwick thought he would have lost his position as the editor the *Spalding Base Ball Guide* had he expressed a more balanced view toward the Players' League and its rebellion. As a sports journalist, Chadwick did not earn much money despite the "public's enormous appetite for baseball." According to David Voigt, Chadwick maintained that despite his extraordinary efforts, he earned only "a modest living, estimated at $1,400 a year in 1900, or considerably less than the salary of a good player." Although journalistic salaries doubled in the 1880s, "top baseball reporters received $15 a week less than police reporters and $25 less than general assignment men."[11] As Voigt put it best, many a sportswriter "answered the call because of the excitement and stylistic freedom that could be enjoyed."[12]

Also, Chadwick may have had some concerns about his economic situation given some issues regarding his health. In early January of 1890, the *Brooklyn Eagle* reported that Chadwick had been very ill and that "a fatal termination was feared."[13] Chadwick, nearing seventy, suffered from jaundice and congestion of the liver, enduring three relapses of the illness within a three-week period.[14] Though *Sporting Life* reported that Chadwick had convalesced from his sickness on the eighth of January, the experience may have made him think more seriously about the future of his family and his estate. Many of Chadwick's close friends owned ball clubs, and he realized that they would be the ones who would be able to assist his family in times of crisis.[15] Chadwick and many other reporters had their freedom to criticize curtailed because of their inability to make enough money so that they could remain independent. After 1900, "club policies were encroaching upon freedom of expression, making reporters truly intellectual prostitutes."[16]

There are class considerations, too, when taking into account Chadwick's position. Chadwick's attitude toward the professional baseball player compares with the hostility that many middle-class people who lived in the city felt toward striking men and women. The social environments of the big American metropolises in the post–Civil War era tended to be more antagonistic toward laborers. In fact, in the big city, "there was almost no sympathy for the city worker among the middle and upper classes."[17] This apathy for the working-class man showed itself at the ballpark, too. At the ball games the owners kept the upper classes and the working classes apart with separate seating arrangements by using ushers and policemen as a means of "protecting" the higher classes from working-class masses.[18]

Though the players' revolt lasted only a year, the American Association could not overcome the financial losses it had incurred during the conflict, and it folded (along with its twenty-five-cent price for admission) late in the 1890 baseball season. With the folding of the American Association, the National League was once again the only professional major league in baseball.[19]

Henry Chadwick remained a loyal Brooklynite despite his five decades of travels across the country and as the game grew outside of Brooklyn and New York's borders while it became the national sport of the United States. Fifty years after he immigrated with his mother and father to the states and settled in Brooklyn, Chadwick was inducted into the Society for Old Brooklynites.[20] He did not always reside in Brooklyn; for a brief period Chadwick lived in Long Island — Sag Harbor to be more correct — but he stayed in Long Island generally in the summer.

Even though he had lived in America for all these years, he still maintained his contact by mail with his older brother, Edwin. He was not physically close to his brother in age or physical distance, and they had not seen each other in fifty-three years; they had corresponded regularly and were true admirers of each other's work.[21]

In fact, Henry had implored Edwin to visit America on at least one occasion. In a letter written in April 1875, Henry enticed his brother to come to the states because he "would be in great demand for lecturing." Henry believed that Edwin could speak to large audiences "in discussions on sanitary subjects," adding "the voyage [to America] would give you a new lease on life."[22] Henry believed that his brother could have been as successful as John Tyndall, the Irish physicist and philosopher, and Richard Proctor, the British astronomer, when they did their talks on visits to America. Henry wrote, "the one lectured on light to thousands and the other on Astronomy to crowded houses." Henry added confidently that Edwin "could do the same."[23] Perhaps Henry hoped that his brother might come to the United States and live like Richard Proctor did.

But Edwin never did venture to America. In early July 1890, Henry received the sad news that his older brother died at the age of ninety at his home in Mortlake, a small suburb located on the outskirts of London. Despite his brother's age, Henry may have been surprised by Edwin's death. Though he had taken ill the past winter, Sir Edwin Chadwick, who had been knighted by Queen Victoria earlier in the year, had convalesced. In his last letter to his American brother, Sir Edwin mentioned the fact "that he had just received a diploma as honorary corresponding member of the Medico Legal Society of New York."[24]

Edwin Chadwick in 1886. Though separated thousands of miles, Henry and Edwin Chadwick maintained a written correspondence until Edwin's death in 1890.

In January, shortly before Edwin's birthday, Henry received a message from his friend, the journalist Newton Crane, the former American consul at Manchester, England, who updated Henry on his brother's condition. Henry had written to Edwin in June of 1899 to let him know that Crane would be coming to England.

> For he is desirous of knowing "England's Sanitary Philosopher." I beg to introduce him to you. He would like to have some of your pamphlets for use by the Southern newspapers.
> Any attention you pay him will be very much appreciated. You will find him thoroughly [up to date] on all American topics which you and I are specially interested and also to be a representative cultured American.[25]

Crane met Edwin Chadwick at his home in Mortlake. He found Sir Edwin sitting at home in the drawing room in an armchair in front of a glowing fire. Edwin rose from the chair to give Crane a "kindly greeting," remembering his name at once and recalling the fact that Crane had once borne a letter from Henry. Mr. Crane was impressed with Edwin's energy and vigor.

> I could hardly realize that he [was] in his 91st year. His figure erect and his leonine head, of massive proportions, [was] covered with white flowing hair, protected by a velvet skull cap.[26]

Indeed, Henry's brother had remained active even in his advanced age. He revealed in an interview published by the *Brooklyn Eagle* that he wanted to build great towers in our cities that would "pump down ozone from above" to purify the air.

> How often my government clerks have asked leave to take home their work, finding it impossible to do anything in the poisoned air of the great public offices. This system, about which I have consulted M. Eifel himself, who thinks very highly of the idea, would affect a revolution in the health of our great cities.[27]

Edwin, in line with his advocacy of soap and water to prevent infectious disease, had even invented a machine for washing children "in which a dozen may be soaped and laved at the cost of one penny."[28]

Truly, Edwin's cult was cleanliness, according to Newton Crane, which Edwin believed was next to godliness. Edwin regarded cleanliness as the salvation of the nation, believing that "[w]herever soap and water are freely used, health, capacity for work and longevity are insured."[29] Doubtlessly, Edwin's work in sanitary reform was finally having an impact in America. In 1889, the convention of the American Sanitary Society "brought permanently into view the vital question of the promotion of sanitary reform in American cities, involving as it does the saving of hundreds of thousands of lives annually, and of millions of dollars of wealth." This American convention on sanitary reform was due to the improvements developed by Edwin Chadwick a half-century earlier in England.[30]

It is remarkable that both brothers were having such a great impact on their respective careers and in their respective countries. Henry truly had an interest in sanitary reform, since it related to health, and in many ways his work as a baseball journalist was linked to this subject. The convention on sanitary reform in America was a great reflection on Edwin Chadwick's influence, one that was only beginning to be felt throughout the world. But it also may have been because of some of Henry's work as well. One year before the convention, Henry had written a letter to Edwin critiquing his brother's attempt at getting his ideas on sanitary reform in the United States into the American newspapers. In the letter, Henry gave Edwin advice:

> Your interesting letter containing your request as to the publication of sanitary papers in [the] United States newspapers reached me.... On reading the article, however, I find that it will not quite fit in for the requirements you aim at, as the introduction is not calculated for the American market, so to speak. I am deeply interested in sanitary reform, and I know that the movement in that direction has taken root here and in time will produce good fruit. Your idea of calling special attention to the subject through the medium of the American newspapers of note is a good one; but to effect the object you aim at it will have to be worked at differently. I know the ins and outs of journalistic matters here thoroughly, and if you will leave it to me to get your facts and statistics supporting your sanitary reforms before the American public through the press I feel sure of [success].[31]

Henry recommended to Edwin how to present sanitary reform to the New York State legislature, suggesting that the "statistical facts" be referred to "as brief as possible." He also advised that his brother focus on cities and towns and "in reformatory, and penal institutions, where high death rates have specially prevailed." Henry also suggested that "an article based on the subject ... will be equally applicable for use in the journals of the country."[32]

One month later, Edwin formulated a plan — "On Sanitary Reform" — addressed "to The Legislature of the State of New York," in which he followed Henry's advice.[33] The following year the convention on sanitary reform in America took place in which Edwin's ideas were put forth. Clearly, there was a connection between Henry's work in promoting baseball and athletics to encourage health and Edwin's sanitary philosophies.

Henry Chadwick, in tribute to his brother, wrote "for the past half century [Edwin] was devoted to the establishment of sanitary reform, the amelioration of the condition of the poor, and the fostering of the education of the masses of Great Britain."[34] Henry was both proud and admiring of his brother's achievements. Edwin's impact on England was great, and his influence had begun to take effect in America. Edwin's beliefs in clean air, clean water, exercise, his love of bathing, and both his advocacy and utilization of statistics to prove his theories and to serve as a tool to implement governmental philosophy also profoundly rubbed off on his brother Henry. While Edwin Chadwick was busy cleaning all of England with soap and water, Henry Chadwick began to lead his adopted nation out of the wilderness of inactivity with his advocacy of sports and games, but most obviously with his crusade to make baseball the national pastime.

Edwin's funeral, unlike that of his master, Jeremy Bentham, who had his body dissected in front of an audience of friends and colleagues, was ordinary, this despite his spectacular career which changed the lives of British citizens.[35] It may have bothered Henry, given his own elaborate funeral later on, that his brother was buried without the pomp and circumstance he deserved. With all the contributions his brother had made in British industrial society and the impact that was beginning to be felt in the United States, Henry may have felt that his brother deserved more. Henry understood the importance of his brother's contribution and saw it reflected in his own work. Henry had changed America with his role as baseball statistician and journalist and proponent of healthy exercise, not to mention his diatribes against gambling and drinking.

Despite his brother's death, the 1890s was a prosperous period for the dean of baseball writers, who was becoming an elderly man. In 1894, the year he turned seventy years of age, Chadwick was made an honorary member of the rules committee of the National League because of his past services to the game. The committee recognized Chadwick as an "authority in all matters pertaining to baseball, and that to him, more than any other individual living is due the credit for the present almost perfect code of rules governing the game."[36]

Two years later, in 1896, Chadwick received a letter dated November 17, from his friend Nicholas E. Young, the president of the National League, informing the dean of baseball writers that the Playing Rules Committee had awarded Chadwick a salary of $50 per month for the rest of his life.[37]

Young was indeed supportive of this motion when the committee put forth the idea of granting Chadwick the lifetime salary. Young, whose history with Chadwick went back to the founding of the National Association and Chadwick's connection to the Washington Baseball Club of the 1860s, knew and saw first-hand Chadwick's great contributions to the game of baseball. In his congratulatory letter to Chadwick, Young spoke in glowing terms of Chadwick's great contributions.

Dear Mr. Chadwick — Republics may be ungrateful, but the representative men of our great American game can prove by their many kind and manly acts that they are truly as great as the manly and honorable sport of which they are recognized champions. At our annual meeting [and] in view of your long service in advancing the best interests of the game with you[r] ready and able pen, and for such services as you may hereafter be able to render the playing rules committee.... That the treasurer be authorized and direct to pay you a salary of fifty ($50) per month during the balance of you[r] natural life. It is hardly necessary for me to add that I heartily supported [the] motion, and it goes without saying that it was unanimously adopted. I can only add that it was a well merited recognition of your long and faithful service as a champion and advocate of clean, honest base ball, and express the hope that a kind Providence will grant me the pleasure of sending you a monthly check for many long years to come.[38]

The message probably came as a great relief to Chadwick, who had certainly paid his dues to garner a salary from the only major league in professional baseball. Unfortunately, there was a negative reaction to his reward when controversial New York Giants owner Andrew Freedman accused Chadwick of greed for accepting it. Freedman was sensitive to comments made about him and his organization and unleashed his venom toward the veteran journalist. Undeterred by Freedman's allegation, Chadwick kept it and decided to shun the Polo Grounds, recommending that others follow his lead for the rest of Freedman's reign.[39] Freedman responded in a letter and accused Chadwick of ingratitude while he was "recipient of its 'bounty'" after Chadwick pointed to certain flagrant abuses in the management of the New York club.[40] Furthermore, Freedman arrogantly took credit for Chadwick's salary and berated the old man as a pauper. Chadwick, in response to Freedman's aggressiveness, boldly published Freedman's letter. It read:

A MONUMENT OF LITTLENESS
NEW YORK, Feb. 14, 1898
Henry Chadwick, ESQ.,
        Sag Harbor, N.Y.
    I have this day written a letter to Mr. Young in which I stated to him yours is the most miserable case of ingratitude I know of. Notwithstanding that you abused the New York Club in your miserable, petty way, you are receiving from our hands a pension upon which I understand you are subsisting. You still abuse and unjustly malign in the public prints a ball player and manager we have, and one whom you have not seen play in years. Your conduct of biting the hand that feed[s] you is too contemptible for me to give further utterance. When you release yourself from the position of pensioner and refuse to accept the pension of the New York Club,

which it has paid you in the past, then you will be freer to unjustly abuse its players.

Yours etc.,
ANDREW FREEDMAN[41]

Part of the reason Chadwick published Freedman's letter was to show how some major league baseball owners were in the practice of bullying members of the press. Chadwick wrote that when he was awarded the annuity, "it was fully understood then and there that my acceptance of the gift was not to involve any forfeiture of independence of publicly-expressed opinion in my base ball letters to the papers." Chadwick added that he had the written support of the Chicago club's president, James A. Hart, who added that "just because you are in receipt of a sum of money annually from the league is not meant to influence your judgment in any way." Hart added, "I take it that you are just as much at liberty to put your thoughts in writing as you ever were."[42]

In response to Freedman's accusation that Chadwick had "abused and unjustly maligned officials and players of the New York club," Chadwick wrote that the claim was entirely "false." He wrote that he had taken:

> Mr. Freedman to task in 1896 for his mistaken policy in being discourteous to members of the press; and I also rebuked the proven blackguardism of his team manager in 1897. These are the offences which called forth the above thoroughly characteristic letter from the president of the New York Club.[43]

Chadwick then declared that if other league managers were of Freedman's mind, he would not accept another penny. None of the owners who responded to the Chadwick request held sympathy with Freedman's point of view, and Chadwick kept his $600-a-year annuity.[44]

It was not the first time that Freedman had a run-in with a journalist. From the beginning of his tenure in 1895, Freedman had an ongoing feud with the press. Sensitive to criticism despite his bold creative mind, Freedman's actions ranged from barring six reporters from the Polo Grounds for criticizing management to punching a *New York Times* reporter when he suggested the team would be better off with a new owner. Given Freedman's temperamental anger and his penchant for fighting with the press, it is not surprising that he and Chadwick would clash.

Because of Freedman's negative reputation and Chadwick's great respect among his fellow writers, other papers immediately rushed to back the dean of baseball writers. The *Pittsburg News* vocalized its support of

Line drawings of some of the great early sportswriters, with Henry Chadwick at center. To the left of Chadwick is Ren Mulford and, above him, Jacob Morse; to the right of Chadwick is O.P. Caylor (Chadwick Scrapbook).

Chadwick, adding that "the National League should feel just a little bit ashamed that it has among its members even one who tries to muzzle criticism even if the method of muzzling were different totally from what it is." Another paper, the *New York Journal*, with its writer Charles Dryden, who had his own run-in with Freedman, also defended Chadwick. Dryden sarcastically described Freedman's correspondence as a "sweet little letter" while noting Chadwick's devotion of "forty years of his life to building up the game." Dryden added that the $600 annuity given by the league to the veteran scribe "aroused the fires of pale blue anger in the soul of Mr. Freedman." Dryden then asked "[w]hat was he paying Mr. Chadwick for but to say nice things about his young men, and here was that viper stinging the bosom that warmed it." Given Chadwick's close proximity to the New York club, as Chadwick lived in Brooklyn, Dryden added that the "Father of Baseball," probably had not heard the last of Freedman. Dryden suggested that Freedman "might in his growing wrath shove the Brooklyn Bridge into the river and tear up the transit facilities of Manhattan to keep the venomous and ungrateful Mr. Chadwick away from the Polo Grounds this Summer."[45]

Despite Chadwick's minor difficulty with Freedman, the incident reminded the public of the respect that Chadwick still garnered among his fellow writers at this time. Fellow journalists clearly understood the role of the press in its role in promoting the game. They also understood Chadwick's great contribution, his literal invention of baseball journalism as well as American sports journalism in general. After all, where would the game and these writers be without Chadwick's great efforts?

However, there was irony to Chadwick's receiving the salary from the National League. True, Chadwick received the pension because of the great work in helping baseball grow. But wasn't it the same Henry Chadwick who had bashed the National League upon its very founding? And had not the National League, in its founding, distanced itself from Chadwick? For sure, Chadwick had come full circle. He was now in the good graces of the league — the same league that had replaced his beloved National Association. He was now to receive a pension and continue his function of editing the official league guide. While most of the owners had supported Chadwick's annuity, as they tacitly approved of his critical eye in matters concerning the league, it was also Chadwick's loyalty that had garnered him the $600 a year for life salary. Chadwick was certainly biased in his observations in many ways and that clearly was the case when he sided with the owners of the National League and the American Association during the players' rebellion. Chadwick's great work, innovations, and promotion of the National Pastime had earned him the lifetime salary, but so had his loyalty to the National League in times of conflict.

This loyalty to the National League was obvious again when a new rival appeared to challenge it. Chadwick used his pen like a sword when the American League rose from the ashes of minor league status to become a major league organization in 1901. Not since the undoing of the American Association in 1891 had there been more than one major league in professional baseball.

Initially, Chadwick announced the formation of the American League with great aplomb. In the July 14, 1900, edition of the *Sporting News*, Chadwick reported "that the American League," then a minor league, "under President Ban Johnson, is laying plans for a 12-club league in 1901 with six clubs from the East and six from the West." Chadwick then wrote prophetically, "Great changes will occur in the professional base ball business in 1901." The American League, under the leadership of a former baseball journalist from the Midwest, Byron Bancroft "Ban" Johnson, signed many of the top National League players, including the likes of Napoleon Lajoie, John McGraw, Hugh Duffy and Wilbert "Uncle Robby" Robinson. The American League snared many of the National League's players because the ten-year agreement, which had been signed by the National League after the strike, expired in 1901. As a result, the Players' Protective Association (an early version of a players' union) encouraged members to take advantage of the expired agreement.

In response to the American League's grabbing some of the National League's best players, Chadwick went on the attack:

> We are approaching what seems to be [a] very interesting time in connection with coming base ball conventions in the professional arena. The topic of interest in the professional base ball world this month has been the sayings and doings of the minor league people as to what their intentions are in the way of organizing for the ensuing professional campaign of 1901. President Ban Johnson, of the American League, seems to have become an expansionist of the class of latest date appropriators. If he does not want the base ball earth he evidently desired to acquire a goodly portion of its occupied territory, I notice, and he proposes to take what he wants "without the consent of the governed."[46]

By calling the American League "expansionists," Chadwick was asking whether they were going to violate the National Agreement. Chadwick even wondered what the Players' Protective Association had to say about all these changes taking place.

Eventually, he suggested "that of securing thorough legislative harmony among the three prominent existing rival organizations ... a permanent settlement."[47] Chadwick said that a meeting was necessary between these three organizations to fend off future difficulty. Chadwick listed the issues that he felt were of great importance to discuss.

> First, that the National Agreement be maintained at all costs. Secondly, that the reserve rule, somewhat modified, be kept as an important plank of the base ball platform. Thirdly, the kicking nuisance [one of Chadwick's favorite issues] be permanently done away with and that a double umpiring system be restored. Without these four planks to stand on, no professional base ball party can hope for success.[48]

Chadwick was clearly agitated with the arrival of the American League, though his suggestion that there be a meeting between the new league, the senior circuit and the Players Protective Association implies that he was resigned to the inevitable. His annoyance at the American League pursuing the National League's players was obviously related to his connection to his long-time employer, the organization that had been paying him an annuity of $600, the same way he had sided with the owners during the players' revolt of 1889 and 1890. What other explanations could there be? He did not raise the same issues when the American Association came into existence back in 1883. The association had proven to be an important counterbalance to the uptight and severe National League.

As the months went by, after the year 1900 came to a close, Chadwick's barbs toward Ban Johnson and the American League became more intense. In early February 1901, Chadwick referred to the American League as the "new" Players' League, writing "that the [athletes] are now the real ruling power of the Johnsonian League." Chadwick chastised what was then termed the "war to the death" between both leagues and wrote how Ban Johnson "will find by the end of the year, that he has made the greatest business mistake of his life by his attempt to down the National League." Chadwick went so far as to say that the new league was determined to alter the playing rules that had been established by the National League to eliminate the game's progress toward a more scientific approach to baseball.[49] What proof Chadwick had in proving the American League's plot to destroy the National League and to alter the game, to make it less scientific, he never offered. Here again, Chadwick, like his loyalty to professional baseball during the players' revolt of 1889 and 1890, had returned to his devious ways of bashing anything that opposed to his beloved National League.

Despite Chadwick's animus toward Johnson and the American League, there were some parallels between both men. Chadwick, back in the 1860s, and Johnson, in the 1890s, had been critical of baseball's playing structure through their respective employers. Johnson worked for the *Cincinnati Commercial-Appeal* and between 1887 and 1894 developed, like Chadwick in the mid 1800s, an "acute knowledge of professional baseball's inner and outer workings."[50] Both Chadwick and Johnson were sportswriters with a reformer's zeal; both sought to improve upon the sport not only on the field, but off the field as well. Johnson, who was born in Norwalk, Ohio, had come from a well-educated family that had emphasized religious study. Though imbued with a religious background, Johnson was to take a much different route in his life than his elders. He had attended two colleges, leaving Oberlin for Marietta College, because he felt that there was too much "emphasis on chapel." Johnson played catcher at both schools, and rather than go into a world of religion, he entered the world of professional sports.[51] Later, Johnson entered the world of journalism and became one of the leading figures in his field, the way Chadwick had made his mark during the 1860s and 1870s. Johnson developed a reputation for being a writer outspoken in his beliefs. Thus, given the similarities between the two men, it is unfortunate that Chadwick had to resort to attacking Johnson when he probably understood Johnson's goals. Given Johnson's reform instincts, it was inevitable that Chadwick would come around to support Johnson.

Chadwick came to Johnson's side in the early summer of 1901 on the subject of kicking umpires, an issue Chadwick had always felt passionately about. Chadwick had always hated when players or managers, when disagreeing with a call, resorted to kicking umpires. Given his role in the game throughout the years, Chadwick had always felt a special bond with the umpires. He had even written several manuals on umpiring. In article that appeared in the *Sporting News* on June 1, 1901, Chadwick criticized the National League by saying that the "kickers rule the roost ... simply because the club managers and captains back them up in their kicking and are even rewarded in their actions." Chadwick added that under such conditions reform is "hopeless." But, when he turned his attention to the other league, Chadwick actually found hope.

All honor say I to President Ban Johnson for the pluck and courage of his convictions he has played in punishing that rowdy kicker, "Mugsy" [John] McGraw, and also that other kicking fellow, [Clark] Giffith, of Chicago, both of whom [were] suspended last week from field service and pay for their violation of American League rules. There has been so much kicking in the American League ranks this month, especially in Baltimore and Chicago, that I began to think that Mr. Johnson had gone back on his record: it was therefore, a great treat to rue when I read that "President Johnson of the American League, today issued a notice of suspension to Manager John McGraw, of the Baltimore team, for a period of five days. The offense was the use of profanity against Umpire Cantillon in the last game played at Baltimore."[52]

Chadwick was certainly pleased with Johnson's actions. He even described McGraw's punishment that prevented him from donning a uniform and a place on the Baltimore bench, adding that he was "nothing higher than a player out of a job or an ordinary 'deadhead' at the game."[53]

Chadwick's initial ire toward baseball's newest Czar, however, was perplexing. Given the fact that Johnson had every intention of cleaning up baseball, why Chadwick would be cynical toward the new league, showed a bias that, unfortunately, the veteran scribe had shown from time to time in the past.

Chadwick favored the National League. Johnson's raiding of certain National League players clearly offended Chadwick and blinded him toward Johnson's goals. Johnson's aim of creating a new league was not purely entrepreneurial and self-serving. In 1893, Johnson, on the advice of his friend Cincinnati manager Charles Comiskey, the retired first baseman and future Hall of Fame owner of the Chicago White Sox, had been convinced to resurrect the failed Western League, a minor league that since its inception in 1879 had been feeding players as a "farm system" to the National League. Comiskey, already important for having innovated the practice of first basemen playing "off the bag to scoop up grounders and throw to covering pitchers," was helping to lay the seeds of a new league that would become the National League's most powerful rival.[54]

Comiskey had convinced his friend Ban Johnson to resurrect the Western League. From the ashes of a minor league circuit, and through several shrewd moves in a span of less than eight seasons, Johnson not only sustained the Western League, but by 1901, had transformed it from a minor league to a major league circuit, renaming it the American League. In creating a new professional league, Johnson sought reform. Johnson aimed at creating a brand of baseball that contrasted with the National League, which had developed a bad reputation: it had become commonplace for players to assault umpires, where riots had become too often the norm. Johnson sought to pattern baseball's new "league along the lines of scholastic contest, to make ability and brains and clean, honorable play."[55]

Surely, these were goals that Chadwick sympathized with. His opposition of the AL clearly stemmed in part to the aggressiveness by which Johnson raided the National League of some its players. Chadwick's sense of moral righteousness was violated when Johnson and the AL acted in such a manner, but he should have displayed his admiration for Johnson sooner in print. Chadwick was nearing 80 and was getting increasingly conservative. His reaction toward the new league may have been due to the swift changes that Johnson had embarked on. However, Chadwick's reaction mirrored his early response to the founding of the National League in 1876. Chadwick had developed an emotional connection to the NL, like he had earlier for the National Association. On the other hand, with the founding of the National League, his response was confusion and hurt rather than outright viciousness. Despite his reputation and his advocacy of propriety and fair play, Chadwick showed that he was all too human when it impinged on his territory. On some level, he could be forgiven for that, after all he was "the father of the game." Besides, as shown, Chadwick did realize, soon enough, with Johnson taking action against McGraw, the American League really did mean business.

The decade of the 1890s was one of great activity for Chadwick. Many of Chadwick's friends, those who had known him since the early years of the game, had true respect for Chadwick's contributions. Among those were his close friend and fellow innovator, Harry Wright. However, Wright was not around to see Chadwick accept his annuity from the rules committee. Chadwick, who had already mourned the death of his brother in 1890, suffered the loss of his friend Harry Wright in 1895. In 1893, Wright completed helping the Philadelphia club become a championship-level team when he left to become chief of umpires of the National League. The following year, Wright began to have health problems. Over the next couple of years, Wright's condition alternated between better and worse. Wright narrowly escaped blindness and was left with an arthritic condition that caused his limbs to bloat for a time. Though he recovered from these ailments, Wright's overall health was worsening. When Wright's sight began to fail him once again, the doctor's diagnosis was catarrhal pneumonia. By this time he was in a sanatorium in Atlantic City, New Jersey, where it was hoped he could heal from his wretched state. Wright's condition ameliorated briefly, but he suffered a relapse and died with his third wife and five children next to him.[56]

Chadwick wrote, "No death among the professional fraternity has occurred which elicited such painful regret" as Wright's passing. In the press he rued that Harry had "gone before me." Chadwick recalled that only a few months earlier, Wright had regained his eyesight and had begun riding a bicycle to his great enjoyment. But now, Chadwick lamented, "he is no more." In a fitting tribute to Wright, Chadwick paid homage to the father of professional baseball and his contributions to the great American game.[57]

> To every worthy young ball player he was a father figure to a son, and to those of older growth, who were deserving of his regard he was the true friend and counselor. In deportment and conduct to umpires in the game he was truly a model manager and captain, not a single one approaching him in this respect. A loving husband, a devoted parent and true friend, Harry Wright's loss is mourned by thousands, while by his sterling integrity of character alone he presented a model every professional ball player can copy from with great gain to this individual reputation, and to public esteem and popularity. Let us trust that in the coming time one may look upon his like again.[58]

After 1891, with no American Association to present its champion to match the National League winner in a world championship series, the National League struggled to create interest in the postseason. With several experiments failing to arouse fan interest, the league could not come up with a suitable way to present a champion. Though there were twelve teams in the league, three clubs essentially dominated the 1890s — Boston, Brooklyn and Baltimore — leaving the other nine to battle in the mud of mediocrity. The absence of competitive teams in New York, Philadelphia and Chicago, three of the most populous cities, financially damaged the National League. Also, the development of Sunday games, made out of necessity with the inclusion in the league of four clubs from the former American Association, meant that some cities played ball on the Sabbath and some did not. Even in Chicago, the original National League morality broke down.

While Chadwick seemed to be positively stimulated by his confrontation with Freedman, other aspects of his life seemed to be going well during this decade. In the first week of August 1898, cards announcing that the 19th of that month would be the fiftieth wedding anniversary of Henry and Jane Chadwick were sent to their friends and relatives. Henry and Jane spent the morning of their anniversary at Trinity Church, the church in which they exchanged their nuptials fifty summers earlier. Henry and Jane then went on a two-week tour, "a sort of second honeymoon," as Chadwick explained to an *Eagle* reporter with a chuckle, to Montreal and Quebec. Chadwick, not one to miss a beat, caught a game, in Montreal, by invitation between the home club and Buffalo. At the conclusion of the trip, on September 5, the Chadwicks returned home to their friends at their residence of 257 Greene Avenue.[59]

In the following year, on the morning of October 28, 1899, Chadwick met with President William McKinley about supplying base ball equipment to the army "at the government's expense."[60] First, Chadwick called on McKinley's secretary, George B. Cortelyou, so he could give the president an editorial written about his proposal in the *Washington Star*, published on the Wednesday, October 25 edition.[61] It read:

> The suggestion which has been recently advanced by Mr. Henry Chadwick, the veteran base ball writer, that the United States troops be furnished gratis with base ball outfits is worthy of consideration by the military authorities. It is well known that soldiers when off duty are eager for some sort of exercise.... The small pay of the soldier does not permit him to contribute much to this purpose, and often it is difficult to secure a proper amount of attention to the games which thus invite the men, because of the lack of equipment.... The training which a man receives on the base ball diamond or the foot ball gridiron is of rare value in maintaining a high state of muscular efficiency, which will be of service when the troops are called into action involving an exposure to fatiguing conditions. Such an enterprise as that suggested would have an excellent moral effect, too, in that it would assure the soldier that the government has a care for them aside from the mere routine of providing them with uniforms and fighting implements.[62]

The president received a letter from Chadwick explaining his proposition, and McKinley expressed interest in it. McKinley "suggested that Mr. Chadwick see Secretary of War" Elihu Root "in regard to the matter."[63] Chadwick suggested that the army get equipped with baseball paraphernalia when he learned that "the Navy Department furnishes Indian clubs, boxing gloves, dumbbells, foils, esc., for the men of the Navy, while on the other hand the soldiers have to pay for their athletic goods of all kinds."[64] Chadwick spoke about his journey, remarking:

> It occurred to me to change the order of things. I saw the President's secretary on Friday and asked him to get me an interview with the President, at the same time leaving an editorial from the *Washington Star* for the President to read. I was then given an appointment for an interview on Saturday at 10 A.M., which was accorded to me.[65]

The *Brooklyn Daily Eagle* building. Chadwick wrote for many publications, but he is still most closely associated with the *Brooklyn Eagle*.

The president was pleased to see Chadwick and welcomed him cordially. "I am very glad to see you, Mr. Chadwick. I know you by name," President McKinley said. The two men shook hands. Chadwick asked if he had read the editorial sent to him and McKinley said he had read it with great interest. Chadwick then asked if he approved of the idea, but McKinley, to Chadwick's disappointment, "said he could not express an opinion, as it was not within his province." McKinley then suggested that Chadwick meet with Root. Unfortunately, Root was not present for Chadwick to meet; instead, Chadwick presented the subject matter to his secretary, Mr. Mason, who would bring it to his attention.[66] Once again, Chadwick was laying groundwork. Baseball was played during the Civil War, but it was not sanctioned by the United States government. Over the next several decades, long after Chadwick was gone, the army would draft major league players for war. Joe DiMaggio, Hank Greenberg, Ted Williams and Bob Feller would all served military time, building on

An aged Henry Chadwick, show here ca. 1900, fighting to stay with the times. He was revered in many circles, but some thought his views, such as his disdain for the home run, were old-fashioned.

Chadwick's belief that baseball and the military should have a relationship.

For the sixty-fourth anniversary of the *Brooklyn Eagle* in 1905, Chadwick recalled the early days of Brooklyn and compared, among other things, sports and pastimes in the 1840s with the present-day sports and pastimes for the young, favoring the latter. He wrote:

We boys of the period were deprived of nearly every facility for recreative exercise in the way of out-door sport such as the boys of the present time now revel in.... In the 1840s there was nothing but horse racing in the way of public sport at command. It is true our English residents had cricket to enjoy, and some of the "old American boys" of the period had a form of baseball which afforded them some field exercise, but we boys of the old time were limited to skating in the winter — and that of the poorer kind — and to "running with the machines" — that is, going to fires after our favorite fire engine.[67]

Though writing for *Sporting Life* and the *Sporting News* may have been beneficial, Chadwick may have grown tired of the demands. As a result, on May 22, 1907, Chadwick returned to the *Eagle* to write and edit exclusively for the paper. He also changed homes, moving from 275 Steuben Street in Greenpoint to *The Glen*, 840 Halsey Street, in Bedford-Stuyvesant.[68]

An indication of Chadwick's fragility was reported on July 28, 1906, when the *Eagle* wrote that Chadwick, stricken with rheumatism, his second attack in over a decade, was confined to his bed. Although the *Eagle* reported that Chadwick had just completed his English baseball guide and that his "Mexican base ball guide was soon to be issued," a representative from *Sporting Life* found the veteran journalist in bed "chafing under the enforced restraint from his customary activities, and every now and then crying out from the terrible spasms of pain he had on moving his rheumatically inflamed limbs."[69] According to the article, Chadwick told the reporter that he had sustained a bad fall on the Fifth Avenue L at the Flatbush and Fulton station, caused by the train being started before he could leave it. He had partially recovered from the effects while going down stairs a week afterward, his knee gave way under him and he had another fall. His great recuperative power enabled the veteran to rally, and in the last week had gotten to work again. On July 19, he visited the Staten Island Cricket Club grounds on the occasion of the intercity match with Philadelphia, Mr. Chadwick acting as scorer for the Americans. The fatigue of that day's trip, however, proved too much for him and that night his physician had to be called. A severe attack of inflammatory rheumatism had developed itself, from which Chadwick was now suffering.

Despite his many ailments, Chadwick remained a seminal figure in baseball circles. But soon, not only would "The Father of Baseball" — as he was being called by then — face physical challenges, he would be aggressively confronted in a different kind of way. In the last years of his life, one of his closest friends, Albert Goodwill Spalding, would pick a fight with the elderly Chadwick that would challenge and overwhelm the Dean of all sportswriters' long-held advocacy that baseball had evolved from rounders. The results of this fight would shape the way the origin of baseball was viewed for the next century and, even more importantly, alter the way Chadwick would be remembered by the public.

CHAPTER 7

Al Spalding and the Origins for a Feud

As the nineteenth century came to a close, as baseball entered its second century of existence as the national game, it had fully matured and progressed as a pastime familiar to every American. Progress would soon be a word familiar to all Americans, too. With the reelection of William McKinley in 1900, Americans throughout the nation had no reason to foresee a new era in American government. However, McKinley's murder in September 1901 by assassin Leon Czolgosz in Buffalo, New York, changed all that. Vice President Theodore Roosevelt, the muckraking governor of New York who had been given the vice presidency to, in effect, stem his progressive political career, ascended to the White House. Now with Roosevelt in charge, changes were to come — a new era in which government would intercede on behalf of its citizens and protect them from the wrath of giant corporate monopolies. Roosevelt would also become the first environmental president, making conservation part of his agenda.

Baseball also was facing a new era. With two major professional leagues fueling the interest of fans across the nation, baseball was headed in a new direction. If baseball in the 1800s was characterized by change, experimentation and evolution, the new century would become characterized by familiarity and tradition. The early century produced baseball's classic confrontation: the World Series. Debuting in 1903, it featured the American League champion, the Boston Americans, battling the National League's best, the Pittsburgh Pirates, in a best-of-nine series. This series was established in an effort to promote unity in baseball since the two major leagues had become fierce rivals. Nine years earlier, when Boston was in the senior circuit, both clubs had met in an experimental postseason, with Boston emerging as the victor, five games to three, to win the Temple Cup, the championship prize awarded to the best team each year in the 1890s. Pirates owner Barney Dreyfuss and Americans owner Henry Killilea agreed to meet in this new edition for a world's championship. Little did Dreyfuss and Killilea foresee what their championship match would create historically for the game of baseball. Led by the great Cy Young, Boston defeated the Pirates and Honus Wagner.[1]

By the turn of the century, with the great era of experimentation over, baseball had developed into a major sport, one that had completely matured. Henry Chadwick's work — his nurturing of baseball, his innovativeness, and his creativity — had certainly borne fruit.

The early twentieth century saw many of his friends and colleagues once again recognize Chadwick's great achievements. At nearly eighty years of age, he was approaching fifty years of baseball journalism. Friends and admirers, among them Spalding; Stewart L. Woodford, the ex-minister to Spain; sportswriters Jacob C. Morse, C.C. Spink and Francis Richter; and National League presidents, both past and present, Nicholas E. Young and Harry C. Pulliam, all wrote to Chadwick to congratulate him on his life and career's work. Spink did the best job in his letter in summing up Chadwick's lifetime of efforts.

> Dear Mr. Chadwick: The splendid service that you have given the Sporting News as correspondent and the success that you have achieved as the Editor of the Spalding Guide, attest to your ability as a journalist, and in tendering to you my congratulations on reaching the eightieth year of your age, and the fiftieth of your professional career, I desire to express the sense of satisfaction I have in the thought that you will entertain and instruct the base ball public for many seasons. You did more than anyone else to popularize baseball, and chiefly through your efforts the game has been almost redeemed from the reign of rowdyism which has handicapped it for years. With a renewal of my congratulations and assurance of my best wishes...
>
> Respectfully, C.C. Spink.

Despite Henry Chadwick's reputation as baseball's "father," and his role in helping to cultivate the game's growth, he became embroiled in baseball's most controversial disputes involving the game's origins. The argument centered on whether the National Pastime had evolved from the

British game of rounders, as Chadwick believed, or whether the game was purely of American origins, a theory supported by former pitching great and current baseball magnate Albert Spalding of Spalding Sporting Goods. Spalding and Chadwick were friends, and Chadwick had worked for Spalding as the editor of the *Spalding Guides* since the early 1880s. However, despite their friendship and long history together, Spalding took a rather aggressive route in challenging Chadwick's contention.

The baseball origins dispute took its most infamous turn when Spalding embraced late Civil War general Abner Doubleday as the game's inventor. Spalding had no real evidence to support his theory other than a letter from Abner Graves of Denver, Colorado, a nut who contended that when he was a small child he saw Doubleday invent the game in Cooperstown, New York. Spalding and Abraham G. Mills tackled the notion with such great enthusiasm that the American public, with the exception of a small few, took the bait cast by the two very powerful, wealthy businessmen and believed the story.

Spalding, in effect, won the argument not so much on the theory's veracity but by his ability to convince the public that Doubleday invented the game. Chadwick was a brilliant man in many ways, but he was overmatched against Spalding's genius for marketing and his business savvy. Harkening back to the days when Spalding dominated hitters with his delivery and clever pitching, Chadwick was clearly dominated and overwhelmed by the public relations moves pulled off by Spalding and the others involved in the story. Spalding's support for this idea was so successful that even after one hundred years, the general public still believes that a Civil War general invented the game.

As has been mentioned in a previous chapter, Chadwick may have been the game's first historian. Throughout the nineteenth century, Henry Chadwick periodically wrote articles on the game's history, making the connection between rounders and baseball. The first appearance of such a claim was in the 1860 *Beadle's Dime Base Ball Guide*. As a youngster in Plymouth, England, Chadwick played rounders and made the logical assumption, given the similarities of the two bat-and-ball games and given America's British cultural heritage, that baseball derived from the British bat-and-ball game.

Later, in an 1867 essay on the game's history, he tried to explain the connection between the two sports by tracing baseball to an earlier version of rounders called *bars*, a game played by English youth in the first half of the fourteenth century, during the reign of King Edward the Third.

Chadwick wrote that the game "consisted in running from one bar or barrier to another." Chadwick injected a bit of historical reference when he added that "it grew so popular that it at last became a nuisance, so that the barons of England, as they went to the Parliament House, were annoyed by the bands of children engaged in playing it." Chadwick explained how the name of the game changed:

> The name of this game was subsequently corrupted to "base".... The skill in this game consisted simply in running with agility and swiftness, in such a way as not to be caught by the opposing party, from one "bar" or "base" to another. After a while somebody thought of uniting with it the game of ball, and thus formed the game of "rounders," "rounder ball," or "base ball." "Rounders" took its name from the fact that the players were obliged to run *round* a sort of circle of bases....[2]

Today there is extensive debate regarding whether rounders and baseball were separate games. In *Baseball Before We Knew It*, David Block refutes that baseball derived from rounders, that the game of baseball even existed in England, predating the British game. Other historians, like Frederick Ivor-Campbell, disagree, writing that while "base ball" precedes the word "rounders," they were essentially the same game, but had different names due to regional customs. Whether the two sports were the same or not, or whether baseball had existed in England prior to rounders, Chadwick, nonetheless, correctly believed that baseball was British in origin. Chadwick summed it up best in his publication the *Ball Player's Chronicle* when, in the July 18, 1867 edition, he wrote how the "whole subject," of the game's origins "needs elucidation, and a careful study of the rural sports of the mother country would undoubtedly throw much light upon the history of base ball."

Regardless of whether Chadwick was correct or incorrect about the game's true origins, he did ignite a debate that others, years after he introduced his theories, began to take part in.

One of the biggest challenges Chadwick faced prior to Spalding was Will Rankin's theories on the game's origins. Rankin was a baseball writer with a deep knowledge of the game that even competed with the encyclopedic brilliance of Chadwick. In 1886, Rankin, a man who had amassed perhaps the greatest library on the national pastime, was the first to doubt the historical connection between rounders and baseball.

It should be noted that Rankin was baseball journalist par excellence. He had a reputation for being thorough and conscientious in his work. A native of southern Pennsylvania, Rankin was born May 23, 1849, but he moved to Brooklyn in 1865 and then to Nyack, in Rockland County, in upstate New York in 1868.[3] Rankin played amateur ball in the mid 1860s, but turned to baseball journalism in 1872 for the *Rockland County Journal*. Later, Rankin would write for many papers, including the *New York Times, Daily Witness, Tribune, Sporting World* and eventually the *New York Clipper*, becoming assistant editor when Chadwick left in 1888. His contribution to this publication was enormous. Under his leadership, Rankin staffed a "number of 'baseball centers' with competent observer-writers," and he "vitalized its coverage and blanketed the major-league world." These reports were not confined to the scores of the game. Not unlike the modern dailies of the twentieth and twenty-first centuries, his reports were filled with gossip of the baseball world. In a way he was like a modern-day Peter Gammons, drawing the public in with rumors on inside wheelings and dealings of the baseball world. By 1894, Rankin became the *Clipper*'s lead sporting editor.[4]

Though Henry Chadwick played a significant role in helping Rankin obtain a job as a city reporter for the *New York Sunday Mercury*, they were to butt heads numerous times, especially after Rankin published his essay on the origins of baseball to counter Henry Chadwick's theories. Rankin's "Our National Game" was printed in nearly every leading paper throughout the country, and it elevated the debate to another level. Rankin defied Chadwick's theory that baseball came from rounders by believing that baseball simply "sprang up." In his challenge he even attacked Charles Darwin, appealing to Christian fundamentalists, when he wrote that both the theory of baseball descending from rounders and Darwin's theory of the origin of man lack "the necessary connecting links to carry out the idea."

Rankin, in an attempt to dispel the relationship between the two ball games, proceeded to highlight the differences between rounders and baseball. He wrote that rounders' bat was flat compared to baseball's round shape, and that the configuration of rounders' field was square to baseball's diamond form. He also noted that rounders still practiced "plugging" or "soaking," the custom of throwing out a runner by hitting him with the ball. Of course, Rankin made a large error with this last point, for baseball, before a change in the rules, used "plugging."[5]

The 1886 challenge was not the only time Rankin disputed Chadwick's theory on baseball's origin. In the *Sporting News* fifteen years after his initial article, Ranking once again laid into Chadwick's theories. This time Rankin espoused his own ideas on the game's origins. Interestingly, this article was placed right next to a Chadwick article, the one in which Chadwick praised Ban Johnson for suspending John McGraw for kicking an umpire. Unlike his earlier piece in which he wrote that baseball just "sprang up," Rankin said the game derived from bat-and-ball games played by Native Americans, writing that "the Mohawks, the Oneidas, the Hurons, the Abuakis, the Seminoles and the Cherokees, and, coming down to a later day, the Sioux, the Creeks, the Comanches and other tribes contended with the ball and bat, tribe against tribe, in friendly rivalry."[6] Rankin's article clearly distanced himself from Chadwick's views.

> The modern game of base ball is an American institution and not, as some people might believe, an exotic of foreign growth which has come to us from older civilizations of Europe and the East. The game from which our present sport is derived ... is as distinctly American as is our wild and boundless Western scenery or the spirit of freedom and independence which animates us as a people.[7]

Rankin is plainly referring to Chadwick. And Rankin ended his article by referring to an October 26, 1861, *New York Clipper* essay in which the writer discussed baseball's roots as being exclusively an American game despite the similarities between the game and rounders. After the paragraph, Rankin wrote, in hidden reference to Chadwick, how:

> The above [article] certainly takes all the romance out of that pipe store which appeared in a Cincinnati paper several months ago, and in part said: "Little did I dream when playing 'rounders' in Plymouth, Devonshire, England, that I should afterward become chief gardener, so to speak, who, from the little English acorn of 'rounders,' helped to cultivate the giant American oak of base ball."[8]

Rankin, in using the famous quote by Chadwick, took a direct stab at "the Father of Baseball" and his theory. Rankin then concluded his long article, which mostly consisted of paragraphs of various articles written about the game's roots, by saying that:

> If there has ever been any doubts about the origin of our national game of base ball or the public has been misled by the belief that it was the outgrowth of "Rounders" or "townball," the above quotations should dispel that allusion and forever settle the question that its origins is American pure and simple.[9]

Rankin, for whatever reason, was clearly at war with Chadwick and his views on the subject. Rankin's initial attack on Chadwick's rounders theory in 1886 began a series of confrontations by other figures driven by nationalism.

Only two years after Rankin's initial swipe at Chadwick's rounders-baseball connection was a challenge issued by John Montgomery Ward. Chadwick and Monte Ward had battled during the players' rebellion; this time they jousted over the game's origins. Ward had his own theories on how baseball came about. In *Base-Ball: How to Become a Player*, the erudite Ward began his book with a history of baseball. In the introduction, one comes away convinced that Ward is indeed an expert on the subject. Entitled "An Inquiry Into the Origin of Base-Ball," Ward's introduction displayed the erudition of a college professor, citing the Greek historian Herodotus and the epic poet Homer when discussing the invention of the first ball used for pastime. But what makes Ward's history compelling is his denial, in the same vein as the eventual Spalding denial, of baseball's British heritage, specifically its derivation from rounders. His attack on Chadwick's theory is especially biting, though he never mentioned the father of baseball by name.

Ward assailed Chadwick and the advocates of baseball's English ancestry by claiming that because of baseball's growth and popularity over cricket in the 1850s, jealousy against the "rising upstart" and snobbery, "the belief everything good and beautiful in the world must be of English origin," led to the theory that baseball had to have descended from an English game.[10]

Ward then fired another salvo by writing that one "of the strongest advocates of the rounder theory, an Englishman-born himself, was the writer for out-door sports on the principal metropolitan publications."[11] Ward began his assault effectively and it became a familiar one, bringing up Chadwick's British-born heritage as a way of undermining the old man's authority. None other than Spalding later echoed this technique against Chadwick when the retired ace leveled his own assault on the rounders-baseball theory.

After faulting Chadwick's British ethnicity, Ward added that Chadwick "has lost no opportunity to advance his pet theory," and that "[s]ubsequent writers have, blindly, it would seem, followed this lead, until now we find it asserted on every hand as a fact established by some indisputable evidence." Finishing off his assault, fittingly given his Columbia legal degree, as if he were a lawyer in a court room, Ward sniffed that "there has never been adduced a particle of proof to support this conclusion."[12]

Ward did, however, refrain from a total attack on Chadwick. He wrote of the great respect he had him, for what Chadwick had done for baseball "both as a journalist and as a man." Ward understood that Henry Chadwick's contribution to the game was enormous and that the national sport owed "him a monument of gratitude for the brave fight he [had] always made against the enemies and abuses of the game."[13]

But while he retreated from his attack on Chadwick momentarily, Ward went back on the warpath by debunking the idea that rounders was the older game, adding that baseball could not have derived from rounders since it predated it. He wrote that there "is ample living testimony to its existence as early perhaps as 1830, but that it was a popular English game before base-ball was played here I am not ready to believe."[14]

Ward also surveyed the history of baseball in America, reporting that old Knickerbocker Colonel Jason Lee, in 1846, at the age of 60, said that he "often played the same game when a boy" and that Dr. Oliver Wendell Holmes, the poet and father of future Supreme Court Justice Oliver Wendell Holmes Jr., a graduate of Harvard in 1829, said to a Boston paper that baseball was "one of the sports of his college days...."[15] Given that Ward traced baseball back that far, one might assume that he would arrive at the same conclusion that Rankin did: that baseball "sprang up." But, Ward had a little surprise. He wrote that baseball derived from old-cat games like one old-cat and two old-cat. Both games, like baseball, Monty pointed out, had a bat and a ball, and a batter, pitcher, catcher and fielders involved in the contests. Then, he declared with great confidence, but without too much documentation to back him up, that "from one-old-cat to base-ball is a short step.... That base-ball actually did develop in this way was the generally accepted theory for many years." Who else held this "accepted" theory Ward failed to mention. In his conclusion, in his final analysis, once again as if he were presenting his final case to the jury, he averred:

> I reassert my belief that our national game is a home production. In the field of out-door sports the American boy is easily capable of devising his own amusements, and until some proof is adduced that base-ball is not his invention I protest against this systematic effort to rob him of his dues.[16]

Chadwick, instead of walking away from a fight, battled back. In the July 1, 1888, edition of the *Brooklyn Eagle*, Chadwick asked, with reference to the connection between baseball and rounders, "Was the former game evolved from the latter?" Chadwick began by presenting an excerpt from the previously discussed 1860 *Beadle's Dime Base Ball* book. In this excerpt, the rules of rounders are explained to show the connection between the two games and to provide the reader with an historical background to lend credence to his argument. Then Chadwick confronted Ward's dispute directly. First he tackled Ward's belief that rounders was a relatively new game and could not have given rise to baseball. Chadwick proclaimed that rounders was a game "I used to play over fifty years ago, as my grandfather had similarly played it a hundred years previous."[17] Afterward, he dismissed Ward's "attempt to make [baseball] a distinctive game of strictly American origin, as Mr. Ward does in his otherwise ably written book on base ball," by writing that the game, being strictly American in origin, "is not in accordance with historical facts, to say the least."[18] What historical facts Chadwick used was absent in his own argument, but he did make a compelling point, and perhaps even a dig at Rankin's weak comparison, when he wrote that baseball "as played in Hoboken over forty years ago had for its rules the old rounders' rule of putting a base runner out by hitting him with a thrown ball."[19]

Chadwick, in response to Ward's book, mocked Ward's legalistic approach, writing, "There is no need of presenting any arguments in the case, as the connection between rounders and base ball is too plain to be mistaken." Chadwick then remarked with great confidence or even with slight arrogance, "[w]hy Mr. Ward should strive to repudiate the ancestry of base ball surprises me." Then Chadwick dispelled Ward's futile attempt to nullify the game's British heritage while defending his own by adding that the "evolution of our grand game of to-day is beyond question American work, and as an Englishman I am proud of the aid I have been able to give in the work."[20]

In the next sentence, Chadwick attempted to foster a sense of patriotism when he added that the "improvement introduced are such as accord with American sports and with Americanized English sports, for we attach new and improved methods of play to every English sport we adopt."[21] In summation, Chadwick finished with a grand conclusion:

> Suffice it to say that base ball as now played, no matter what its origin, is a distinctive American game, alike in its rules and its method of play, even though its origin can be readily traced to the English schoolboy game above mentioned.[22]

Luckily, Chadwick was not alone in his rounders-to-baseball theory. In a December 1888 article in the *Brooklyn Eagle*, announcing the death of astronomer Richard Proctor the paper printed his views on the subject. Chadwick knew Proctor and cited him in his letter to Edwin. Proctor was the first man to publish a complete map of the surface of Mars. How much attention the public gave Proctor's opinion is difficult to gauge, but what he had going for him could have worked against him as well. Highly educated, Proctor, like Chadwick, was English-born but eventually became an American citizen.[23] Therefore, Proctor had thorough knowledge of the rules of both games. And, like Chadwick, Proctor played rounders as a child, saw the connections between the two games, and was convinced that baseball and rounders were linked.[24] However, given Proctor's British heritage and scholarly viewpoint, his views may not have been taken seriously by the average American man. The article, like Chadwick's in July, rebuked Ward. Proctor simply regarded "the two games as one and the same," and observed that the difference between baseball and rounders in name was a "mere accident."[25] Proctor explained that rounders got its name "because it depends on making the round of the bases ... whereas when it became established in America it was called base ball because it depends on bases being circuited." Proctor used an historical analogy to make the point that "American independence was won by British colonists..." and that every "Briton is as fully and justly entitled to be proud of George Washington (who was not only of purely British blood ... bred under the British flag) as of Oliver Cromwell." The difference in name between baseball and rounders, Proctor added:

> No more makes the War of Independence different in kind from the Civil War in the old country that the name "base ball" make the game differ from our British "rounders." But to say this is not to claim from Americans what is their due; it is simply an expression of the sense of oneness of British blood on both sides of the Atlantic which every Briton and every American ... ought to feel.[26]

Despite his knowledge of history, Proctor did undermine himself, inadvertently, when he presented this British viewpoint. Furthermore, Proctor admitted that he had no shred of evidence "that the name rounders is as old as, for instance, the settlement of Virginia," though he claimed "hearing an old man of 80" four decades earlier "speak of rounders as played at Harrow when he was a boy."[27]

However truthful or not the arguments were on both sides of the issue, however slanted and biased those involved in the arguments were, the debate was only heating up. Spalding began espousing his own theory of baseball origins. Spalding's initial premise was closer to the truth than his later theories. At an address before the Public Schools Athletic League of Greater New York, Spalding said that "base ball is of American origin, was born in New York City, and the first base ball ground was located about where Madison Square Garden stands."[28]

The controversy over baseball origins took on a whole different meaning the following year. In March 1889, at a posh banquet held at New York's finest restaurant, Delmonico's, located on 5th Avenue and 26th Street in Manhattan, the baseball origins controversy escalated to new levels. The dinner was held to celebrate the return of Albert Spalding and "his troupe of ball players from an around-the-world tour" to promote the national game. Luminaries such as Mark Twain and a rising political figure named Theodore Roosevelt were in attendance when former National League president Abraham G. Mills announced, once and for all, that the combination of "patriotism and research determined that baseball had no foreign origin.[29] The audience responded, "No rounders! No rounders!"[30]

It was common, even for sophisticated men like Spalding, Mills, and even Roosevelt, to echo such nationalistic tones. Leading American thinkers in the late nineteenth century began to espouse nationalistic philosophies about the origins of American culture. Among them was Frederick Jackson Turner, who, in 1893, while a professor of history at the University of Wisconsin, composed one of the most important historical treatises on Western civilization, "The Frontier Thesis." While the main thrust of his thesis was his point that the American frontier had closed and that "American energy will continually demand a wider field for its exercise" — a statement welcomed by expansionists — he stressed that, among other things, the ever-expanding continental frontier in America had formed a unique character, a distinctive American character, one that had no connection to foreign elements past or present. As Turner wrote in his work:

> Behind institutions, behind constitutional forms and modifications, lie the vital forces that call these organs into life and shape them to meet changing conditions. The peculiarity of American institutions is the fact that they have been compelled to adapt themselves to the changes involved in crossing a continent, in winning a wilderness and in developing at each area of this progress out of the primitive political conditions of the frontier into the complexity of city life.[31]

Other factors contributed to this need to create the desire of a highly distinctive American culture. The Industrial Revolution and a new wave of immigration, consisting of eastern and southern Europeans who, when arriving in the United States, worked in factories with poor ventilation and low wages, further complicated matters. The strain caused by these two realties led many to fear that social tensions would turn to violence.[32] Many immigrants turned to spectator sports, and baseball was especially attractive, as it was the American pastime, a game that gave immigrants a feeling of belonging. As a result, many of baseball's leaders took it upon themselves to promote the game as an indigenous American sport. Albert Goodwill Spalding, in particular, was one of these men. Spalding, like Ward and Rankin, beginning in the 1870s and continuing through the early 1900s, espoused the nativist theory about baseball's heritage, even though Spalding had at one time accepted Chadwick's argument that baseball came from rounders. Spalding and the others may have been promoting this new idea in response to the new wave of immigration. Spalding's promotion of the national game as being purely of American derivation was an attempt to foster a sense of belonging to all Americans, new and old. Spalding stated that baseball was a completely indigenous sport originating in the countryside and that it espoused American values. This was another example of Spalding's genius for marketing baseball. Part of his promotion consisted of "portraying the owners as benevolent citizens who operated their franchises out of concern for the public interest, that players came from rural regions, and that the sport was open to anyone with talent and perseverance. Two of the principal functions ascribed to baseball were that it would teach children traditional American values and that it would help newcomers assimilate into the dominant WASP culture through their participation in the sport's rituals."[33] In many ways, Chadwick bought into this ideology himself. His role during the great players' rebellion in 1990 that led to the formation of the Players' League was a good example of this philosophy.

Despite his role in the players' rebellion and his own belief in the "benevolence" of baseball's executives, Chadwick stuck with his rounders theory. And though he disagreed with Spalding and knew that his boss's theory about baseball's origins was a myth, he sympathized, like he always had, with those who sought to portray baseball as a purely American game. Chadwick skirted his differences with Spalding and mollified his readers by saying that baseball was indigenous to America because it was in this country that the game was organized and standardized, even though it had originated as an English ballgame.[34] While Chadwick sympathized with Spalding's quest to prove baseball's origins as being American on the one hand, there was another part of Chadwick that could not understand Spalding's persistent need to prove baseball's American origins. The fact that the game had originated in England did not "detract one iota from the merit of its being unquestionably a thoroughly American field sport, and a game too, which is fully adapted to the American character."[35]

Once again, the debate was reopened when Spalding requested that Chadwick write an article on baseball's origins. When the "Father of Baseball" naturally traced the game's ancestry to rounders, Spalding decided an official debate was necessary.[36] In the 1905 edition of *Spalding's Official Baseball Guide*, Albert Spalding and Henry Chadwick went head-to-head to debate the true origins of baseball.

In the 1905 *Guide*, Spalding wrote that though "Mr. Chadwick's Rounder theory is entitled to much weight because of his long connection with Base Ball and the magnificent work he had done in the upbuilding of the game for upwards of fifty years, yet [he was] unwilling longer to accept his Rounder theory without something more convincing than his oft-repeated assertion that 'Base Ball did originate from Rounders.'"[37]

Spalding spelled out what he intends to do to his friend of forty years.

> For the purpose of settling this question I hereby challenge the Grand Old Man of Baseball to produce his proofs and demonstrate in some tangible way, if he can, that our national game derived from Rounders.[38]

In his challenge, Spalding insinuated, echoing Ward's accusation, that Chadwick was unfairly biased because he "is of English birth, and was rocked in a 'Rounders' cradle."[39] He then remarked that the game had not evolved from rounders, but had instead, mirroring Ward's idea, "evolved from a colonial American game called one-old-cat, maturing into its present form thanks to the ingenuity and creativity of succeeding generations of American youth."[40] Not completely satisfied with his own ideas, Spalding then proposed that a commission be established to once and for all determine the true origins of the game.[41]

He further proposed that his old friend Abraham (a.k.a. A.G.) Mills chair a commission to decide how baseball came about. The Mills Commission consisted of several prominent men, all with some involvement with baseball. First was Arthur P. Gorman, a United States Senator from Maryland who was an amateur baseball player and ex-president of the old National Baseball Club of Washington. Next, Morgan Bulkeley, the former governor of Connecticut, was the first president of the National League. Then there was Nick E. Young, one of the founders of the National Association. Young was also an ex-player and was the fourth president of the National League. The other members were Al Reach, an old time ballplayer turned sportswriter; George Wright, Harry's brother, an exshortstop for Cincinnati and Boston who had become a successful businessman; and James E. Sullivan of New York, president of the American Sports Publishing Company. Sullivan was appointed secretary of the commission.

Then there was the chairman himself. Abraham Gilbert Mills, like Spalding, was no stranger to marketing and promotion. A Civil War veteran who received his law degree in Washington, D.C., at Columbian Law School (now George Washington Law School), Colonel Mills excelled in sales, joining the Hale Elevator Company. After the Otis Elevator Company bought Hale, Mills rose to the level of vice president, spending thirty-five years with the corporation. But it was his work in baseball that truly gave Mills his status. He served three years, from 1882 to 1885, as president of the National League. It was Mills who authored the National Agreement, signed between the National League and the American Association in 1883, which brought success and harmony to the game.[42] Mills, in a letter to Albert Spalding dated March 1, 1905, had his own recollections of early ball games. Mills remembered playing one-old-cat and two-old-cat in New York City, where he grew up, also adding that he played town ball, too, at Union Hall Academy, located on Jamaica, Long Island (present-day Jamaica, Queens). And though he admitted that he had never heard of rounders "until Chadwick claimed that it was the origin of the American game of baseball," Mills "never thought it worthwhile to dispute this claim of Mr. Chadwick's."[43] Regarding Chadwick's theory, Mills initially advised Spalding to wait.

> Chadwick is a feeble old man now, and I am inclined to advise you not to be too hard on him. In the course of nature, he will pass away soon and then it will be time enough to wipe up the floor with his particular theories.[44]

Spalding probably liked what he heard from Mills, but obviously did not want to wait until Chadwick's death to get the ball rolling. It was not in Spalding's nature to be patient. After all, it was Chadwick who had said that Spalding was like "stirring Western merchant, full of ... nerve, pluck, independence, and push."[45]

In light of the theories being bandied between Mills and Spalding, there is another aspect to the baseball origins debate that needs to be examined. In an 1894 article on baseball's beginnings, on this subject, eleven years before the issue became a hot topic of discussion, Chadwick wrote:

> [n]ext Tuesday will be the anniversary of the first match game of baseball ever played, which took place at Hoboken, N.J. on June 19, 1846. The

game of baseball had originated nearly nine months before. It had gradually grown out of the old English school-boy game of rounders. *Like man, baseball is the result of evolution* [emphasis added].[46]

This sentence reveals not only Chadwick's views of baseball history; it also reveals Chadwick's views on religion and science, and adds another aspect to the game's origins debate. Chadwick, like many progressive and reform-minded people of his age, accepted the "new science" regarding man's evolution put forth by Charles Darwin in his books, *Origin of Species* and *The Descent of Man*. Chadwick, as was written earlier, was much like his father and brother, accepting and often using scientific methods. Of course, not everyone agreed with the theory of evolution. Christian fundamentalists, naturally, were against it. And as mentioned earlier, Will Rankin had taken a swipe at Darwin's theories to espouse his own views on baseball's development.

Surprisingly, the baseball origins debate, to a large extent, is analogous to the debate on the origins of man. As Chadwick's evolutionary theory of baseball was an analogy for man's evolution, so too was Spalding's theory of baseball origins as being a strictly American creation, an analogy to biblical creation. Spalding proposed that the game was spontaneously invented in New York, and had not evolved from town ball and the British game of rounders. That is similar to the biblical story of Adam and Eve, where creation was spontaneous.

In its attempts at proving baseball's origins, the Mills Commission turned out to be a failure. Initially, what the commission tried to do was to make a connection with the Knickerbocker club; they toyed with several possibilities involving a Cooperstown-Knickerbocker connection, investigating one premise that "a member of the Knickerbocker Club had lived in Cooperstown, and although that connection was never established, the Commission concluded that baseball had originated in that hamlet."[47] The next question, however, remained with the game's invention.

Despite the initial difficulties encountered by this group, new life was injected into the study when Spalding came up with the answer himself. Spalding received a letter written by Abner Graves, a former mining engineer, of Denver, Colorado. Graves had grown up in Cooperstown and claimed to have witnessed a young Abner Doubleday, in 1839, invent the game of baseball before his eyes. While playing marbles behind a local tailor shop, Graves claimed that Doubleday "interrupted the game and drew a baseball diamond while he explained the game and gave it a name." Doubleday eventually joined the army and later fought in the Civil War, rising to the rank of major general. With his distinguished career as a Civil War hero, Graves wrote that Doubleday would be an "ideal candidate to be the inventor of baseball," since his tour of duty and service to his country "certainly appeals to an American's pride to have had the great national game of Baseball created and named by a Major-General in the United States Army."[48]

Interviewing former members of the Knickerbocker club, the Mills Commission attempted to find out if there were any players who originated from Cooperstown in an attempt to determine if "'Doubleday at Cooperstown and the beginning of the game in New York could be established.'" Though the link was never discovered and never documented, the Mills Commission concluded "that baseball had been invented in Cooperstown by Abner Doubleday."[49]

And, of course, there were other reasons, not just the Graves' letter, which made Doubleday an enticing figure to both Mills and Spalding, the two central men behind the story. For Mills, it was the Civil War connection. Both Mills and Doubleday were war heroes: Mills, a colonel, and Doubleday, a decorated general. In fact, Mills and Doubleday were members of the Civil War veteran's organization, the New York post of the Grand Army of the Republic. When Doubleday's body lay in state in New York's City Hall on January 30, 1893, Mills was responsible for "assembling the military honor guard that attended" Doubleday's remains.[50] Spalding, Mills and many other Americans knew of Doubleday's exploits as a soldier in the Civil War because he had written several books and numerous articles on his various roles in defeating the Confederacy. It seemed in battle that Doubleday was everywhere. A graduate of West Point, Doubleday aimed the first guns fired at Fort Sumter to begin the Civil War. He also played a pivotal role in Gettysburg, replacing General Joshua Reynolds after his death on the first day of battle. Finally, Doubleday led troops to repulse Pickett's Charge.[51]

While Mills' connection to Doubleday was through the armed forces, it was Spalding's connection to Doubleday via the Theosophy Society that helped propel the late Civil War general from war hero to baseball immortality. Unknown to the public, both Spalding and Doubleday were members of this liberal organization devoted to human solidarity, cultural understanding and self-development. While Doubleday clearly had an interest in the society's esoteric teaching — he joined the Theosophists in 1878, three years after its founding — Spalding only became involved because his second wife, Elizabeth, had been a member since 1890, when she was known as Elizabeth Mayer, and was most likely aware of Abner Doubleday since she worked for William Quan Judge, Doubleday's former associate and one of the founders of the Theosophical Society in New York. Doubleday served as interim president of the society for a time.[52]

Perhaps in an effort to impress his wife, Spalding, two years before the Mills Commission, anointed Doubleday as baseball's inventor, giving the late major general his role in the game's founding. On August 13, 1905, only four months after the Graves letter was signed, an obituary of Doubleday's death that had originally appeared in 1893 in the *Path*, a Theosophical journal, was republished in the *New Century Path*, the Theosophical Society's weekly magazine of the Point Loma, California, community to which Spalding belonged. The issue contained the obituary, word for word, from the original, but it added something in the end that the 1893 article did not include — ascribing Doubleday the role of giving baseball its name and "in large degree its development from a simpler sport; or indeed ... its *very invention*."[53]

Whether Henry Chadwick knew of Spalding's prior connection to Doubleday is unclear. There is no evidence in any of Chadwick's correspondence to suggest that Chadwick had known of Spalding's relationship to Doubleday, although he knew of Mills' connection with the Civil War general, given Doubleday's public burial ceremony and the fact that Chadwick knew Mills well and was aware of Mills' own Civil War background. Also, that Chadwick owned a mounted postcard of Abner Doubleday on which he scribbled two separate notes in pencil. The one above refers to Graves and the bottom note says, "Friend of A.G. Mills died 1893."

The results of the Mills Commission's "findings" were published in March 1908 in the *Spalding's Base Ball Guide*. The *Guide* published Chadwick's letter to the Mills Commission, reiterating his belief that baseball came from rounders. Chadwick's letter was "brief and to the point" and was much shorter than the other letters printed by the guide: one by Spalding, one by John Montgomery Ward, and one by A.G. Mills that related the final decision of the Mills Commission.

Had Chadwick been aware of the length and depth of the other's letters, he might have wanted to write a longer one. But given his knowledge of Spalding's anti-rounders theory and being aware of the bias of the members of the commission against his own beliefs, he may not have deemed it necessary to write a long letter. He may have felt that no matter what kind of letter he wrote, the Mills Commission was going to find fault with his theories anyway. Also, given Chadwick's advanced age, perhaps he did not have the energy to commit to writing a long, time-consuming letter.

Another possibility may have been overconfidence or even arrogance, that Chadwick was so confident in his rounders-baseball theory that he felt it was unnecessary to write anything longer. Still, whatever his perspective was, Chadwick did attempt to refute some of his opponent's beliefs in private and in public. Chadwick's private refutation carried more venom. In a letter to his friend Sam Crane, the old second baseman who had become a baseball journalist, and who supported Chadwick's views, Chadwick wrote that he was grateful for his backing, thanking Crane "for [his] support of my arguments in the controversy between Al Spalding and myself...." Chadwick then goes on to add, "Spalding must realize that the rounder argument overwhelms the ridiculous fraud of Mr. Graves and the findings of the commission which are inherently flawed." Chadwick was clearly correct in this particular point. He clearly knew that Graves' letter was a bogus scheme, one that Spalding erroneously pursued. Chadwick concludes his brief letter writing how "'Young Albert' is overzealous in his patriotism to a fault. Indeed," Chadwick adds, "baseball is a truly American game — but it evolved — and I am old enough to bear witness to this like my old friends Mr. [Andrew] Peck and Mr. [Duncan] Curry." In his more public view, Chadwick was more civil. Chadwick wrote that the two games' different rules of play served as evidence that the games were not connected. Chadwick insisted that baseball was not played during the colonial period. In his letter to the Mills Commission he wrote:

> As to the various methods of playing the two games, and the difference in their respective details of play, that matter in no way affects the question of the origin of the American game of Base Ball.
>
> In regard to the point, made by the opposing counsel, in which he refers to the game of ball played in "Colonial" days, I claim that the Canadian national game of "Lacrosse," a game played by the aborigines of North America, and the old English game of Cricket, played in New York as far back as 1751, were the only games of ball known to our Colonial ancestry in the old revolutionary period he refers to. So [Spalding's] argument in that regard falls to the ground "as dead as a door nail," as the saying is.
>
> On this statement of incontrovertible facts I present my clients' case to your final judgment, feeling confident that your decision will be in my favor.
>
> Very respectfully yours,
Henry Chadwick,
>
> Counsel for the Defense[54]

Chadwick's letter was followed by Albert Spalding's, who made his case for baseball's origins. In contrast to Chadwick's short letter, Spalding's was long, taking several pages. In it Spalding, as in his previous critique of Chadwick's theory, goes after Chadwick rounders-baseball connection.

> I am aware that quite a general impression exists in the public mind that Base Ball had its origin in the English schoolboy game of rounders, which has been occasioned largely, if not entirely, by the very able Base Ball writings of my esteemed venerable friend, Mr. Henry Chadwick, who for the past forty years has continued to make the assertion that Base Ball had its origin in "Rounders," without as yet producing any satisfactory evidence to sustain his theory. Mr. Chadwick has done so much for Base Ball, especially in its early struggling days, that I regret the necessity of disagreeing with him on any Base Ball subject, but my American birth and love of the game would not permit me to let his *absurd* [emphasis added] theory pass unchallenged.[55]

Like his earlier attack on Chadwick's belief, Spalding cleverly tied Chadwick's British birth to his rounders-baseball connection, writing that "if Mr. Chadwick had been bourn in this country, and not in England, he might be as totally ignorant of Rounders as the rest of us," adding that "he had possibly played in a game of Rounders, but I do not recall that he claims to have ever seen or played a game of Rounders since his arrival in America, nor have I ever seen or heard of his producing any convincing proof in support of his contention."[56] Spalding went on to discuss his theory on baseball's evolution, copying John Montgomery Ward's "old cat" theories by tying it in with the development of town ball, adding that in the early 1850s, in Massachusetts, "this 'Town Ball' games was changed in name to 'Base Ball,' and in those early days it was referred to as the 'Massachusetts game of Base Ball,' in contradistinction to the 'New York game of Base Ball,' the latter being the present game of Base Ball."[57] Spalding also added that in 1860, the Massachusetts version of baseball died out and was supplanted by the New York game and "at present is the only game of 'Base Ball' now played anywhere in the world."[58]

In the next paragraph, Spalding segued into the Abner Doubleday theory of baseball's invention, calling "special attention of the Commission to the letters received from Mr. Abner Graves." Spalding explained the Graves' connection to Doubleday and concluded that:

> I am very much impressed with the straightforward, positive, and apparently accurate manner in which Mr. Graves writes his narrative. I am strongly inclined to the belief that Cooperstown, N.Y., is the birthplace of

the present American game of Base Ball, and that Major General Abner Doubleday was the originator of the game.[59]

John Montgomery Ward's letter followed Spalding's. Ward, as in his previous essay on baseball's origins, discussed the differences between rounders and baseball and recounted much of the ground he had already covered in a previous essay on the subject in his book. Certainly, Spalding and Ward's printed correspondence are important. But it is the letter that follows Ward's that has the most lasting impact on what most baseball fans understand as baseball history today. A.G. Mills, one of the most underrated figures of nineteenth century baseball, is perhaps the most pivotal figure in the Doubleday saga. Mills, who headed the commission that bore his name, finally released the findings to the public in a letter dated December 30, 1907. Mills, the former president of the National League, did not rush into matters. He instead gave his views on the debate before presenting the final decision to back the fabricated Abner Doubleday invention of baseball theory.

Mills' presentation is different than Ward's and Spalding's because, as in his words, of his willingness to give credit to our "Anglo-Saxon kinsmen" regarding the nation's tardiness in adapting a culture of exercise and love for field sports, for in his "opinion we owe much [to them] for their example." Then, Mills added that he had no difficulty "if the fact could be established by evidence that our national game, 'Base Ball,' was devised in England, I do not think that it would be any the less admirable nor welcome on that account."[60] Mills went as far as to cite the British game of cricket's long history in the United States, as a game that he respected and admired.

But Mills' letter, despite his embrace and acknowledgement of England's influence on America's athletic culture, has plenty of negative things to say about Chadwick's views. While admitting that he and "'Father' Chadwick" had not always agreed on a variety of subjects, Mills wrote that he "always had respect for [Chadwick's] opinions and admiration for his inflexible honesty or purpose." Perhaps because of his respect for Chadwick, he "endeavored to give full weight to this contention that Base Ball is of English origin." Despite his "respect" for Chadwick, Mills wrote that he could not see a connection between the two games. Mills ridiculed Chadwick's baseball-rounders connection, writing that its basis rests "chiefly upon the fact" that the both games rely on the same implements — the tossing of a ball to "striking it with some kind of stick."[61] These claims, Mills wrote, are inadequate since if that were the case:

then "Father" Chadwick would certainly have to go far back of Anglo-Saxon civilization — beyond Rome, beyond Greece, at least to the palmy days of the Chaldean empire! Nor does it seem to me that he can any more successfully maintain the argument because of the employment, by the English schoolboy of the past, of the implements of the materials of the game.[62]

Mills added that he believed baseball had its beginnings with the Knickerbocker club in 1845, but that Spalding, "in the interesting and pertinent testimony for which we are indebted," provides evidence that Mills describes as "circumstantial by a reputable gentleman, " referring obviously to Graves, that Abner Doubleday, the old Civil War general, had invented the original diagram of the game.[63] Mills somehow made a connection, albeit a weak one, with Doubleday's design and the Knickerbockers formalizing their rules. Mills seemed satisfied with this link, declaring that it "is possible that a connection more or less direct can be traced between the diagram drawn by Doubleday in 1839 and that by [Louis Fenn] Wadsworth [who was a member of the Knickerbockers] in 1845."[64] In summation, Mills declared that baseball had its origin in the United States, and not England, as Chadwick claimed, and that "according to the best evidence obtainable to date," the game of baseball was "devised by Abner Doubleday at Cooperstown, N.Y., in 1839."[65] With Mills' statement and signature, along with signatures of the other members of the commission, history was made. The public bought into the claims made by Spalding and Mills, along with the tacit support of the other members of the commission, who went along for the ride.

Chadwick had two known reactions to the findings of the Mills Commission. In his own copy of the Spalding guide, Chadwick scribbled in blue pencil a terse message: "Commission's findings unfounded." The other response was in a letter Chadwick penned to the man who led the commission himself. In March 1908 Chadwick wrote to A.G. Mills that the Mills Commission report was "a masterly piece of special pleading which lets my old friend Albert escape a bad defeat," noting also that the baseball origins debate was a "joke between Albert and myself."[66]

Joke or not, the seriousness by which the public took to the "findings" of the Mills Commission was remarkable. And still is. Peter Levine, in his biography on Albert Spalding, wrote how "no one today, not even baseball's officialdom, recognizes Abner Doubleday as the inventor of baseball." This is false. There is still wide acceptance that Doubleday invented the game. Given Chadwick's weak letter and diminished state, and the fact that his words of reason were overshadowed by the whirlwind of nationalism and an American public in need of heroes, it was not surprising that Chadwick lost this battle.

The irony of the whole matter is while Spalding was making mincemeat of Chadwick's theories, he and Chadwick were in serious discussion about a book on baseball's history that the "Father of Baseball" would write himself. In November 1905, Chadwick made the suggestion that rather than include a history of the game at the beginning of the 1906 *Spalding Baseball Guide*, Chadwick would pen a book on the game's history, independent of the guide. Though Spalding was in the process of formulating Chadwick's views on baseball's evolution, he, interestingly enough, responded well to Chadwick's suggestion.[67] Already thrilled with Chadwick's preliminary work for the 1906 baseball guide, Spalding, in a November 25, 1905, letter, was excited with Chadwick's ideas of "eliminating from the 1906 Guide all reference of the origin of the game...."[68] Spalding agreed with Chadwick that a book was needed because the volume of work would overwhelm a small guide, adding, "I don't know of any one that is so well fitted to write such a history as Henry Chadwick, and I don't know of a better monument he can leave than to edit such a work."[69] Already mindful of Chadwick's age, Spalding's comment showed that he was even sensitive on some level of his friend's legacy. Initially, Spalding asked if Chadwick was physically up to the task. "Are you sure," Spalding questioned, "that such a work will not tax your strength beyond what it should be taxed?"[70] In fact, Spalding even offered "to supply [him] with an assistant, [even] a stenographer," asking if Chadwick was "accustomed to dictating to a stenographer, or would you prefer to write it out in long hand? Or by your own typewriter."[71] When Chadwick responded and wrote that he was able to do the manuscript, Spalding replied quickly and with typical furor developed an outline for the book. Spalding even referred to the project in terms of "our" and "we" rather than "yours."

In his usually aggressive way, Spalding commanded, only several days after Chadwick agreed to the task at hand, to stop whatever he was doing and "get busy, get action and give me the manuscript for a first class history on Baseball, both professional and amateur, in this country and the rest of the world."[72] Chadwick said he would start writing the manuscript and would "be prepared to take up this work after" the 1906 guide was finished, but Spalding would have none of that.

What other work do you refer to? Unless it is very important, it seems to me you had better start right in on this history business as soon as you finish the matter for the 1906 Guide, for I fear that if we defer it too long, it will get out of mind. Then again, remember that you are not going to live forever, and you owe it to Base Ball as well as yourself to see that a complete history, under your editorship, is left for future generations.[73]

Did Spalding expect Chadwick to bring up his rounders theory? The answer is uncertain, but it is doubtful that Spalding would have left that section for Chadwick to write without his approval. In fact, it would explain why Spalding controlled the process from the start; in writing an outline, Spalding included chapters beginning not with baseball's evolution or from the "days" of Abner Doubleday, but rather from the "Knickerbocker Era." Here is the outline that Spalding presented to Chadwick:

Commence the work with the origin of the game, giving in detail all the information bearing on the subject.

Then divide the history into eras on some such plan as this:

1. Knickerbocker Era, 1845 to 1857 inclusive.
2. National Association of Amateur Players, 1858 to 1870 inclusive
3. National Association of Prof. Base Ball Players, 1871 inclusive.
4. National Association of Prof. B.B. Clubs, 1876 to 1906 inclusive.[74]

Spalding also told Chadwick to avoid statistics, at least those of specific players, because he wanted the work to focus on "a history of the game with principal reference to its government and development." In other words, Spalding wanted Chadwick to focus on the things that would have brought Spalding and men like him into focus regarding the structure of the National League.

The question of Chadwick was time. Already in his early eighties, baseball's greatest scribe was slowing down and feeling the effects of old age. That is why, two years after Spalding offered Chadwick the monumental task of writing what Chadwick entitled "The Rise, Progress, and History of our American National Game," Chadwick informed his friend in a letter written on May 28, 1907, that the could not complete the great undertaking.[75] Though tempered somewhat by the fact that Chadwick had entrusted his massive baseball library to him, and acknowledging his delight "with [Chadwick's] magnificent gift of [his] unique and valuable Base Ball Library," Spalding was deeply disappointed.[76] Spalding even admitted his intimidation at Chadwick's request that Spalding complete the book.

"Great Scott!" Spalding exclaimed. "I am not a literary genius, and do not feel myself competent to undertake a work so entirely out of my line of previous effort."[77] Spalding clearly seemed nervous about the giant task.

> You say that you will gladly assist me in such a work in any way you can. Now, if you will guarantee to live until the book is completed, and blue pencil my manuscript, I might undertake the job, but if you should up and die before the work was completed, my own lease of life I think I would be shortened. I won't follow my present inclination at this time and say "No" to your proposition, nor will I say "Yes" today, but I will mull it over and as the Judges are wont to put it, "I will take it under advisement."[78]

It is hard to imagine, given Spalding's incredible self-confidence and huge ego that he would have a problem finishing such a task, which he ultimately did in 1915, entitling the work *Base Ball: America's National Game, 1839–1915*. Chadwick, for his part, may have been tired of Spalding's heavy-handedness and wanted to focus his energies on things he could complete. Like many elderly men his age who battle with illness, and who think deeply about their legacy, and have a need to focus on posterity, Chadwick turned to one of his other trusted friends, sportswriter Sam Crane. Crane had been a major league second baseman in the 1880s, but he made his lasting reputation as a journalist, eventually becoming the sports editor for the *Brooklyn Eagle* for a number of years. In a touching letter written on February 27, 1908, Chadwick wistfully admits that he is "nearing the end of my days." Enclosed with the letter were an undetermined number of "historic items" that Chadwick believed Crane "more than others will preserve." Among them were "Frank Queen's gold ball from use campaign of 1868 — and the ball I played with at Hoboken with the Knicks in '47."[79]

Despite the fact that he was "nearing the end of my days," Chadwick continued to work hard as if he were still in his prime. He had always been incredibly disciplined, remaining an active worker, as he was still editing away at the annual Spalding Guides as he had done since the early 1880s. He still prepared himself every day for work. His determination was reflected in his ability to wake up every morning at 5 A.M. to take a cold morning bath to prepare for the day ahead. Despite his age, Chadwick was determined to live a long life like his brother, who lived until 90 years, and his grandfather, who lived to 100. His morning plunge was related to his fascination with Turkish baths. Chadwick began taking Turkish baths in the 1870s and attributed his relative good health to the baths themselves.[80] A Turkish bath is distinguished by its continuous flow of very high dry heat in which the bather sweats profusely in a room, followed by a full body wash; it is sometimes even followed by a plunge into cold water. After exposing the body to the extremes in temperatures, from hot to cold, the person gets a massage followed by a period of relaxation in a cooling area.

Chadwick truly believed in Turkish baths and even wrote about it in the *Sporting News*. In 1900, when Chadwick was 76 years old, he wrote how "he stood by the heating range in the hottest place of the bath under a temperature of 212 degrees for five minutes without any ill effects."[81] He certainly endorsed the hot air baths and felt they were the best thing for athletic conditioning and training.

> The effects of a Turkish bath are that it relaxes the tissues of the body, quickens and equalizes the circulation of the blood, which necessarily becomes ... perfectly oxygenated; it arouses the most remote capillaries of the dormant parts to their normal actions, and carries the newly vitalized blood to every section of the body. The secretions are increased, the excretions are stimulated, and, in short, every function of the body, including the lungs, liver, kidneys and bowels, is brought to the highest standard. The senses and all the mental operations are quickened. The skin is made more active as a breathing organ, and assumes its natural, roseate complexion, indicative of the generally improved condition. In fact, this bath opens every pore of the skin, and hence comes a perfect sewage of the body.[82]

Chadwick clearly liked to push himself, for he truly believed that any type of exercise, or any way to push the body, was the way toward health. But was it wise for Chadwick to always push himself? On April 14, 1908, the opening of the new baseball season, Chadwick planned to attend the first game at Washington Park between his beloved Brooklyn Superbas and the Boston Braves. He planned to do this despite his 83-year-old body and a minor scalp wound inflicted after falling against his piano in his apartment at The Glen, 840 Halsey Street, in Bedford Stuyvesant, Brooklyn, and a slight cough he had caught a week earlier while attending an exhibition game at the Polo Grounds. Chadwick, with typical great determination, would not to miss the season opener. And why shouldn't he? After all, he was the "Father of Baseball." How could the game's father miss opening day? Each opener was like the dawning of the first days of spring, when the scent of the air seemed new and fresh, with the anticipation of summer and the warm weather. Chadwick must have been especially proud. After all, he had seen the game grow from its early days during the mid 1800s, when it was a local sport with little prestige. He saw the game when it was generally a gentleman's sport, consisting primarily of white-collar professionals, doctors and lawyers, men who could afford to take time away from work, men who played the game not for the laurels of victory, but for health and recreation and gentlemanly pleasure. Chadwick was there decades before the game had solidified itself. He was there in the early years to shape the game like a sculptor with a wet piece of clay. Chadwick was like a witness to all the changes in baseball — from its primitive form to its growth and evolution, as it slowly came under the spell of the rest of the country, as it became professionalized, a game played and watched by many Americans.

Yet, he was more than an eyewitness. Chadwick was the man responsible for helping baseball grow with his work as a journalist, a statistician, as a proponent of health and recreation, a genius and a visionary who believed, when no one else believed, it could become the national game. He was there when there was only one professional league, when there were labor battles, when baseball had its struggles. It was often Chadwick's steady hand that guided the sport. Now that 1908 was here, baseball, thanks to Chadwick's direction, had woven itself into the fabric of the American psyche.

By 1908, because of Papa Chadwick's great contributions, baseball did not need such promotion. By 1908, opening day of the new baseball season was a time-honored event, one that Chadwick, like any other American, would not want to miss. So, as Chadwick would rise in the morning hours of April 14, perhaps with nervous anticipation of the new season, he would do as he traditionally did, as reported in the *Washington Star*, by partaking in a light breakfast and then heading straight to his typewriter.[83]

These were not easy days for "old Chad," as he was affectionately called by his colleagues and baseball men, and by the young generation of ballplayers of that era, players like pitchers Cy Young and Christy Mathewson, and hitters Ty Cobb and Honus Wagner. There was a time when Chadwick's presence on the ball field commanded respect. After all, he invented a way to tabulate the score of a game. He was, at that time, virtually the only person who could do that. He even umpired some games in those early years, providing unbiased observations for competing clubs.

Despite his father-of-baseball status, Chadwick, over the recent decades, had lost touch with the average player and the average fan, not to mention the average sportswriter. He had become an object of derision and snide remarks by the modern players, the young sportswriters, and even the fans, which may have been naïve about Chadwick's contributions or may have perceived, somewhat justifiably, that he was no longer in sync with modern baseball. Some believed that Chadwick was an old man from another time, that he belonged to another era in which sportsmanship, sobriety, and honesty were an integral part of manliness. Ironically, it was the fans, the players and the journalists who owed a great debt of gratitude to Chadwick and who, without his contributions in the decades past, would not have been witnessing the same game, nor reaping the benefits of his contributions that provided salaries to both players and journalists alike.

But, despite all of his deeds and contributions, Chadwick had become unappreciated. What made matters worse was that like many elderly men, Chadwick had been battling a variety of injuries and ills. In the previous winter, he was knocked down by a slow moving automobile and was laid up for several weeks. Years earlier, in the 1890s, Chadwick suffered from a serious case of rheumatism that almost led to his death. Luckily, with the help of several friends and the loving care of his wife, Jane, he successfully healed and was able to continue his work. There also were some professional problems. Chadwick was being pushed aside for his historical views on baseball by one of his closest friends. As discussed earlier in this chapter, in establishing the Mills Commission, along with its subsequent "findings," Albert Spalding had railroaded Chadwick, even though he was one of the few voices that correctly claimed the game had British roots and was, in fact, not of strictly American origin.

Despite his expertise in early ball games, his upfront eyewitness of baseball's evolution and his well of historical knowledge, Chadwick's words of reason were overshadowed by Spalding and by the powerful men who promoted the great American baseball myth.

Despite the limitations of old age, Henry remained an active and even an admired worker. He was still editing the *Spalding Base Ball Guides*, and writing columns called "Chadwick's Chat" for the *Brooklyn Daily Eagle*. He augmented those duties by writing and editing books on other sports and games, like football, cricket and chess. And in addition to his "Chadwick's Chat," he authored another column for the *Eagle* under the pseudonym "Uncle Harry," which appealed to young people but was also read with pleasure by adults. Regarding the subject of exercise and good parenting, Chadwick wrote:

That advice about "deep breathing walks," which valuable exercise in the open air is what the general class of society of girls are in great need of, for it yields, as you say, "fine red cheeks and bright eyes," and drives away dullness of thought, school headaches and low spirits, which are largely induced by the want of pure oxygen in the air, where at school rooms or at office desks.[84]

Chadwick remained a participator of different sports. His other interests included "less strenuous pursuits like fishing, billiards and chess." In fact, he was believed "to be a chess player of some ability being a member of the Bensonhurst Chess Coterie and [was] often seen in across-the-board play at the Brooklyn and Queens County Clubs." As a billiard player, Chadwick was adept enough to execute three cushion caroms and bank shots. The results sometimes were quite amusing when he tried other sports. One afternoon, Chadwick attempted:

to put on ... roller skates and slid on his back eleven feet before the slivers stopped him. When he went home that night and wanted his back rubbed with salve, [Jane] shrieked at the display. "For mercy's sake," she screamed, "what ails your back?" Calmly he made response, "Wrinkles." "Wrinkles!" echoed his wife: "do you call great welts and scratches and lumps 'wrinkles'?" "Yes," he said, with a stifled sigh, "skating wrinkles."[85]

It was the same determination that kept him active, that drove him toward physical challenges, like putting his body in 212 degree temperature or attempting to learn how to roller skate despite his periodic bouts with sickness that compelled him to attend an exhibition game at the Polo Grounds one week before the season opener in Brooklyn. Clearly, his advice to women to get fresh air reflected his belief, as much as it was his joy and excitement of finally seeing baseball for the first time since the fall. Yet, it was his presence at the exhibition between the New York Giants and Yale University the week before that had weakened Chadwick's health. "I do like to see college Base Ball and Yale always has had a fascination for me," he said.[86]

According to newspaper accounts, the weather at the Polo Grounds was raw and cold, and "though well protected with heavy wraps, the grand old man took cold."[87] Prior to the match, Chadwick had noted the improvement of the college players in the proficiency in the game, calling attention, in particular, to the "excellence" of Yale catcher Tad Jones' work. Chadwick was astonished at what progress was made by the college men, remarking that they had "acquired the finer points of the sport almost to the equal of the professionals who make a thorough study of the game."[88]

After the contest's conclusion, Chadwick stayed until sundown. He began to cough slightly, and it was suggested to him "that it might be foolish if he remained too long, as the Polo Grounds is inclined to be damp in the spring."[89] He agreed. "Yes, I must be going," Chadwick said, "but I want to say a word to [New York Giants manager John] McGraw before I start." McGraw, after spotting Chadwick, "walked across the field to where Chadwick was seated." Although Chadwick had criticized the former infielder who had starred for the great Baltimore Orioles teams of the 1890s for kicking umpires and his overall rowdyism, Chadwick must have also recognized by now the good McGraw had done for the game as one of the better managers to ever don a uniform. After greeting McGraw with open arms, he complimented McGraw on the "fine showing of the Giants," and as he said goodbye, he wished the diminutive manager well and luck for the upcoming season, though he admitted that he would be in Brooklyn, not in Manhattan's Polo Grounds, for the opener.[90] After saying his goodbyes, Chadwick, who was likely carrying his famous walking stick, left the grounds for the last time.

With stubborn determination and against the advice of his friends, Chadwick had every intention of attending opening day, even though he was "warned that he was running a dangerous chance."[91] Maybe he thought the fresh air would ameliorate his condition. Or perhaps he thought that being among the multitude of spectators attending the game at the newly renovated Washington Park would raise his spirits.

The game was set to begin at 4 P.M., but as early as 1 o'clock, long lines of men and boys were gathered at the entrance to the bleachers, and "before two o'clock, the lines from this gate stretched in each direction, along First Street and Fourth Avenue and Third Avenue and Third Street, for a full block and a half."[92]

By 3:15 P.M. the real excitement came when players of the two teams, all in one line, took position behind the Twenty-Third Regiment Band, which had been playing for more than two hours, for the parade across the field.

Down the field from the clubhouse to the pitcher's box, the *Brooklyn Eagle* reported, the parades marched, then executed a ninety-degree turn to the right and walked straight to the front of the press box. There a long rope was lying on the ground and each player picked up a portion of it. The rope raised to the top of the staff at the front of the grandstand a beautiful American flag, held in gaskets. As the flag reached the top of the pole, the pulling of a light cord released its silken folds, which waved proudly forth. Every spectator was on his feet then, and as the band began to play the "Star Spangled Banner," every hat was doffed and every man, woman and child present stood silent and at attention until the last chord of the national anthem was played.[93]

Perhaps at that moment Chadwick flashed back to those first days in America, the ones he spent in the cabins of the ship that carried him to his new home. Or perhaps he reflected on how American he had become. After all, only three years earlier, he had been acknowledged by President Theodore Roosevelt. Chadwick received a letter from the president (whom Chadwick referred to as my young friend Theodore). It said:

> FROM THE PRESIDENT OF THE UNITED STATES
> White House,
> (Personal.)   Washington, D.C., January 18, 1904.
> My Dear Chadwick: I congratulate you on your eightieth year and your fiftieth year in journalism. It is given to but few men to enjoy the privilege of active participation in the affairs of life so long a period, and you are entitled to the good wishes of all for that part you have taken in behalf of decent sport.[94]

Perhaps, as the "Star Spangled Banner" played, he reflected on how much America had changed over the nearly seventy years, from a largely agrarian nation, divided slave and free, to a truly industrial *United* States of America. Perhaps he realized how American he had become, though imbued with English attitudes toward sport.

Then there came a mighty cheer from the roughly 21,000 spectators present, and the crowd settled into their seats to await the ceremonial first pitch to be thrown by a local minister.[95]

As soon as the opening pitch was thrown, much of the immense crowd that showed up at the gates began to get unruly. Probably to Chadwick's chagrin, who always in his writings had advocated crowd control and measures to keep the roughs away from the game, "many in the field stands jumped the fences and rushed out and seated themselves on the grass a few yards behind the base lines."[96]

Immediately, Boston answered the bell with two runs in the first inning. But in the second inning, first baseman Tim Jordan of the Superbas smashed a solo home run, which cleared the right field fence. As he turned third base, manager Pat Donovan, showing appreciation, shook hands with his slugger as he finished his jaunt around the bases. Chadwick was probably a little dismayed with this show of power. He never liked the home run. Chadwick felt that the home run was too much an expenditure of energy. Rather, he much preferred the ball in play, where he believed the true beauty of baseball lay. While he may have been ambivalent about how the Superbas scored their run, Chadwick must have been appreciative when shortstop Phil Lewis robbed Boston's Bill Sweeney of a hit in the opening inning. Lewis threw himself at full length on the dirt, and from the ground tossed the ball to Harry Pattee at second, who relayed to first for a double play. Despite another defensive stop by shortstop Phil Lewis — who also contributed a run batted in — the Superbas could not muster the offense needed to defeat Joe Kelley's boys from Boston. Brooklyn fell on this opening day by the score of 9 to 3.

Though Chadwick courageously remained for the entire game, he sat at the top of the grandstand, where the frigid air and a cold breeze blew directly against his back. Chadwick was already sick from his attendance at the Polo Grounds, and the raw weather conditions led to him catching "severe cold."[97] Though he suffered from the affect of an illness, the next morning Chadwick composed a touching letter to his friend Jacob Morse of *Baseball Magazine*, describing the state of his overall condition on personal matters.

> Please bear in mind, my old friend, that here I am, at 84 years of age, with lots of dear relatives to look after and working harder and for less than I did forty years ago. You are probably unaware that I live in a fourth floor flat of a four-story apartment house, and have no servant, two of my grandchildren serving as housekeepers alternatively, winter and summer ... but fourtunately my mental powers have withstood the attacks of age and physical incapacity ... blessed with a treasure of a wife I have been enabled to get along thus far on comparatively small means. So you see how necessary it is for me to avail myself of every chance to earn money by my pen.[98]

It was painfully obvious that Chadwick had to push himself at a very old age, to write other columns, when he should have been enjoying retirement and the writing of his final treatise: a comprehensive history of the game, the one that Spalding had commissioned him to write. Yet, despite his physical limitations, despite the severity of his cold, Chadwick continued with his regular activities. On Friday afternoon, the nineteenth, Chadwick once again was pushing himself physically when he should have remained in bed recovering from a cold. He began, innocently enough, to move some light furniture "from his apartments on the fourth floor to the second floor, [when] he overtaxed his heart and fell to the floor unconscious." Chadwick was found lying on the floor by one of his granddaughters, who summoned Henry's physician, Dr. Arnold Caitlin, who had seen

Chadwick the day before. Noting the obvious severity of Chadwick's wretched condition, Dr. Caitlin ordered the granddaughter to send for her grandmother, Henry's beloved wife of sixty years, Jane, and their two daughters from Blue Point, Long Island, at once.[99]

Chadwick's condition was reported in the newspapers. Both the *Brooklyn Eagle*, the paper where he worked for over fifty years, and the *Brooklyn Standard Union* had articles on Chadwick's sickness. His cold had progressed into pneumonia, complicated by heart failure. He lost consciousness until that Saturday when he rallied, awakening from his unconscious state to inquire eagerly about the results of the game between Brooklyn and New York. When he was told the Giants had defeated the Superbas, 4–0, behind Christy Mathewson's typical brilliance, he sighed regretfully and relapsed into unconsciousness.[100] Chadwick managed to survive through the night and into the morning hours of April 20, 1908. Dr. Caitlin finished another thorough examination of Chadwick and confirmed to Jane Chadwick that Henry's lungs had filled with congestion. A few minutes after 12 P.M. Henry Chadwick took his last breath.[101]

A.G. Spalding, having been told of Henry Chadwick's demise, sent a telegram to August Herrman, chairman of the National Base Ball Commission, located in Cincinnati, Ohio. It read:

> The death of Mr. Henry Chadwick removes from Base Ball its oldest and most prominent writer and upbuilder of the game especially in its earlier days. It would seem a deserving tribute and very appropriate for the National Base Ball Commission to take the initiative in providing some suitable tribute to Mr. Chadwick's memory as a token of the esteem in which Mr. Chadwick was held in the Base Ball world. I would respectfully suggest for the consideration of the Commission that on the day of his funeral a flag be hung at half-mast on all ball grounds throughout the country.

Numerous tributes from the publishing and baseball worlds filled the pages of newspapers throughout the country. Papers like the *Brooklyn Eagle* and the *New York Times*, both former employers of Chadwick, and the *Boston Herald*, paid homage to the great baseball scribe; men like Harry Pulliam, the president of the National League, and former big leaguer and current journalist T.H. Murname gave tributes to their late baseball comrade. Others like Francis Richter of the *Sporting News*, Ren Mulford, the veteran baseball scribe from Cincinnati, and Henry P. Edwards, baseball editor of the *Cleveland Plain Dealer*, were mourners who willingly delivered written eulogies on behalf of the late Henry Chadwick.

Mulford's eulogy may have been the most truthful.

Henry Chadwick's name is linked with Base Ball to live as long as the game itself lives. The patriarch among diamond historians ... no one did more in the infancy of the sport than he for its well-being and permanency. There never was a word in all the miles of copy that Henry Chadwick has written that was not penned for the betterment of the game as he saw it.[102]

An American League umpire named Frank O'Loughlin paid another eulogy to Chadwick.

I always loved Father Chadwick, for it was he who gave me my first encouraging words when I started out as an umpire. It was in Wilkes-Barre, Pa., in 1898, that Mr. Chadwick saw me.... After the game he called on me, complimented and congratulated me on my work, and told me to stick to umpiring. I followed his advice. That's the reason I'm an arbitrator today.[103]

P.T. Powers, president of the National Association of Base Ball Leagues, of which Chadwick was a lifetime member, gave the order to have all the flags at half-mast in ballparks throughout the country. Powers also set up a collection program to pay for a monument to be placed above Chadwick's grave that consisted of "each club in organized base ball donate a suitable sum, and that each and every professional base ball player contribute one dollar."[104] Powers also suggested that "in the near future a day be set aside in each park known as the Henry Chadwick Day, and that the public who will certainly be interested in the erection of this monument be given a chance to contribute their mite to the Chadwick Memorial Fund."[105] While the proposed fund was never carried out, it showed the deep love that the sporting world held for Chadwick. The mission to fund his graveside monument was led by Charles Ebbets. Ebbets served in the dual capacity as executor of Chadwick's will and chairman of the committee that raised needed funds, which totaled a lofty $600, to erect Chadwick's gravesite monument.[106]

The Reverend Thomas Edward Potterton conducted the funeral services held at the Universalist Church of Our Father (located on the corner of Lefferts Place and Grand Avenue) on Thursday, April 23, in Brooklyn. His wife, Jane, his two daughters, Susan Eldridge and Helen Chadwick Edwards, and their respective husbands Thomas S. Eldridge and William Edwards (who, along with Spalding, was an executor of Chadwick's will), numerous grandchildren, Thomas, Harry, Louis, Bessie, Eugenie, and Helen Eldridge, Richard Litton Edwards, Jennie Pugsley, Avis Mortimer

Worden, Kate Lewis and Elsie Scofield, and great-grandchildren, as well as many friends from the sporting world ("base ball men, chess devotees, athletes — in fact, representatives of every sport he ardently supported") came to pay their respects to the author of many sporting books and articles that helped promote their respective games.[107] Among those in attendance were Harry Pulliam, Charles H. Ebbets, president of the Brooklyn club, and St. Clair McKelway, editor-in-chief of the *Brooklyn Eagle*, whom, among others, acted as pallbearers.[108] Spalding "purchased a burial plot in Greenwood Cemetery, as a testimonial of his personal regard for the "Father of the Game."[109] Spalding, unable to attend because of the long distance of travel from San Diego, "sent a floral arrangement of white immortelles in the shape of a baseball."[110]

When the casket was brought into the church, the congregation rose and the honorary pallbearers entered, followed by the family. The flower-covered coffin was placed in front of the pulpit platform, and the many floral tributes placed nearby almost obscured the view of Potterton. The *Brooklyn Eagle* described the services as simple and impressive. It began with the hymn "Lead Kindly Light," sung by a quartet of two men and two women.

Potterton spoke of Chadwick in a personal way, remarking that the funeral "was an expression of the sympathy for the family of 'Father' Chadwick and their love for him and pride for his achievements." The reverend added that Chadwick always built his life toward being a man of character, which was his great desire, and read from Chadwick's latest published work, which said, "place premium on character." He added:

> Mr. Chadwick was a man thoroughly imbued with a fine ethical sense. He did things because he deemed them right. And once ... Father Chadwick had determined a course to be right, nothing could swerve him from the path of duty. The voice of conscience was the voice of God, and he would be obedient.

In closing the reverend said, "He was a kind old man, and when he reached the end of life he had the wealth of your love and the riches of your respect to carry away with him to a peaceful rest."

After the quartet sang "Safe in the Arms of Jesus," the burial service was read and a prayer ended the funeral service. Chadwick's casket was taken to Green-Wood Cemetery for internment.[111]

A touching tribute by Spalding, published several days after Chadwick's death, reiterated the contributions that Chadwick made to baseball:

Chadwick's baseball-themed memorial at Green-Wood Cemetery (photograph by author).

it was not to Mr. Chadwick's love for Base Ball, great as it was; not to his ability as a writer, forceful and graceful as his literary efforts were ever acknowledged to be; not to his accuracy as a statistician, perfect as were his achievements along those lines; but to his indomitable energy and sublime courage in behalf of the integrity of Base Ball that our national game is most indebted for its high standing in the estimation of the American people.[112]

The following month, on the one-year anniversary of his burial, the Ebbets-funded monument was erected at Green-Wood Cemetery. Along with the monument, which is topped by a granite sphere carved to look like a baseball, stones etched to resemble bases marked the four corners of Chadwick's lot. The monument, at its center, is also adorned with a bronze version of a catcher's mask, a baseball glove and crossed bats — a fitting monument to the father of the game.[113]

On March 27, 1910, during Easter services at the Church of Our

Father, Potterton dedicated a stain glass window to the memory of Henry Chadwick. The sponsors of the memorial window were members of the church, led by Potterton, and members of the baseball world, led by Charles H. Ebbetts. When the Easter Sunday sermon concluded, Potterton stood in front of the altar rail, extended the right hand of fellowship and welcomed several new members of the church, eulogized Mr. Chadwick, and then walked across the church to stand under the window to formally dedicate it. Then Potterton dropped the curtain and disclosed the window to the audience. The window was a reproduction of Holman Hunt's painting of "The Light of the World," and it depicted Jesus knocking at the door of humanity with the words in bold relief, "Behold, I stand at the door and knock." In attendance were Henry's ninety-one-year-old wife Jane and their two daughters along with their husbands. Charles Ebbetts also attended the ceremony. Under the window bore the inscription:

HENRY CHADWICK,
Father of Baseball,
By His Friends.[114]

Chadwick was a visionary. Not only did he help to usher in a new era in American history, he helped to shape baseball while America was transforming itself into an industrial society. Perhaps the most touching tribute to Chadwick came from his dear friend and frequent philosophical opponent Albert Goodwill Spalding.

> I knew Mr. Chadwick intimately for over forty years, and can attest to his sterling worth, honesty of purpose and great ability as a journalist. His aid in the upbuilding of baseball has been invaluable and the present great popularity of the game is largely due to this efforts. I don't believe the old gentleman had an enemy in the world, and I am sure I voice the sentiment of every one interested in baseball and clean sports, when I say that he loved so well and did so much for, and he will ever be remembered as the "Father of Baseball."[115]

In 1938, as a testimony to Chadwick's services toward the game, he was elected to Baseball's Hall of Fame in Cooperstown, New York, where he is enshrined near his friends A.G. Spalding and Harry Wright, and along with other ball playing greats of the game, those who benefited from his contributions.[116]

Appendix 1: Writings by Henry Chadwick

Henry Chadwick was a prolific writer. He wrote numerous guides and books related to sports, and contributed to many other publications.

Baseball

The Art of Base Ball Batting (1885)
The Art of Base Running (1886)
The Art of Batting and Base Running (1886)
The Art of Pitching (1885)
The Art of Pitching and Fielding (1886–1887)
Introduction by Henry Chadwick. *Athletic Sports in America, England and Australia* by Harry Clay Palmer, J.A. Eynes and W.I. Harris (1889)
The Base Ball Book of Reference for Umpires and Scorers (1866–1872)
Base Ball Umpire's Guide: A Complete Book of Instruction to the Umpires of the Professional and Amateur Leagues (1876)
Beadle's Dime Base Ball Player (1860–1881)
DeWitt's Base Ball Guide (1868–1880)
DeWitt's Base Ball Umpire's Guide: A Complete Book of Instructions to the Umpires ... (1875)
The Game of Base Ball: How to Learn It, How to Play It, and How to Teach it, with Sketches of Noted Players (1868)
Haney's Book of Reference (1866–1872)
Spalding's Official Baseball Guide (1880–1908)

Football

The Game of Football (1887)

Chess

The Game of Chess: A Work Designed Exclusively for Novices in Chess (1895)

Other Sports and Pastimes

Beadle's Dime Book of Pedestrianism: Giving The Rules for Training and Practice in Walking and Running (1867)
The Game of Lawn Bowls as Played Under the Code of Rules of the Scottish Bowling Association (1895)
Handbook of Winter Sports Embracing skating (on the Ice and on rollers) rinkball, curling, etc (1879)
The Sports and Pastimes of American Boys: A Guide and Text-Book of Games of the Playground (1884)
Yachting and Rowing: A Complete Manual of the Science and Practice of the Two Pastimes

Appendix 2: What Has Been Said About Chadwick

Over the last several decades, much has been written on baseball history. Most of the game's history has focused on baseball's development during the nineteenth century. Written works on baseball include books and articles on the growth of nineteenth-century sports, and baseball history books that examine the game's emergence in the 1800s within a social context. In this appendix I shall examine various books and articles and discuss what has or has not been said about Henry Chadwick.

Fred Ivor-Campbell has written two brief biographies that focus exclusively on Henry Chadwick. "Henry Chadwick" and "Henry Chadwick (Chad, Father of Base Ball)" are essays that raise awareness about Chadwick's contributions to the game. In the latter work, Ivor-Campbell lists many of the publications that Chadwick wrote for, giving the reader a greater understanding of how much influence Chadwick had regarding the spread of baseball and sports in general. In the former article, Ivor-Campbell writes that Chadwick "covered baseball for more than twenty newspapers and magazines and wrote a number of books and pamphlets for players and spectators (including an explanation of the game for Britishers)."[1] Although Ivor-Campbell does not look at the larger historical issues connected to Chadwick's contribution, and baseball's growth *per se*, he does provide important insight into Chadwick's achievements and the respect he garnered among fellow journalists and athletes alike.

Several books have been written about the rise of sports in the nineteenth century. Melvin Adelman's *A Sporting Time: New York City and the Rise of Modern Athletics, 1820–1870* devotes two chapters to baseball. Adelman mentions Chadwick's important views on gambling, the fly ball rule, and the admission fee.

George B. Kirsch's *The Creation of American Team Sports: Baseball and Cricket, 1838–72* centers on baseball's and cricket's histories as organized team sports. Like Adelman, Kirsch gives the reader some of Chadwick's reactions to the controversies and changes that occurred in nineteenth century baseball and shows how Chadwick participated in the debate over whether baseball was purely an American invention or whether it evolved from the British games of rounders and cricket.

Warren Goldstein and Elliot J. Gorn wrote *A Brief History of American Sports* which examines the growth of sports from colonial times to the present. It also looks at the cultural, religious and socioeconomic forces that influenced individuals to play or watch certain organized sports. They write that during the Gilded Age:

> baseball's infatuation with statistics developed, not out of consensus that accurate and detailed records benefited everyone, but from a variety of particular constituencies gamblers could handicap games more reliably, owners and athletes could measure the quality of play more effectively in their never-ending labor disputes, journalists could give fans a better feel for the game.[2]

Given this analysis, it is surprising that these authors do not connect Chadwick's contribution to baseball and other sports as well. In fact, Gorn and Goldstein do not discuss Chadwick's role as a significant voice in the rise of nineteenth century sports and place it within a historical context as they do with other figures.

Baseball essays that examine the growth of the game within a historical context help to explain the role of the game's advocates in promoting baseball. Melvin Adelman's "Baseball, Business, and the Workplace: Gelber's Thesis Reexamined" discusses the pros and cons of two different theories used to explain baseball's emerging popularity in the nineteenth century. Here, Adelman writes about Henry Chadwick's role in encouraging a more scientific approach to the game, and his encouragement of better conditioning for the athletes.[3]

Steven Riess's book *Touching Base: Professional Baseball and American Culture in the Progressive Era*, acknowledges the role that sports journalists like Chadwick played in baseball's growth, but does not go beyond this analysis to show the crucial role that Chadwick played, nor is it biographical.

Chadwick and other journalists helped to promote the game not only as sportswriters, but also as a meaningful authority for an American audience. According to Warren Goldstein, the author of *Playing for Keeps: A History of Early Baseball*:

> baseball writers were intimately involved in the baseball world of their day. They played the game sometimes [or] belonged to a club. They participated in baseball politics, attended club social affairs, and [went with] clubs on visits to other cities. The most vocal promoters of the newly organized game, they expected — and received — privileged treatment from players and clubs.[4]

In the second chapter of Jules Tygiel's *Past Time: Baseball as History*, the author examines the cultural significance of baseball by looking at the importance of statistics. Entitled "The Mortar of Which Baseball Is Held Together: Henry Chadwick and the Invention of Baseball Statistics" examines Chadwick's statistical contributions within a historical and cultural framework. Tygiel comes closest to this author in his attempt to examine Chadwick's significant contributions and reveals some biographical information about the man.

Another important book covering the early period of baseball is David Quentin Voigt's *American Baseball: From Gentleman's Sport to the Commissioner System*. Voigt calls Chadwick "the most productive and authoritative of the early baseball writers." Voigt writes that along with Francis C. Richter, also a notable baseball writer and editor of that period, Chadwick believed that baseball derived from British ball games like rounders and cricket. Though Voigt provides only the most elementary information about Chadwick's life, he does convey great enthusiasm about Chadwick's role in baseball's growing popularity, writing that Chadwick's "tireless efficiency ... won him the editorship of most of the early baseball guides ... as his reputation as the leading authority and critic on baseball matters grew."

Benjamin Rader's *Baseball: A History of America's Game* is an examination of the game's history from 1840 to 1990, and its connection to American cultural society. While Rader acknowledges Chadwick's role as a promoter of the sport and as a journalist who was a moral voice for the game, he does not treat Chadwick front and center as an important figure in baseball nor as a voice in Victorian society.[5]

Baseball in America, by Robert Smith, is a vividly written book on baseball history from its beginnings in the 1840s to 1960. In this work Smith describes some of Chadwick's suggestions, such as the proper batting order and the correct approach to hitting and fielding. Smith also acknowledges Chadwick's contribution, calling him the "[s]enior officer of the game of baseball." Smith mentions, without citation, that Chadwick was a pitcher for a team called the Nationals when in actuality he was only an honorary member and traveled with the team for a brief period. More importantly, he writes that Chadwick was "the first sportswriter to devote his full time to baseball. [That] Chadwick invented a 'photographic' (i.e., shorthand) method of keeping score and was the acknowledged final authority on rules and behavior."[6] Smith also credits Chadwick for embracing the professional game after the formation of the Cincinnati Red Stockings in 1869 because it would lessen the influence of gamblers and pool sellers on baseball.

Harold Peterson's *The Man Who Invented Baseball* is a book that credits Alexander Cartwright, the captain of the New York Knickerbockers base ball club, for "inventing" the game of baseball. He provides diagrams of the variety of ball games that preceded baseball before Cartwright's contribution. Peterson credits Chadwick with being the first sportswriter to cover baseball. But he is profoundly mistaken when he confines Chadwick to being "only a sportswriter," thereby undervaluing Chadwick journalistic and statistical contributions.[7] Of course, Chadwick was more than a sportswriter. He was the first and most vocal proponent of baseball and ball games (having played rounders as a child and cricket and baseball as an adult), a rule maker, a statistician, an innovator and probably the most legitimate voice on sports, other than the athletes themselves.

Peterson is not the only author to believe that Cartwright was the father of baseball. *How Baseball Began: The Long Overlooked Truth About the Birth of Baseball*, written by Ron McCulloch, supports Peterson's notion that Cartwright invented baseball. While the evidence he presents concerning Cartwright's invention is dubious, he does help to dispel the false notion that Abner Doubleday invented the game. *How Baseball Began* is an easy-to-read book with outstanding photos of baseball in the nineteenth century. In fact, it contains the best photojournalism of the period when compared to other works of this kind. However, McCulloch discusses Chadwick only concerning his role in the baseball origins controversy. He writes only that Chadwick "is acknowledged to be the first full-time baseball writer, and is credited as the inventor of the box score."[8]

Like Peterson, he neglects to mention Chadwick's role on the rules committee in the 1870s and 1880s and being the man primarily responsible for promoting the sport in the 1860s. He also neglects to mention how Chadwick believed that baseball was not invented by anyone in particular, that the game just evolved. In fact, McCulloch unknowingly lends credence to Chadwick's theory by calling him "a very credible source" on baseball's origins.[9]

Ball, Bat and Bishop: The Origin of Ball Games by Robert Henderson is probably the most unique work of all the books and articles mentioned in this appendix. Henderson traces the history of ball games from their pagan and religious origins to their more recent secular status. The author examines ball games in a variety of cultures throughout the world and, naturally, dedicates several chapters to baseball, covering the years from 1800 through 1900. The book dedicates several pages to Chadwick and his contribution to baseball.

Henderson vividly describes the disagreement between Chadwick and Albert Spalding regarding the baseball origins debate. According to Henderson, it was Spalding who felt the issue should be resolved by a commission. Spalding argued that it was a sport of strictly American origins, whereas Chadwick argued that the game derived from the British game of rounders.[10] Henderson's account of this issue is the closest to a biographical portrait about an aspect of Chadwick's life that any of the writers come to.

Henderson is not the only author to focus on Chadwick's role in the baseball origins debate with Spalding. G. Edward White, a law and history professor at the University of Virginia, wrote *Creating the National Pastime: Baseball Transforms Itself, 1903–1953*. White looks at baseball's transformation in the first half of the twentieth century in an attempt to understand and explain modern-day baseball in the 1990s. White does a fine job, like Henderson, in explaining the controversy, but unlike Henderson, White footnotes his work.

Koppett's Concise History of Major League Baseball by Leonard Koppett is a thorough history of the game from the late 1800s to modern times. It is the only book where Henry Chadwick is mentioned in the same work that includes a discussion regarding the phenomena of domed stadiums and interleague play. Like the two aforementioned books, Koppett writes on the baseball origins debate. His unique contribution to the Chadwick story, however, is his description of the proper batting technique accepted by "conventional wisdom, from baseball's beginning to 1920," as described by Henry Chadwick.[11] Without going into great detail, "[g]ood hitting, [Chadwick] wrote, consisted of *forwarding runners on bases.*"[12]

While there are many books written about baseball in the nineteenth century, there are two that focus on Chadwick's friends. First is Peter Levine's *A.G. Spalding and the Rise of Baseball: The Promise of American Sport.* While the book obviously does not center on Chadwick, Levine quotes him often and does focus, like the White and Henderson's book, on the baseball origins controversy. Levine's book is superb, and he acknowledges Chadwick's contribution in helping to modernize the game, touting Chadwick as the "most knowledgeable baseball writer in America."[13]

The second biography that focuses on another one of Chadwick's friends is Christopher Devine's *Harry Wright: The Father of Professional Baseball.* Devine traces Wright's early years in New York to his role in developing professional baseball in Cincinnati. Devine acknowledges Chadwick's important role in developing the national game, recognizing both Wright's and Chadwick's mutual influence in the nineteenth century rulebook. While Devine writes that while "20th century achievements and events" have influenced "opinions to change over time," he recognized Chadwick for being "America's original sportswriter," adding that the profession of sportswriting has "been applauded for its use in popularizing base ball across the country with an in-depth coverage of the game, a style originated by Chadwick."[14]

Two other books related to baseball's early history center on the formation of the National League. The first is Tom Melville's *Early Baseball and the Rise of the National League,* and the other is Neil MacDonald's *The League That Lasted: 1876 and the Founding of the National League of Professional Base Ball Clubs.*

Melville's book is an excellent work that focuses its attention not only on how the National League came about, but its important exploration of baseball's development from a non-competitive local game in New York to its rise as a competitive, truly national game. While Melville barely mentions Chadwick, referring to Chadwick as the "Dean of Baseball writers," he does understand the role that the press in New York played in the growth of the "New York" game outside of New York. While writing that journalists like Chadwick discovered baseball, as it was already growing in popularity among its followers, the "sporting press," he writes, "played a more important role in carrying baseball out and away from its urban environment to other areas of the country."[15] As excellent as his point is, along with the rest of his well-written and researched document regarding baseball's development, he understates in many ways Chadwick's single-handed promotion of the sport as a journalist, statistician and rule maker. Nonetheless, Melville's work is an outstanding treatise on the early development of baseball.

In the other book on baseball's rise of the National League, Neil MacDonald chronicles the founding of the new league as it rose from the ashes of the crumbling National Association. While not a book that focuses on Chadwick's life per se, it does explore the animosity of National League founder William Hulbert regarding Chadwick's role in various controversial issues during the 1870s. It also details Chadwick's feeling on the formation of the National League. This work demonstrates that not every individual in baseball appreciated Chadwick's efforts, nor was everyone enamored with the great journalist's personality, despite his enormous reputation as the dean of baseball writers. The most important thing that *The League That Lasted* provides is great sources — letters about and regarding Chadwick written by Hulbert and others involved with Chadwick's personal and professional life. It is especially important in understanding Chadwick's vision of baseball and how and why it contrasted with Hulbert's.

The next work is Alan Schwarz's *The Numbers Game: Baseball's Lifelong Fascination with Statistics*, a superb book on the history of baseball's statistics. Opposite Schwarz's first chapter, fittingly, is a photo Henry Chadwick. The chapter is dedicated to the nineteenth century baseball statistics. While Schwarz gives some basic biographical detail on Chadwick's personal life, his analysis focuses on his statistical contributions, detailing Chadwick's early statistical contribution to the game of baseball and his later ones as well. *The Numbers Game* is a lively, compact, yet richly detailed analysis of baseball statistical history and gives full credit to Chadwick's contributions, though it focuses only on those efforts and not his other important work, like his role on the rules committee and the impact of his early writings.

Another work that focuses on the game's numbers is the national bestseller *Moneyball* by Michael Lewis. This book centers on the recent success of the Oakland A's and their general manager, Billy Beane, who has used modern statistics to help build a competitive club despite a low payroll. In discussing these matters, Lewis goes back and examines Chadwick's contribution to the game and astutely states that Chadwick's cricket background influenced his thinking. But Lewis takes too many swipes at Chadwick's work.

"How could baseball statistics be so screwed up," Henry Chadwick was usually the beginning, and occasionally the end of the answer.... Chadwick was better at popularizing statistics than thinking through their meaning.

In two sentences, Lewis displays his complete ignorance of Chadwick's writings and intellectual ideas, the ones that helped to make the game great. Lewis portrays Chadwick as having an overly moralistic approach to statistics. As it related to his events that affected the game off the field, like gambling and alcoholism, Lewis writes "he [was] never tired of complaining." If Lewis has a problem with Chadwick's too many complaints over alcoholism and gambling, would he have tired of Chadwick's concern over the modern ballplayers' cocaine abuse in the eighties and steroid use during the late 1990s to the present? Who does Lewis think laid the moral groundwork for professional and collegiate baseball? It was Chadwick's determination during the mid 1800s to rid the game of impurities he felt would rightly damage baseball in the eyes of the public. It is the same moral calls of impropriety that need to be echoed today in this modern world, that are being voiced today by those calling attention to the rampant steroid use by today's "heroes." I suppose Hulbert would have agreed with Lewis' complaints over Chadwick's overly righteous attitude, but Hulbert didn't seem to have problems firing players for their impropriety.

Then, to illustrate "the absurdity" of Chadwick's opinions on statistics, Lewis writes that Chadwick disliked the walk because he believed this category was a reflection of bad pitching rather than effective hitting, adding that Chadwick even gave a pitcher an error for the mistake in one of his box scores. As Chadwick got older, he from time to time was old-fashioned in his ideas. But what Chadwick was doing was attempting to improve the game with good intentions. To say that Chadwick did a "better job of popularizing statistics than thinking through its meaning" is nonsense. Lewis was looking back at Chadwick's career in hindsight, through the eyes of a twenty-first century writer, rather than having looked at Chadwick from the perspective of what Chadwick was: a nineteenth century journalist trying to make sense of a game that was constantly changing.

It's easy to criticize someone with the perspective of 150 years of baseball history, but I suppose Lewis also would have had a problem with Copernicus not knowing the theory of relativity. Perhaps he is justifiably annoyed at Chadwick's overly righteous and overbearing morality, but I bet Chadwick would have been justifiably disgusted by someone as smug and ignorant as Lewis seems to be.

Chadwick was present in baseball's early years in the nineteenth century and was developing statistics to suit the game at that particular time. Some of his statistics stuck, some did not. But he got the ball rolling so that others could help the game move forward, as he did, when he as a young British-born journalist making his way in a strange land in a strange time, pushing and prodding baseball, the sport he adopted when it was virtually unknown to the rest of the world. "How can baseball statistics be so screwed up?" Lewis asks. The question, however, should ask how did Lewis' opinions get to be so screwed up? What Lewis fails to mention is the game has survived for over one hundred and fifty years because of Chadwick "screwing up" statistics. Many clubs' successes and failures were not because Chadwick's statistics "were inadequate." It was not the statistics so much as those who utilized them or misused them. Chadwick obviously had his opinions, and some of those points of view seem out of place when viewed through eyes of a twenty-first century writer. There is no question that Chadwick, particularly as he got older, became more conservative in his views, and there was no doubt that others, even his contemporaries, grew frustrated with some of his old-fashioned ideas. After all, Chadwick was from a different era, something that Lewis fails to take into account. Lewis is devaluing a nineteenth-century thinker in a twenty-first century world.

Another important work related to baseball history that involves a discussion of Henry Chadwick is David Block's *Baseball Before We Knew It: A Search for the Roots of the Game*. This book dispels previously understood notions regarding baseball's heritage and provides valuable insight into the origins of the Doubleday myth, previously unknown. His focus on Chadwick, while not biographical, is important for it relates to the baseball origins debate that Chadwick participated in with the likes of contemporaries Will Rankin, John Montgomery Ward and Albert Spalding. While Block disagrees with Chadwick's belief on baseball's origin, he does place proper emphasis on Chadwick's role in the debate and how important his ideas actually were.

Chapter Notes

Introduction

1. John Rickards Betts, "The Technological Revolution and the Rise of Sport, 1850–1900," *The Mississippi Valley Historical Review*, 232.

2. *The Sporting News*, April 21, 1908.

3. Harry Wright to William Hulbert, November 1875. Wright's correspondence, VI, Society for American Baseball Research library (emphasis added).

4. "Henry Chadwick — The Father of Baseball," *Washington Star*, July 2, 1906, Chadwick Scrapbooks, 18.

5. Henry Chadwick, "Papa Chadwick Writes About '69 Reds," *Enquirer*, March 29, 1901, Chadwick Scrapbooks.

6. David Quentin Voigt, *American Baseball: From Gentleman's Sport to the Commissioner System* (Norman, Oklahoma: University of Oklahoma Press, 1966), 91.

7. *Ibid.*

8. Richard Topp, in his essay "Demographics," located in the 1989 version of *Total Baseball* (John Thorn and Peter Palmer, eds.), writes that most big league rookies stood slightly under five feet, ten inches and weighed 170 pounds. Also see, *A Clever Base-Ballist: The Life and Times of John Montgomery Ward* by Bryan Di Salvatore. For example, Di Salvatore writes that John Montgomery Ward stood only at five feet, seven and one-half inches (some had him at five feet, eight inches), Brooklyn Atlantic Joe Start, five feet, nine inches and

Mike McGeary, five feet, seven inches, p. 415.

9. Edward J. Tassinari, "Henry Chadwick: 'Father of Baseball,' Friend of Chess," in *Lasker and His Contemporaries*, 5 (1997): 49.

Chapter 1

1. Henry Chadwick, *The Game of Base Ball: How to Learn It, How to Play It and How to Teach It* (New York: George Munro, 1868), 10.

2. Henry Chadwick, "Henry Chadwick: The Father of Baseball," newspaper by Guy T. Viskniskki from the Chadwick Scrapbooks, 8. Frederick Ivor-Campbell, "Henry Chadwick," *Harvard Magazine*, 90, no. 1 (September October, 1987).

3. Corey Seeman, *Elysian Fields*, Encyclopedia of New Jersey, Maxine N. Laurie and Marc Mappen, eds. (New Brunswick, New Jersey: Rutgers University Press, 2004), 251.

4. John Cox Stevens was the son of John Stevens, a lawyer, engineer and an inventor who bought land at a public auction from the State of New Jersey that eventually became the city of Hoboken.

5. Seeman, *Elysian Fields*, 251.

6. "Henry Chadwick: The Father of Baseball," Chadwick Scrapbooks.

7. Chadwick, *The Game of Base Ball*, 10. Quoted in Ivor-Campbell, "Henry Chadwick."

8. *Ibid.*

9. Jules Tygiel, *Past Time: Baseball As History* (New York: Oxford University Press, 2000), 7.

10. *Ibid.*

11. "Base Ball in the Central Park," *New York Clipper*, March 7, 1856, 362.

12. "Inning 1: Our Game, 1840s–1900," *Baseball: A Film by Ken Burns*, DVD, directed by Ken Burns (1994; the Baseball Film Project: Time Warner Entertainment Company, 2000).

13. Henry Chadwick, *New York Daily Times*, July 10, 1856, 6.

14. Other sports covered in the *Clipper* included yachting, curling, boxing, chess, and other games that were more obscure. Once a week, when a new edition hit the newsstands, the *Clipper* would print the rules and regulations of various games, in addition to summaries and statistics of assorted sporting events occurring over the week. According to Betts, Queen hailed from Philadelphia and was born to working-class parents in 1823. Later, he became a printer's apprentice and ran a stationary store and newspaper stand until he ventured into the newspaper business in New York. Queen, with Harrison Trent, founded the *Clipper* in 1853.

15. Henry Chadwick, "An Early Base-Ball Reminiscence," 1895, Chadwick Scrapbooks, 3.

16. Dan Schlossberg, *The Baseball Catalog* (New York: Jonathan David Publishers, 2000), 2.

17. Chadwick, *The Game of Base Ball*, 9.

18. Henry Chadwick, *1860 Beadle's Dime Book of Cricket* (New York: Irwin P. Beadle, 1860), 9–10.

19. *Ibid.*

20. Chadwick had written numerous articles and guides on cricket, discussing the game's history.

21. New York Public Library records on ship arrivals, 1837.

22. Oliver Allen, *New York, New York: A History of the World's Most Exhilarating and Challenging City* (New York: Antheneum, 1990), 131.

23. Robert Ernst, *Immigrant Life in New York City, 1825 to 1863* (New York: Columbia University Press, 1949), 27.

24. New York Public Library records on ship arrivals, 1837.

25. Robert V. Remini, *Henry Clay: Statesman for the Union* (New York: W.W. Norton, 1991), 497.

26. "The Epic of New York City," 244.

27. Allen, *New York, New York*, 137.

28. Peter J. Nash's Henry Chadwick Collection of letters and documents of Cooperstown, New York. Peter Nash is a collector of nineteenth century baseball memorabilia and is an avid collector of Henry Chadwick materials, including Chadwick's old walking stick.

29. Letter from Theresa Chadwick to Henry Chadwick, 1836, Peter Nash Chadwick Collection.

30. "Old Time Games: Henry Chadwick's Recollections of Many Years Ago," *Brooklyn Eagle*, May 16, 1888.

31. "Henry Chadwick Recalls Brooklyn 60 Years Ago: Sixty-Fourth Anniversary of the Eagle Puts the Father in Reminiscent Mood," *Brooklyn Eagle*, approx. November 2, 1905, from the Peter Nash Collection.

32. "The Epic of New York City," 251.

33. They lived there for two years. *The 1839–39 Brooklyn Directory*, Brooklyn Public Library. From 1840–1841, the Chadwicks lived on High and Fulton. In 1841 and 1842, they lived on Clove Road near Bedford Avenue. Between 1842 and 1844, the family resided at 16 Hicks Street in Brooklyn Heights. Between 1844 and 1850, they lived at 68 Middagh, also in Brooklyn Heights.

34. "Old Time Games," *Brooklyn Eagle*, May 11, 1888.

35. Denton's Mill Pond is located in present-day Bergen Hill. Henry Chadwick, "Old Time Games." The Luquer Mill was named after Nicholas Luquer. It was "a long, low, and cozy looking homestead ... surrounded by trees, through whose branches a pleasant breeze seemed always to play. It fronted the mill-pond, wherein Mr. Luquer, a thin French-looking man, raised oysters of extraordinary size and delicacy. Luquer's mill was used in grinding grain for the purpose of supplying Henry Pierrepont's distillery...." See Henry R. Stiles, *A History of the City of Brooklyn, Including the Old Town and Village of Brooklyn, the Town of Bushwick, and the Village and City of Williamsburgh*, originally published by Subscription, in 1869 (Facsimile Reprint, Heritage Books, Bowie, Maryland, 1993), 158.

36. "Old Time Games," *Brooklyn Eagle*, May 11, 1888.

37. *Ibid.*

38. Cricket was among the earliest field sports in Brooklyn.

39. "Old Time Games," *Brooklyn Eagle*, May 11, 1888.

40. James Chadwick diary entry entitled "For the Transcript," January 28, 1839, 38–39.

41. Benjamin Ward Richardson, *The Health of Nations: A Review of the Works of Edwin Chadwick with a Biographical Dissertation* (London: Longmans, Green, 1887), taken from a website from the Department of Epidemiology, University of California, Los Angeles, School of Public Heath, http://www.ph.ucla.edu/EPI/snow/chadwick/chadwick_chapt2.html, 2.

42. Many people rank Manchester to be England's second city, not only because of its historical reputation, but due also due to is serving as a center that is home to the arts, media, high education and big business. The origin Manchester name comes from *Mamuciam*, an old Roman name believed to be Latinized from the original Celtic name which (thought to be *mamm*, which means "breast" or "breast-like hill") along with *ceaster*, Old English coming from the Latin *castra*, meaning "camp." According to http://www.manchester2002-uk.com/history/roman.html, the city got its name from the Roman General Julius Agricola (40–93 AD), who after invading instantly built a wooden fortress. According to this website, it was Agricola who named the area "mamucian" for "breast-like hill."

43. Rochdale consists of four divisions: Hundersfield, Spotland, Castleton, and Butterworth. These four areas are further subdivided, with Chadwick being one of the subdivisions of Spotland. Henry Fishwick, *History of the Parish of Rochdale*, http://www.rochdale.gov.uk/living/libraries.asp?url=ebookHOR, 2.

44. Richardson, *The Health of Nations*, 1. Ethel Bader Cage, "The Chadwicks of England and America, Hemet, California, August 1952," available online at http://home.bak.rr.com/russellhome/Histories/Chadwick%20History%20Report.htm, 2.

45. Cage, "The Chadwicks of England and America," 2. England is actually derived from the Angler.

46. *Ibid.*

47. Fishwick, *History of the Parish of Rochdale*, http://www.rochdale.gov.uk/living/libraries.asp?url=ebookHOR.

48. "The Chadwicks of Guelph and Toronto and Their Cousins," http://www.antonymaitland.com/emctext/emcprintd.htm, 5.

49. *Ibid.*

50. Anthony Brundage, *England's "Prussian Minister": Edwin Chadwick and the Politics of Government Growth, 1832–1854* (University Park, Pennsylvania: Pennsylvania State University, 1988), 4; Richardson, II, 1.

51. E. P. Thompson, *The Making of the Working Class* (New York: Pantheon Books, 1964), 38.

52. Gertrude Himmelfarb, *The Roads to Modernity: The British, French and American Enlightenments* (New York: Vintage Books, 2004), 125. In Himmelfarb's work, the author takes author E.P. Thompson to task for labeling John Wesley and his movement anti-intellectual. Thompson believed that Methodism prevented England from having a revolution, one that would overthrow the monarchy, because it was repressive and kept the English working class from pursuing its true interests.

53. Brundage, *England's "Prussian Minister,"* 4. James Chadwick's birthday could be found in his diary entry in Brooklyn, December 2, 1852. The diary is in the hands of Peter J. Nash, who received it from Fran Henry of Massachusetts, a direct descendant of Henry Chadwick

54. Richardson, II, 1.

55. *Ibid.*

56. *Ibid.* Joel Barlow (1754–1812) was born in Redding, Connecticut, and in his early years was part of a group of writers known as the Connecticut Wits. A poet and author, Barlow served in the Revolutionary Army as a chaplain during America's War of Independence and later traveled to Europe, going to both France and England. In Paris he became a liberal in religious matters and a strong republican and after publishing some radical essays in England, namely *Advice to the Privileged Orders* in 1792, he became a French citizen. When he was in England, he became friends with Thomas Paine, and when Paine was imprisoned in Paris, Barlow helped effect the publishing of *The Age of Reason*. Barlow served in diplomatic roles, securing the release of American prisoners

and negotiating treaties with Algiers, Tunis and Tripoli.

57. Thompson, *The Making of the English Working Class.*

58. "Henry Chadwick, the Father of Baseball," *Washington Star,* July 2, 1906, Chadwick Scrapbook, vol. 18. Tygiel, *Past Time,* 17. Henry Chadwick's mother's first name and his sister's first name were discovered on passenger lists from their arrival at New York aboard the ship *Philadelphia,* located at the New York Public Library. His father was fifteen years older than his second wife, Therese, who was forty-five at the time of the arrival.

59. America has always been seen as a land of opportunity, a virtual frontier where individuals could reinvent themselves and provide the kind of opportunities for their children that they would not have had back in the mother country.

60. Marjorie Bloy, Ph.D., Senior Research Fellow, National University of Singapore, www.victorianweb.org/history/chad1.html., 1.

61. James Chadwick diary entry, "For the Transcript," January 28, 1839, 38–39. Peter J. Nash Chadwick Collection.

62. *Ibid.,* 39.

63. According to the B.W. Richardson biography, Edwin's mother was of the "family of Greenlees of Cheshire," England, 2.

64. Bloy, www.victorianweb.org/history/chad1.html., 1.

65. "At Ninety Years: Interview with the 'Father of Sanitary Science,'" *Brooklyn Eagle,* December 22, 1889, 7. It should be noted that the *Eagle* published this interview that was conducted by the *London Pall Mall Gazette.*

66. Brundage, *England's "Prussian Minister,"* 1.

67. Bloy, www.victorianweb.org/history/chad1.html., 1.

68. In 1842, he published his "Report into the Sanitary Conditions of the Labouring Population of Great Britain." The report showed that the life expectancy was much lower in the town where all the factories were than in the countryside. More importantly, Chadwick's report challenged the *laissez faire* philosophy popular at the time as he argued that it was possible for the government to improve people's lives by bringing about reform. Chadwick files, the Albert

Spalding Collection. BBC 1 Website, history, Society and Economy.

69. "At Ninety Years," 7.

70. *Ibid.*

71. "Fiftieth Year of Journalism: Henry Chadwick's Long Service in the Cause of American Sports," 3, Chadwick Scrapbooks. The Asylum, actually, had been formed back in 1833 to house the children whose parents died of Cholera during an outbreak that swept through the cities of New York and Brooklyn. Edwin G. Burrows and Mike Wallace, *Gotham: A History of New York City to 1898* (New York: Oxford University Press, 1999), 593.

72. *Ibid.*

73. Later, according to Frederick Ivor-Campbell, he reviewed music and theater, and he covered the early days of the Civil War for the *New York Tribune.* His father also taught music. According to an 1845 Brooklyn directory, both father and son used the title of "Professor of Music" to list their occupations.

74. James M. DiClerico and Barry J. Pavelec, *The Jersey Game: The History of Modern Baseball from Its Birth to the Big Leagues in the Garden State* (New Brunswick, New Jersey: Rutgers University Press, 1991), 1.

75. "Henry Chadwick Recalls Brooklyn 60 Years Ago," Brooklyn *Eagle.* The *Star* was located on 57 Fulton Street, opposite of Hicks Street; the *Eagle,* 53 Fulton Street; and the *Daily News,* No. 1 Front Street.

76. Burrows and Wallace, *Gotham,* 676–677.

77. "Father and Mrs. Chadwick Celebrate Their Fifty-Eighth Anniversary of Their Wedding Day," August 25, 1906, Chadwick Files of the National Baseball Hall of Fame and Museum.

78. The American System, as devised by Clay, was essentially a variation of the Hamiltonian system that endorsed the idea of using taxes and tariff dollars, supported by a central bank, as a source of revenue for the federal government to be used in developing and improving upon the infrastructure of the United States and as a means of creating greater national unity. See Remini, *Henry Clay.*

79. http://www.famousamericans.net/johnminorbotts/; Chadwick Scrapbooks, 8.

80. The Chadwick Collection. Benjamin and his wife Jane (her maiden name was

Tyler) lost their lives when the Richmond Theater was burned in 1811. Also, according to a *Brooklyn Eagle* article commemorating her 82nd birthday, Mrs. Chadwick, through her mother, is descended from the "Princess Pocahontas."

81. "Tells of Seeing Aaron Burr: Mrs. Henry Chadwick's One Glimpse of Him, of an Annuity for $500 for Life—Documentary Evidence That Burr Did Not Die in Poverty," *New York Sun*, May 17, 1903, 8.

82. *Ibid.*

83. *Ibid.* According to the article, Mrs. Chadwick has her father's day book and ledger in which each payment was entered. "The first entry was in 1833: 'Cash to Col. Burr, $500,' the last in 1836, followed by the note, 'Col. Burr died in September, 1836.' In all, $2,300 appears to have been paid him."

84. *Ibid.*

85. Letter from the Peter Nash Chadwick Collection.

86. 1860 Census, 11th Ward, District 3, 727, New York Public Library.

87. Peter Nash Chadwick Collection.

88. James Chadwick diary entry in Brooklyn, December 2, 1852. Peter Nash Chadwick Collection.

89. Harold Coffin Syrett, *The City of Brooklyn, 1865–1898: A Political History* (New York: Columbia University Press, 1944), 12.

90. Burrows and Wallace, *Gotham*, 736–738.

91. New York Public Library records on ship arrivals, 1837.

92. Robert Ernst, *Immigrant Life in New York City, 1825 to 1863* (New York: Columbia University Press, 1949), 27.

93. Jacob Judd, "The History of Brooklyn, 1834–1855: Political and Administrative Aspects," PhD. Dissertation, New York University, April 1959, 119–120.

94. *Ibid.*, 790.

95. Burrows and Wallace, *Gothams*, 784–785.

96. Judd, "The History of Brooklyn, 1834–1855," 152–154. It is another indication that Brooklyn's political leaders were more responsive to the needs of its citizens.

97. Harvey Green, *Fit for America: Health Fitness and Sport and American Society* (New York: Pantheon Books, 1986), 136.

98. *Ibid.*, 790–791.

99. Roy Rosenzweig and Elizabeth Black-

mar, *The Park and the People: A History of Central Park* (Ithaca, New York: Cornell University Press), 24.

100. *Ibid.*, 24.

101. Green, *Fit for America*, 104.

102. *Ibid.*, 776.

103. Green-Wood Cemetery records of death.

Chapter 2

1. Don E. Fehrenbacher, *Prelude to Greatness: Lincoln in the 1850's* (Stanford, California: Stanford University Press, 1962), 20–21.

2. Melvin Adelman, *A Sporting Time: New York City and the Rise of Modern Athletics, 1820–70* (Chicago: University of Illinois Press, 1986), 115.

3. Adelman, *A Sporting Time*, 46.

4. Steven A. Riess, ed., "Sport and the Redefinition of American Middle Class Masculinity, 1840–1900," *Major Problems in American Sport* (New York: Houghton Mifflin, 1997), 189.

5. Green, *Fit for America*, 89.

6. *Ibid.*, 89. Jim Moore and Natalie Vermilyea, *Earnest Thayer's "Casey at the Bat": Background and Characters of Baseball's Most Famous Poem* (Jefferson, North Carolina: McFarland, 1994), 10.

7. "Importance of Recreation," printed speech by Edward Everett, *New York Clipper*, July 5, 1856, 81. Edward Everett, a professor of classics at Harvard, preceded Abraham Lincoln's address at Gettysburg with a two-hour speech honoring the dead in the tradition of the ancient Greek soldier Pericles.

8. Foster Rehea Dulles, *A History of Recreation: America Learns to Play* (New York: Meredith Corporation, 1965), 183.

9. Henry Chadwick, *The Ball Player's Chronicle*, New York, June 37, 1867, from the Special Collections Division of the Brooklyn Public Library.

10. Riess, *Major Problems in American Sport*, 189.

11. Chadwick, *The Ball Player's Chronicle*, June 37, 1867.

12. "Physical Advantages of Drill," *Brooklyn Eagle*, November 8, 1860, 1.

13. Henry Chadwick, *New York Clipper*, July 27, 1858.

14. R.C. Adams, "Mailbox: On Base-

ball When the Game Was Very New," biography of Dr. Daniel "Doc" Adams, written in 1939 by his son and submitted by his great-great-grandson Nathan Adams Downey of New York, *New York Times*, April 13, 1980. From the Doc Adams Collection of the Baseball Hall of Fame and Museum in Cooperstown, New York.

15. Adams, "Mailbox: On Baseball When the Game Was Very New."

16. Among the teams that played in Brooklyn were the Atlantics, Baltics, Charter Oaks, Mohawks, Putnams, Powhatan and Newsho of New Utrect. The ball fields were located in Wheat Hill in Williamsburg, Park Avenue and Ryerson Street, Fifth Avenue and Warren Street, DeKalb and Claremont Avenues, Biddle Grove, Grand Avenue and Bedford Avenue.

17. Tom Melville, *Early Baseball and the Rise of the National League* (Jefferson, North Carolina: McFarland, 2003), 12–13.

18. "Henry Chadwick: The Father of Baseball," Chadwick Scrapbooks, 8.

19. John Thorn, Thornpricks (weblog), http://thornpricks.blogspot.com/2005/07/four-fathers-of-baseball.html,3.

20. Melville, *Early Baseball and the Rise of the National League*, 12.

21. http://thornpircks.blogspot.com/2005/07/four-fathers-of-baseball.html, p.3.

22. John Thorn, "Daniel Lucius Adams 'Doc,'" *Baseball's First Stars*, Frederick Ivor-Campbell, Robert L. Tiemann and Mark Rucker, eds. (Cleveland: The American Society for Baseball Research, 1996), 1.

23. "Henry Chadwick: The Father of Baseball," Chadwick Scrapbooks, 8.

24. See Henry Eckford's biography in www.famousamericans.net. In 1820, Eckford moved to Brooklyn because he was appointed head naval constructor and proceeded to design some of the most powerful war ships in the world, the first of these being the *Ohio*.

25. Irving A. Leitner, *Baseball: Diamond in the Rough* (New York: Criterion Books, 1972), 53. Leitner also points out that the Eckfords' record was "no less remarkable since baseball clubs at the time usually played no more than ten or twelve matches each per season."

26. Ellen M. Snyder-Grenier, *Brooklyn! An Illustrated History for the Brooklyn Historical Society* (Philadelphia: Temple University Press, 1996), 224–225.

27. Christopher Devine, *Harry Wright: The Father of Professional Base Ball* (Jefferson, North Carolina: McFarland, 2003), 22. Also see Chadwick Scrapbooks.

28. Robert H. Schaefer, "The Great Base Ball Match of 1858: Base Ball's First All-Star Game," January 20, 2004, 8.

29. *Ibid.*

30. *New York Daily Times*, July 20, 1858.

31. Chadwick, *The Game of Base Ball*, 11.

32. Tygiel, *Past Time*, 12.

33. Chadwick, *The Game of Base Ball*, 11.

34. Adelman, *A Sporting Time*, 131.

35. "Base Ball," *Brooklyn Eagle*, August 6, 1860, 2, from www.eagle.brooklynpublic library.org/Archive.

36. "Base Ball: The Fly Game Versus the Bound," *New York Clipper*, November 10, 1860, 234.

37. Adams, "Mailbox: On Baseball When the Game Was Very New."

38. *New York Evening Express*, Aug. 3, 1859, 1.

39. Chadwick, *Beadle's Dime Book of Cricket*, 7–8.

40. *Ibid.*, 49; Henry Chadwick, *Beadle's Dime Base-Ball Player: A Compendium of the Game, Comprising Elementary Instructions of This Game of Ball* (New York: Irving P. Beadle, 1860), 26–27.

41. While it can be argued whether catching a baseball on the fly is a manly act, it cannot be argued whether it was a painful one; the players were playing without gloves.

42. "Ball Play: The Next Convention, the Fly Game vs. the Bound," *New York Clipper*, November 19, 1864, 250.

43. *Ibid.*

44. *Ibid.*

45. *Ibid.*

46. "Ball Play: The Base Ball Convention, the Fly Rule Adopted by a Large Majority," *New York Clipper*, December 23, 1864.

Chapter 3

1. http://www.niulib.niu.edu/badndp/chap6.html.

2. Henry Chadwick, "Base Ball and Rounders: Was the Former Game Evolved from the Latter?" *Brooklyn Eagle*, July 1, 1881, 7.

3. David Block, *Baseball Before We Knew It: A Search for the Roots of the Game* (Lincoln: University of Nebraska Press, 2005), 1.

4. Chadwick, *1860 Beadle's Dime Base-Ball Player*, 8–9.

5. *Ibid.*, 18.

6. *Ibid.*, 19.

7. *Ibid.*, 21.

8. Henry Chadwick, *1869 Beadle's Dime Base-Ball Manual* (New York: Beadle, 1869), 53.

9. *Ibid.*, 55.

10. *Ibid.*, 55.

11. *Ibid.*, 57–58.

12. *Ibid.*, 58.

13. While the only remaining symbol left from Chadwick's innovation is the "K" in strikeout, his standardization of the scoring system still remains. Tygiel, *Past Time*, 23.

14. Chadwick, *1869 Beadle's Dime Base-Ball Player*, 55–56.

15. *Ibid.*, 54.

16. *Ibid.*

17. *Ibid.*, 55.

18. Tygiel, *Past Time*, 21.

19. Fox Butterfield, "Cooperstown? Hoboken? Try New York City," *New York Times*, October 4, 1990. "An excerpt and box score from an 1845 account in the *New York Morning News* that is the earliest known report of a baseball game."

20. Chadwick Scrapbooks, taken from a box score published in *Sunday Mercury*, August 1862.

21. *New York Clipper*, August 30, 1856, 149.

22. *New York Clipper*, August 19, 1871. The parentheses inserted after Spalding's name in the box score is to indicate that the *Clipper* mistakenly listed him as center fielder when in fact he most likely pitched, as player-manager Harry Wright roamed the vast territory of center field.

23. Chadwick, *1869 Beadle's Dime Base-Ball Player*, 50.

24. *Ibid.*

25. Chadwick Scrapbooks, 1.

26. Cricketers' Averages for 1857, *New York Clipper*, October 31, 1857, 220.

27. "Ball Play: Averages for the Atlantic Club for 1861," *New York Clipper*, November 16, 1861, 247.

28. Patricia Cline Cohen, *A Calculating People: The Spread of Numeracy in Early America* (Chicago: University of Chicago Press, 1983; Routledge, 1999), 154.

29. Tygiel, *Past Time*, 17–18.

30. Tygiel, *Past Time*, 22. Quote taken from Chadwick, *The Game of Base Ball*, 11–12.

31. Cohen, *A Calculating People*, 144. It was not just the "primacy of business principals" that spawned the birth of player-statistics. Sporting statistics existed before the game became professionalized, as cricket followers had always kept extensive statistics.

32. Chadwick, *Beadle's* (1864), 59–60.

33. Chadwick's Chat, *Sporting News*, January 12, 1887.

34. Alan Schwarz, *The Numbers Game: Baseball's Lifelong Fascination with Statistics* (New York: Thomas Dunne Books, 2004), 24.

35. Tygiel, *Past Time*, 21.

36. Henry Chadwick, *New York Clipper*, September 1, 1860, 7.

37. *Ibid.*

38. Steven A. Riess, *Touching Base: Professional Baseball and American Culture in the Progressive Era* (Westport, Connecticut: Greenwood Press, 1980), 3.

39. Henry Chadwick, "The Model Base Ball Player," *New York Clipper*, November 9, 1861.

Chapter 4

1. Leitner, *Baseball: Diamond in the Rough*, 49. Also see "Out-Door Sports: Base Ball," *Brooklyn Eagle*, 2.

2. Chadwick, *1862 Beadle's Dime Base-Ball Player*, 40.

3. *Ibid.*, 59–60.

4. Donald, David Herbert. *Lincoln.* New York: Simon and Schuster, 1995, 569.

5. Leitner, *Baseball: Diamond in the Rough*, 59. According to Lincoln biographer David Herbert Donald, "Shakespeare's plays appealed to him most ... [and] he had never seen Shakespeare performed on the stage until he became President."

*Ford's Theatre, located on Tenth Street, between E and F Streets, was only a few blocks from Grovers Theatre, located on E Street between Thirteenth and Fourteenth Street. See Donald, *Lincoln*, 568–569.

6. Donald, *Lincoln*, 567.

7. *Ibid.*, 567–568.

8. Henry Chadwick, *Brooklyn Eagle*, June 6, 1868.

9. *Ibid.*

10. E. Anthony Rotundo, *American Manhood: Transformations in Masculinity from the Revolution to the Modern Era* (New York: Basic Books, 1993), 239; Howard Mumford Jones, *The Age of Energy: The Varieties of American Experience: 1865–1915* (New York: Viking Press, 1971), 104.

11. Adelman, *A Sporting Time*, 134.

12. http://bioproj.sabr.org/bioproj.cfm?a=v&v=1&pid=16900&bid=770. "James Creighton," John Thorne, The Baseball Biography Project, from www.sabr.org.

13. Peter J. Nash, *Baseball Legends of Brooklyn's Green-Wood Cemetery* (Portsmouth, New Hampshire: Arcadia, 2003), 64.

14. "Base Ball," *Brooklyn Eagle*, August 6, 1860, 2.

15. *Ibid.*

16. Nash, *Baseball Legends of Brooklyn's Green-Wood Cemetery*, 64–65.

17. "Ball Play: The Death of James Creighton," *The New York Clipper*, October 25, 1862, 219.

18. Nash, *Baseball Legends of Brooklyn's Green-Wood Cemetery*, 128.

19. *Ibid.*

20. *Ibid.*, 2.

21. "Base Ball," *Brooklyn Eagle*, April 30, 1860, 2.

22. "Ball Play: Third Grand Match at Base Ball, the Game Broken Up by Rowdies," *New York Clipper*, September 1, 1860, 154.

23. "The Base Ball Match Between the Atlantics and Excelsiors," *New York Clipper*, Saturday, September 8, 1860, 164.

24. *Ibid.*

25. Burrows and Wallace, *Gotham*, 832.

26. *Ibid.*, 888–895.

27. Kirsch, *Base Ball Players' Chronicle*, 236.

28. *Ibid.*, 235.

29. David Nasaw, *Going Out: The Rise and Fall of Popular Amusements* (New York: Basic Books, 1993), 26; Kathy Peiss, *Cheap Amusements: Working Women and Leisure in Turn-of-the-Century New York* (Philadelphia: Temple University Press, 1986), 142.

30. Chadwick Scrapbooks, 27.

31. *Ibid.*

32. Snyder-Grenier, *Brooklyn!*, 224–225.

33. Henry Chadwick, "Base-Ball Matters: The Grand Base-Ball Tournament," *Wilkes Spirit of the Times*, 294.

34. Henry Chadwick, "A.G. Spalding," 7, 90, Chadwick Scrapbooks.

35. John B. Foster, "Henry Chadwick 'The Father of Base Ball,'" *Spalding's Official Base Ball Guide* (New York: 1909), 14.

36. Frank Ceresi and Carol McMains, *Early Baseball in Washington, D.C.: How the Washington Nationals Helped Develop America's Game*, paper from http://www.fcassociates.com/aboutus.htm.

37. *Ibid.*

38. *Ibid.*

39. Henry Chadwick, "Arthur P. Gorman, Esq.," *The Ball Players' Chronicle*, New York, July 11, 1867, 4.

40. "Mr. Henry Chadwick: Modestly Disclaims the Paternity of the National Game," *Brooklyn Eagle*, March 16, 1888, 2.

41. *Ibid.*

42. *Ibid.*

43. "Out-door Sports: Base Ball," *New York Times*, Saturday, July 7, 1866, 2.

44. *Ibid.*

45. "Sports and Pastimes: Base Ball," *Brooklyn Eagle*, July 6, 1866, 2.

46. *Ibid.*

47. *Ibid.*

48. Leitner, *Baseball: Diamond in the Rough*, 76.

49. Ceresi and McMains, *Early Baseball in Washington, D.C.*

50. Henry Chadwick, "Base Ball: The Game in the West: The Grand Western Tour of the National Club, Their Visit to Columbus," *The Ball Players Chronicle*, New York, July 18, 1867, 1.

51. *Ibid.*

52. "The Nationals Trip Forty Years Ago," 18, 30, Chadwick Scrapbooks.

53. "Base Ball: The Second Game of the Series: National vs. Cincinnati," *The Ball Players' Chronicle*, July 25, 1867, 1.

54. "Base Ball: The Greatest Victory of the Tour: National vs. Excelsior of Chicago," *The Ball Players' Chronicle*, 1, No. 10, 1.

55. *Ibid.*

56. *Ibid.*

57. *Ibid.*

58. *Ibid.*

59. *Ibid.*

60. *Ibid.*

61. *Ibid.*

62. *Ibid.*

63. *Ibid.*
64. *Ibid.*
65. *Ibid.*
66. *Ibid.*
67. *Ibid.*
68. *Ibid.*, 6.
69. Devine, *Harry Wright*, 12.
70. Devine, *Harry Wright*, 34–36. Also see Lee Allen, *100 Years of Baseball: The Intimate and Dramatic Story of Modern Baseball from the Game's Beginnings Up to the Present Day* (New York: Bartholomew House, 1950), 13; and Andrew Schiff, "Wright, William Henry ("Harry")," *The Scribner Encyclopedia of American Lives: Sports Figures,* Kenneth T. Jackson, ed. (New York: 2002), 518.
71. Devine, *Harry Wright*, 12. Also see Chadwick Scrapbooks.
72. William Ryczek, *When Johnny Comes Sliding Home* (Jefferson, North Carolina: McFarland, 1995), 139.
73. Albert G. Spalding, *Base Ball: America's National Game* (New York: American Sports Publications, 1911), 149.
74. *Ibid.*, 149–150.
75. "The Cincinnati Club in the Metropolis: Their Defeat by the Atlantics," *New York Clipper,* June 25, 1870, 3.
76. *Ibid.*
77. *Ibid.*
78. Goldstein, 214, and Adelman, *A Sporting Time,* 125. During the 1860s many of the baseball clubs consisted of certain shops or workplaces, like the Eckford Club of Brooklyn, which consisted of highly paid shipwrights and mechanics of Henry Eckford's shipyards.
79. Andrew Jay Schiff, "Labor and Baseball History, A Historiography," *Clio: The History Journal of the Chi Delta Chapter of Phi Alpha Theta* (University at Albany, Volume 2, Spring 1995), 39; Steven Gelber, "Their Hands Are All Out Playing: Business and Amateur Baseball, 1845–1918," *Journal of Sport History* (Spring, 1984), 6.
80. "Business and Recreation," 1871, Chadwick Scrapbooks.
81. Crosset, Todd, "Masculinity, Sexuality, and the Development of Early Modern Sport," 52–54.
82. Adelman, *A Sporting Time,* 283. Also see John Kasson, *Rudeness and Civility,* 112–146, and Rotundo, *American Manhood,* 71–74; Wilma J. Pesavento, "Sport and Recreation in the Pullman Experiment,

1880–1900," *Journal of Sport History* (Summer, 1982), 38: The best and most well-known example of sports used within a corporate environment was the social experiment of railroad magnate George Pullman's community town between 1880 and 1900. Built on the shores of Lake Calumet, in Illinois, the town, which consisted of members of Pullman's factory workers, came equipped with sports facilities. Baseball, as well as other sports, were an integral part of the success of the town and the happiness of its resident workers.
83. Chadwick Scrapbooks, 7.
84. Kirsch, *The Creation of American Team Sports,* 238.
85. Kirsch, *The Creation of American Team Sports,* 110–111. The Excelsiors, predominately consisting of white-collar professionals, stopped "hiring players and dropped out of championship competition" during and after the Civil War.
86. Henry Chadwick, "Professionals Seize Control of the NABBP," *New York Clipper,* December 18, 1869. Sullivan, Dean A. *Early Innings: A Documentary History of Baseball, 1825–1908* (Lincoln, Nebraska: University of Nebraska Press, 1995), 77.
87. Kirsch, *The Creation of American Team Sports,* 251.
88. "Sports and Pastimes: Baseball," Chadwick Scrapbooks, 1.
89. "Base-Ball," *New York Times,* February, 29, 1871, 6.
90. "The Father of Baseball," Chadwick Scrapbooks, 18.
91. Henry Chadwick, *New York Clipper,* April 3, 1858.
92. *Ibid.*
93. "The Father of Baseball," *Washington Star,* 1906, Chadwick Scrapbooks.
94. *New York Clipper,* December, 29 1873, 3.
95. *Ibid.*, 3
96. Robert Schaefer, *The Lost Art of Fair-Foul Hitting,* June 1, 1999, 1.
97. Chadwick Scrapbook, 1.
98. Ryczek, William J. *Blackguards and Redstockings: A History of Baseball's National Association, 1871–1875* (Jefferson, NC: McFarland, 1999), 143.
99. "A Ten Inning Game," *New York Clipper,* January 3, 1874, 315.
100. *Ibid.*
101. *Ibid.*
102. "Our National Game, Ten Men

and Ten Innings: A Foolish Opposition to It," Chadwick Scrapbooks, 1.

103. Ryczek, *Blackguards and Red Stockings*, 144.

104. Schaefer, 10.

105. Schaefer, 9–10.

106. *Ibid.*, 6.

107. *Ibid.*

108. "The Science of Batting," Chadwick Scrapbooks.

109. Henry Chadwick, *The Sporting Life*, August 9, 1890.

110. H.I. Horton, "Chadwick Disagreed With," *The Sporting Life*, August 16, 1890, taken from the Chadwick folder at the National Baseball Hall of Fame and Museum.

111. *Ibid.*

112. *Ibid.*

113. "Chadwick Elaborates on Willie Keeler's Treatise on Batting," *Brooklyn Eagle*, August 27, 1901, 12.

114. *Ibid.*

115. Ibid, 2.

116. Ibid, 7

117. Ibid, 10.

118. Ryczek, *Blackguards and Red Stockings*, 144.

Chapter 5

1. Ryczek, *Blackguards and Red Stockings*, 219.

2. Allen, *100 Years of Baseball*, 28.

3. Ryczek, *Blackguards and Red Stockings*, 214.

4. Obituary, "William A. Hulbert, President of the Chicago Base-Ball Club and of the National League," *Chicago Tribune*, April 11, 1882, unspecified page. William A. Hulbert collection of the National Baseball Hall of Fame in Cooperstown, New York.

5. Ryczek, *Blackguards and Red Stockings*, 133–134.

6. Voigt, *American Baseball*, 52.

7. "The Diamond Squared: An Honest Base-Ball Association Born into the World," *The Chicago Tribune*, Friday, February 4, 1876, 5.

8. Neil MacDonald, *The League That Lasted*, 17.

9. Chadwick Scrapbooks.

10. Minutes of Chicago White Stockings Shareholders Meeting held at C.S. Bartlett's Residence, evening of July 3, 1875, 7–9.

11. *Ibid.*, 59.

12. *Ibid.*

13. MacDonald, *The League That Lasted*, 17. *Albert Goodwill Spalding*, William McMahon, *Baseball's First Stars*, Frederick Ivor-Campbell, Robert L. Tiemann, Mark Rucker, eds. Cleveland: SABR, 1985), 115.

14. Ryczek, *Blackguards and Red Stockings*, 187–189.

15. *Ibid.*, 256.

16. Melville, *Early Baseball and the Rise of the National League*, 72–73.

17. Hulbert letter to Chadwick, February 10, 1875.

18. Melville, *Early Baseball and the Rise of the National League*, 73.

19. Benjamin Rader, *Baseball: A History of America's Game*, 2nd Edition (Chicago: University of Illinois Press, 2002), 43.

20. "Baseball: National League of Professional Clubs Formed: A Startling Coup d' Etat," 1876, Chadwick Scrapbooks, 3.

21. Hulbert correspondence to N.T. Apollonio, February 9, 1876.

22. Voigt, *American Baseball*, 62.

23. Wright to Hulbert, March 23, December 30, 1875. Wright's correspondence, VI, from the library of the Society for American Baseball Research.

24. *Ibid.*

25. Hulbert to Wright, Chicago, January 12, 1876.

26. *Ibid.*

27. *Ibid.*

28. "Facts Concerning the Downfall of the 'Father of the Game,'" *Chicago Tribune*, April 2, 1876, s5.

29. *Ibid.*

30. Albert Goodwill Spalding to Henry Chadwick, February 27, 1876, reprinted in *Spalding's Official Base Ball Guide*, 1908, 19–20.

31. Chadwick Scrapbooks, 1.

32. *Ibid.*

33. *Ibid.*

34. *Ibid.*

35. *Ibid.*

36. *Ibid.*

37. *Ibid.*

38. *Ibid.*

39. "The Amateur Season of 1876," Chadwick Scrapbooks, 3.

40. "Sports in Brooklyn: Henry Chadwick Talks About the Old Times," vol. 3. Circa 1890s, Chadwick Scrapbooks.

41. David Pietrusza, *Major Leagues: 18*

Professional Baseball Organizations, 1871 to Present (Jefferson, North Carolina: McFarland), p. 34.

42. *Ibid.*, 35.

43. *Ibid.*, 36.

44. Spalding, *Base Ball: America's National Game,* 226.

45. *Ibid*, 38.

46. Chadwick Scrapbooks, 1.

47. Ryczek, *Blackguards and Red Stockings*, 65; Peter Morris, *A Game of Inches: The Stories Behind the Innovations That Shaped Baseball* (Chicago: Ivan R. Dee Press, 2006), 470.

48. Chadwick Scrapbooks, 1.

49. *Ibid.*

50. *Ibid.*

51. *Ibid.*

52. Spalding, *Base Ball: America's National Game,* 141.

53. *Ibid.*

54. Henry Chadwick, ed., *De Witt's Base-Ball Guide for 1879: A Complete Manual of the National Game* (New York: Clinton T. De Witt, Publisher, 1879), 44.

55. Voigt, *American Baseball,* 92.

56. *Ibid.*, 201.

57. Frank V. Phelps, "Oliver Perry Caylor (O.P.)," *Baseball's First Stars,* Frederick Ivor-Campbell, Robert L. Tiemann, Mark Rucker, eds. Cleveland: SABR, 1985), 25.

58. "Chadwick's Chat: A Valecdictory on Caylor's Gazette, " *Sporting Life,* May 11, 1887, page unknown.

59. Phelps, *Baseball's First Stars,* 25.

60. Chadwick's Chat: A Valecdictory on Caylor's Gazette," *Sporting Life.*

61. *Ibid.*

62. Spalding, *Base Ball: America's National Game,* 241.

63. Chadwick Scrapbooks, 3.

64. *Ibid.*

65. "In Memoriam," *Spalding's Official Base Ball Guide for 1879* (A.G. Spalding, Chicago), 3.

66. Henry Chadwick, *Spalding's Official Base Ball Guide of 1883,* 5.

67. Henry Chadwick, *Spalding's Official Baseball Guide,* 1881, introduction.

68. *Ibid.*

69. Voigt, *American Baseball,* 199. Frank V. Phelps, "Oliver Perry Caylor (O.P.)," 25.

70. *Ibid.*, 4.

71. Spalding, *Base Ball: America's National Game,* 223.

72. *Ibid.*, 224.

73. Chadwick, *Spalding's Official Base Ball Guide,* 17.

74. *Ibid.*

75. *Ibid.*, p 16.

76. Henry Chadwick, "Chadwick's Chat," *Sporting Life,* 1890.

77. Voigt, *American Baseball,* 198.

78. *Ibid.*, 196–197.

79. John Allen Gable, *Theodore Roosevelt: America's 26th President,* Famous American Series (Eastern National, 2003), 9.

Chapter 6

1. Gable, *Theodore Roosevelt,* 9.

2. Rader, *Baseball: A History of America's Game,* 53.

3. John Montgomery Ward, "Is the Base-Ball Player a Chattel?" *Lippincott Magazine* 40 (May 1887): 310–19. Riess, *Major Problems in American Sport,* 216–218.

4. Rader, *Baseball: A History of America's Game,* 57.

5. Henry Chadwick, "Chadwick's Chat," *Sporting Life,* 1890.

6. Henry Chadwick, "Chadwick's Chat," *Sporting News,* October 18, 1890.

7. *Ibid.*, 165

8. Rader, *Baseball: A History of America's Game,* 61.

9. Voight, *American Baseball,* 167; Rader, *Baseball: A History of America's Game,* 61.

10. Voigt, *American Baseball,* 162.

11. *Ibid.*, 196.

12. *Ibid.*, 195.

13. *Sporting Life,* January 15, 1890.

14. *Ibid.*

15. Indeed, it was Spalding who subsequently paid for Chadwick's burial plot and tombstone.

16. Voigt, *American Baseball,* 197.

17. Herbert G. Gutman, "The Workers' Search for Power," *The Gilded Age,* H. Wayne Morgan, ed., 33.

18. Nasaw, *Going Out,* 99.

19. Several American Association clubs were absorbed into the National League: St. Louis, Baltimore, Washington and Louisville; the National League now had 12 teams. The other Association clubs were bought out for $135,000 each. See David Nemec's *The Beer and Whiskey League: The Illustrated History of the American Association — Baseball's Renegade Major League*

(Gilford, CT: The Lyons Press, 2004), 234–235.

20. "Chadwick Honored: Compliments to Be Paid the Noted American Sportswriter," tribute by Mr. St. Claire McElway. *The Brooklyn Eagle,* unidentified date in 1887.

21. *Ibid.*

22. Henry Chadwick correspondence to Edwin Chadwick written from the *Brooklyn Eagle* office, April 19, 1875, 3.

23. *Ibid.* Richard Proctor eventually moved to America and got involved in the baseball origins debate, siding with Chadwick. See Chapter 9. When Tyndall died in 1893, a crater on Mars was named in his honor. Chadwick only spelled Tyndall's name with one l in the letter.

24. "Sir Edwin Chadwick, K.C.B: The Father of Sanitary Science Dies at a Ripe Old Age," *Brooklyn Eagle,* July 7, 1890, 4.

25. Henry Chadwick letter to Edwin Chadwick, June 6, 1889. Chadwick wrote the letter from his residence on 21 Grove Place.

26. "Base Ball in England: It Is Becoming a Popular Pastime in Great Britain, A Letter to the Father of the Great American Game — Sir Edwin Chadwick's Hobby — The Inventor of a Machine for Washing Children," *Brooklyn Eagle,* January 19. 1889, 4.

27. "At Ninety Years," 7. When Edwin Chadwick refers to ozone, he most likely is not referring to the modern understanding of ozone, but probably oxygen.

28. "Base Ball in England," *Brooklyn Eagle,* January 19, 1889, 4.

29. *Ibid.,* 4.

30. "Sir Edwin Chadwick, K.C.B.," 4.

31. Henry Chadwick to Edwin Chadwick, November 13, 1888, 1.

32. *Ibid.,* 2.

33. "On Sanitary Reform," Edwin Chadwick letter to the Legislature of the State of New York, December 1888.

34. "Chadwick's Chat," *Sporting Life,* November 1, 1890.

35. Brundage, *England's "Prussian Minister,"* 172.

36. "Henry Chadwick," Chadwick Scrapbooks, 3.

37. *Ibid.*

38. "Chadwick Officially Notified: President Young's Letter on the Recent Action of the League Magnates," *Brooklyn Eagle,* November 18, 1896, 12.

39. Nicholas Accocella and Donald Dewey, *The Biographical History of Baseball* (New York: Caroll and Graf), 70.

40. Spalding, *Base Ball: America's National Game,* 194.

41. "About His Size: Freedman's Affront to Mr. Chadwick, The Culmination of a Long Series of Insults to Newspapermen," *Sporting News,* March 28, 1898, Chadwick Scrapbooks.

42. *Ibid.*

43. *Ibid.*

44. Spalding, *Base Ball: America's National Game,* 194.

45. Chadwick Scrapbooks.

46. "Chadwick's Tips: Maintain National Agreement at Any Cost," *Sporting News,* December 8, 1900, 3.

47. *Ibid.*

48. *Ibid.*

49. "Troubles Which Beset the Baseball World," *Sporting News,* February 9, 2001. 3.

50. Rader, *Baseball: A History of America's Game,* 86.

51. Johnson was succeed by Moses Fleetwood Walker, the first black player in the major leagues.

52. "Praises Johnson," *Sporting News,* June 1, 1901, 6.

53. *Ibid.*

54. Voigt, *American Baseball,* 312–314; Lee Allen, *The American League Story* (New York: Hill and Wang, 1965), 4–5; Glenn Dickey, *The History of the American League, Since 1901* (New York: Stein and Day, 1980), 2.

55. http://entertainment.howstuffworks.com/ban-johnson-hof.htm.

56. Chris Devine, *Harry Wright,* 166–167. Also see Andrew Schiff, *Wright, William Henry ("Harry"), The Scribner Encyclopedia of American Lives: Sports Figures,* Volume 2 (New York: Scribner's. 2002), 519.

57. *Ibid.,* 167.

58. *Ibid.,* 167.

59. "Their Golden Wedding: Mr. and Mrs. Henry Chadwick Will Celebrate Fifty Years of Wedded Life on August 19," *Brooklyn Eagle,* August, 8, 1898.

60. "Chadwick See the President," *Brooklyn Eagle,* October 29, 2006, 10.

61. "Veteran Chadwick See the President," *Washington Star,* Saturday, October 28, 1899, 25.

62. "Sport for the Troops," *Washington Star,* Wednesday, October 25, 1899, 4.

63. *Ibid.*

64. "Base Ball in the Army: Henry Chadwick Is Trying to Secure Free Outfits for the Soldier Boys," *Brooklyn Eagle,* October 31, 1899, 5.

65. *Ibid.*

66. *Ibid.*

67. "Henry Chadwick Recalls Brooklyn 60 Years Ago: Sixty-Fourth Anniversary of the Eagle Puts the Father in Reminiscent Mood," *Brooklyn Eagle,* approx. November 2, 1905.

68. "Long Life Ended: Chadwick Called Out by Great Umpire," *Sporting News,* April 23, 1908.

*Chadwick's final residence may have been 106 Howard Avenue, as reported on his death card from the Greenwood cemetery library.

**Prior to his residence on Halsey Street, Chadwick lived at 245 Steuben Street, in the Fort Greene section of Brooklyn, located in the North West Corner of the city. He lived on Steuben Street as late as 1906.

69. *Ibid.*

Chapter 7

1. www.baseball-almanac.com/ws/yr 1903ws.shtml

2. *Ibid.,* 60.

3. Rockland County is an hour from Manhattan by car.

4. "William M, Rankin," *Baseball's First Stars,* edited by Frederick Ivor-Campbell, Robert L. Tiemann, and Mark Rucker (Cleveland: The Society of American Baseball Research, 1996), 134; Nash, *Baseball Legends of Brooklyn's Green-Wood Cemetery,* 106–107.

5. Block, *Baseball Before We Knew It,* 4–5.

6. "Base Ball's Birth: Evolution of the Game Played by Indians," *Sporting News,* June 1, 1901, 6.

7. *Ibid.*

8. *Ibid.*

9. *Ibid.*

10. John Montgomery Ward, *Base-Ball: How to Become a Player* (Philadelphia: Penn Publishing, 1990), 11. The original publication of this book was in 1888. Also see, Block, *Baseball Before We Knew It,* 6–7.

11. *Ibid.*

12. *Ibid.,* 12.

13. *Ibid.,* 12.

14. *Ibid.,* 15.

15. *Ibid.,* 13.

16. *Ibid.,* 23.

17. "Base Ball and Rounders: Was the Former Game Evolved from the Latter?" *Brooklyn Eagle,* July 1, 1888, 7.

18. *Ibid.*

19. *Ibid.*

20. *Ibid.*

21. *Ibid.*

22. *Ibid.*

23. Block, *Baseball Before We Knew It,* 8.

24. *Ibid.*

25. "What Is Said of Sports: The Late Richard A. Proctor on Base Ball," *Brooklyn Eagle,* December 30, 1888, 7.

26. *Ibid.*

27. *Ibid.* Also see Block, *Baseball Before We Knew It,* 8.

28. "Mr. A.G. Spalding's Address before the Public Schools Athletic League of Greater New York, Tuesday afternoon, May 22, 1906, on the occasion of the Presentation of the Spalding Trophy to Public School No. 46, Manhattan, Winners of the Base Ball Championship of 1905," Chadwick Scrapbook, 10.

29. K.D. Cook and Joseph T. Basile, "Baseball Has Two Daddies: Here's a story about the inception of the game that comes straight from Brooklyn, the borough of perpetual baseball mourning," *New York Newsday,* Monday September 12, 2000.

30. Rader, *Baseball: A History of America's Game,* 94.

31. Frederick Jackson Turner, *The Frontier in American History* (Mineola, New York: Dover Publications), 2.

32. H. Wayne Morgan, "Toward National Unity," *The Gilded Age,* H. Wayne Morgan, ed. (Syracuse, New York: Syracuse University Press, 1970), 2.

33. Riess, *Major Problems in American Sport,* 7. See Albert G. Spalding, *Base Ball: America's National Game, 1839–1915, Baseball's First Official Bible,* revised and re-edited by Sam Coombs and Bob West (San Francisco: Halo Book, 1991).

34. Adelman, *A Sporting Time* (Chicago: University of Illinois Press, 1986), 136; Chadwick, *Beadle Dime Base Ball Player* (1860), 137; Chadwick Scrapbooks, 7.

35. *Sporting News,* March 5, 1887. See also Peter Levine, *A.G. Spalding and the Rise of Baseball: The Promise of American Sport*

(New York: Oxford University Press, 1985), 113.

36. G. Edward White, *Creating the National Pastime: Baseball Transforms Itself, 1903–1953* (Princeton, New Jersey: Princeton University Press, 1996), 123.

37. *Spalding's Official Base Ball Guide*, 1905, 3. See also Robert H. Henderson, *Ball, Bat and Bishop: The Origin of Ball Games* (New York: Rockport Press, 1947), 172–173.

38. *Ibid.*, 3.

39. *Ibid.*, 5.

40. *Ibid.*, 11.

41. *Ibid.*, 13.

42. A.G. Mills, *The Winged Foot*, October 1929, 13, Abraham G. Mills papers.

43. A.G. Mills letter to A.G. Spalding, March 1, 1905 from the Doyle Papers of the National Baseball Hall of Fame.

44. *Ibid.*

45. Levine, *A.G. Spalding*, 115.

46. Henry Chadwick, "The Birthday of Baseball: Forty-Eight Years Ago Next Tuesday the First Game Was Played by the Knickerbockers and New Yorks: Rounders, Townball, Then Baseball," Chadwick Scrapbooks, 10.

47. *Ibid.*, 123.

48. White, *Creating the National Pastime*, 124. Levine, *A.G. Spalding*, 114.

49. *Ibid.*, 24.

50. Block, *Baseball Before We Knew It*, 33.

51. *Ibid.*, 34.

52. *Ibid.*, 37, 39–40.

53. *Ibid.*, 43. The article gave Abner Graves credit for this story but, more importantly, it also acknowledged another member of the society that influenced baseball's development: A.G. Spalding. Though this article was published two years before the existence of the Mills Commission, which eventually gave Doubleday credit for the game's invention, it does show that Spalding was aware of Doubleday's connection to the Theosophical Society. Why it took nearly two years for Spalding to actually anoint Doubleday as the game's inventor might have had something to do his own doubt about the veracity of the letter or even fears that he would have been discovered as a fraud, given the Theosophical ties to Doubleday. His letter to the Mills commission, dated July 28, 1907, never mentions Spalding's connection with Doubleday, whereas, for his part, Mills was unabashed at claiming his war connection with Doubleday.

54. *Spalding's Official Base Ball Guide* (New York: Spalding, 1908), 37.

55. *Ibid.*, 39.

56. *Ibid.*

57. *Ibid.*, 41.

58. *Ibid.*

59. *Ibid.*, 42.

60. *Ibid.*, 46.

61. *Ibid.*

62. *Ibid.*

63. *Ibid.*, 47.

64. *Ibid.*, 48.

65. *Ibid.*

66. Henry Chadwick letter to A.G. Mills, March 20, 1908, Mills papers.

67. Albert Goodwill Spalding letter to Henry Chadwick, November 25, 1905.

68. *Ibid.*

69. *Ibid.*

70. *Ibid.*

71. Albert Goodwill Spalding letter to Henry Chadwick, November 28, 1905.

72. *Ibid.*

73. *Ibid.*

74. *Ibid.*

75. "Turkish Baths," *Sporting News*, February 17, 1900, 3.

76. *Ibid.*

77. *Ibid.*

78. "The Father of Baseball," *Washington Star*, July 2, 1906.

79. Henry Chadwick, "Uncle Harry's Letter," January 9, 1908, Chadwick Scrapbooks.

80. Chadwick Scrapbooks, 9.

81. *Spalding's Official Base Ball Guide*, 1909, 7.

82. "Time Strikes Out Chadwick, Father of Baseball: Aged Journalist, Who Helped Make the National Game Recreation of Millions, Dies."

83. Foster, 7.

84. *Ibid.*

85. *Ibid.*

86. *Ibid.*

87. "Opening of the Baseball Season Witnessed by Thousands of Rooters: Superbas Start Off With a Defeat Before Nearly Twenty-two Thousand Enthusiasts — Both New York Teams Score Victories. World's Champions Take Great Uphill Battle. Story of the Washington Park Contest," *Brooklyn Eagle*, April 15, 1908.

88. "Opening of the Baseball Season Witnessed by Thousands of Rooters," *Brooklyn Eagle*, April 14, 1908. It should be noted that although the U.S. Army and the U.S. Navy considered it to be our national anthem, it was not until 1931, by an act of Congress, that it was made the official national anthem. Information provided by Harry Higham.

89. "Father Chadwick's Eightieth Year" and see, "In Memory of Henry Chadwick, 'Father of Baseball,'" *Baseball Magazine*, June 1908, 11.

90. "Opening of the Baseball Season Witnessed by Thousands of Rooters," *Brooklyn Eagle*, April 14, 1908.

91. "Big Crowd in Brooklyn: But Superbas Are Severely Trounced by the Boston Team," *New York Times*, Wednesday, April 15, 1908.

92. "Baseball's Devotion Cost Chadwick's Life: Refused Friend's Counsel," Source unknown.

93. "In Memory of Henry Chadwick, 'Father of Baseball,'" *Baseball Magazine*, June 1908, 11. Also see quote in Tygiel, *Past Time*.

94. "The Father of Baseball Dead in His 84th Year: Henry Chadwick Succumbs to Pneumonia and Heart Disease at His Home in Howard Avenue," *Standard Union*, April 20, 1908, from Chadwick Collection.

95. *Ibid.*

96. *Ibid.*

97. *Spalding's Official Base Ball Guide*, 1909, 19.

98. *Ibid.*

99. P.T. Powers, "In Chadwick's Memory: Monument to be Erected Over Grave of Father of Base Ball." Source unknown. April 1908.

100. *Ibid.*

101. Cook and Basile, "Baseball Has Two Daddies."

102. Last Will and Testament of Jane Botts Chadwick, from the basement of the Supreme Court of New York State. Jane Chadwick died in 1915. She lived her last years in Noyac, Long Island in Suffolk County with one of her grandchildren, Louis Eldridge.

103. "Honored in Death: Chadwick's Bier Covered with Flowers," April 23, 1908, Chadwick File.

104. Francis Richter, "Well-Deserved Honors," Chadwick Scrapbooks, 18.

105. Tygiel, *Past Time*, 33.

106. "'Father' Chadwick at Rest: Eulogized by Pastor of Church of Our Father," *Brooklyn Eagle*, April 23, 1908.

107. Spalding, *Base Ball: America's National Game*, 219.

108. Tygiel, *Past Time*, 33.

109. Jeffrey Richman, *Brooklyn's Green-Wood Cemetery: New York's Buried Treasure* (Vermont: Stinehour Press, 1998), 183.

110. "Henry Chadwick Memorial: Window in Church of Our Father Dedicated in Honor of Father of Baseball," *Brooklyn Eagle*, March 1910.

111. A.G. Spalding, "Spalding's Tribute to Father of Baseball: Noted Writer Had No Enemy," *San Diego Sun*, April, 1908, 7.

112. Chadwick is the only sportswriter with a plaque in the hall among the ballplayers. His induction preceded the Spink Award, created in order to give separate recognition to sports journalists who, after the creation of the award, have their own section.

Appendix 2

1. Frederick Ivor-Campbell, "Henry Chadwick," *Harvard Magazine*, 90, No. 1 (Sept.-Oct. 1987), 60.

2. Elliot Gorn and Warren Goldstein, *A Brief History of American Sports* (New York: Hill and Wang, 1993), 112.

3. Melvin L. Adelman, "Baseball, Business and the Workplace: Gelber's Thesis Reexamined" (*Journal of Social History*, Winter 1989), 289.

4. Goldstein, *Playing for Keeps*, 9.

5. Rader, *Baseball: A History of America's Game*, xvi.

6. Robert Smith, *Baseball in America* (New York: Holt, Rhinehart and Winston, 1961), 21–22.

7. Harold Peterson, *The Man Who Invented Baseball* (New York: Scribner's, 1973), 10.

8. Ron McCulloch, *How Baseball Began: The Long Overlooked Truth About the Birth of Baseball* (Los Angeles: Warwick Publishing, 1995), 105.

9. *Ibid.*, 105.

10. Robert H. Henderson, *Ball, Bat and Bishop: The Origin of Ball Games* (New York: Rockport Press, 1947), p. 170–181.

11. Leonard Koppett, *Koppett's Concise*

History of Major League Baseball (Princeton, New Jersey: Princeton University Press, 1998), 148.

12. *Ibid.*, 148.

13. Peter Levine, *A.G. Spalding and the Rise of Baseball: The Promise of American*

Sport (New York: Oxford University Press, 1985), 8.

14. Devine, pp. 10–11.

15. Tom Melville, *Early Baseball and the Rise of the National League* (Jefferson, North Carolina: McFarland, 2001), 17.

Bibliography

Books

Accocella, Nicholas, and Donald Dewey. *The Biographical History of Baseball.* New York: Carrol and Graf, 1995.

Adelman, Melvin. *A Sporting Time: New York City and the Rise of Modern Athletics, 1820–70.* Chicago: University of Illinois Press, 1986.

Allen, Lee. *The American League Story.* New York: Hill and Wang, 1965.

_____. *100 Years of Baseball: The Intimate and Dramatic Story of Modern Baseball from the Game's Beginnings Up to the Present Day.* New York: Bartholomew House, 1950.

Allen, Oliver. *New York, New York: A History of the World's Most Exhilarating and Challenging City.* New York: Atheneum, 1990.

Block, David. *Baseball Before We Knew It: A Search for the Roots of the Game.* Lincoln: University of Nebraska Press, 2005.

Bowman, John, and Joel Zoss. *Diamonds in the Rough: The Untold Story of Baseball.* New York: Macmillan, 1989.

_____, _____, Nicholas Accocella, and Donald Dewey. *The Biographical History of Baseball.* New York: Carrol and Graf, 1995.

Brundage, Anthony. *England's "Prussian Minister": Edwin Chadwick and the Politics of Government Growth, 1832–1854.* University Park, Pennsylvania: Pennsylvania State University Press, 1988.

Devine, Christopher. *Harry Wright, The Father of Professional Base Ball.* Jefferson, North Carolina: McFarland, 2003.

Dickey, Glenn. *The History of American League Baseball Since 1901.* New York: Stein and Day, 1980.

DiClerico, James M., and Barry J. Pavelec. *The Jersey Game: The History of Modern Baseball from Its Birth to the Big League in the Garden State.* New Brunswick, New Jersey: Rutgers University Press, 1991.

Di Salvatore, Bryan. *A Clever Base-Ballist: The Life and Times of John Montgomery Ward.* Baltimore: Johns Hopkins University Press, 1989.

Donald, David Herbert. *Lincoln.* New York: Simon and Schuster, 1995.

253

Dulles, Foster Rhea. *A History of Recreation: America Learns to Play*. New York: Meredith, 1965.

Fehrenbacher, Don E. *Prelude to Greatness: Lincoln in the 1850s*. Stanford, California: Stanford University Press, 1962.

Garraty, John A., and Mark C. Carnes. *American National Biography*. 24 volumes. New York: Oxford University Press, 1999.

Goldstein, Richard. *Superstars and Screwballs: 100 Years of Brooklyn Baseball*. New York: Dutton, 1991.

Goldstein, Warren. *Playing for Keeps: A History of Early Baseball*. Ithaca: Cornell University Press, 1989.

_____, and Elliott J. Gorn. *A Brief History of American Sports*. New York: Hill and Wang, 1993.

Green, Harvey. *Fit for America: Health Fitness and Sport and American Society*. New York: Pantheon Books, 1986.

Hays, Samuel P. *The Response to Industrialism: 1885–1914*. Chicago: University of Chicago Press, 1975.

Henderson, Robert W. *Ball, Bat and Bishop: The Origin of Ball Games*. New York: Rockport Press, 1947.

Jones, Howard Mumford. *The Age of Energy: Varieties of American Experience, 1865–1915*. New York: Viking Press, 1971.

Koppett, Leonard. *Koppett's Concise History of Major League Baseball*. Philadelphia: Temple University Press, 1998.

Kirsch, George B. *The Creation of American Team Sports: Baseball and Cricket, 1838–72*. Chicago: University of Illinois Press, 1989.

Lears, T.J. Jackson. *No Place of Grace: Antimodernism and the Transformation of American Culture, 1880–1920*. Chicago: University of Chicago Press, 1994.

Leitner, Irving A. *Baseball: Diamond in the Rough*. New York: Criterion Books, 1972.

Levine, Peter A. *A.G. Spalding and the Rise of Baseball: The Promise of American Sport*. New York: Oxford University Press, 1985.

Lyman, Susan Elizabeth. *The Story of New York: An Informal History of the City from the First Settlement to the Present Day*. New York: Crown, 1975.

MacDonald, Neil W. *The League That Lasted: 1876 and the Founding of the National League of Professional Base Ball Clubs*. Jefferson, North Carolina: McFarland, 2004.

McCulloch, Ron. *How Baseball Began: The Long Overlooked Truth About the Birth of Baseball*. Los Angeles: Warwick, 1995.

Messner, Michael A., and Donald F. Sabo. *Sport, Men, and the Gender Order: Critical Feminist Perspectives*. Champaign, Illinois: Human Kinetics Books, 1990.

Melville, Tom. *Early Baseball and the Rise of the National League*. Jefferson, North Carolina: McFarland, 2003.

Melville, Tom. *The Tented Field: A History of Cricket in America*. Bowling Green, Ohio: Bowling Green State University Popular Press, 1998.

Moore, Jim, and Natalie Vermilyea. *Earnest Thayer's "Casey at the Bat": Background and Characters of Baseball's Most Famous Poem*. Jefferson, North Carolina: McFarland, 1994.

Morgan, H. Wayne, ed. *The Gilded Age*. Syracuse, New York: Syracuse University Press, 1970.

Morris, Peter. *A Game of Inches: The Stories Behind the Innovations That Shaped Baseball*. Chicago, Illinois: Ivan R. Dee Press, 2006.

Nasaw, David. *Going Out: The Rise and Fall of Popular Amusements*. New York: Basic Books, 1993.

Patten, William, and J. Walker McSpadden, eds. *The Book of Baseball: The National Game from the Earliest Days to the Present Season*. New York: P.F. Collier, 1911.

Peiss, Kathy. *Cheap Amusements: Working Women and Leisure in Turn-of-the-Century New York*. Philadelphia: Temple University Press, 1986.

Perry, Marvin. *Western Civilization: A Brief History, Volume II from the 1400s*. New York: Houghton Mifflin, 1997.

Peterson, Harold. *The Man Who Invented Baseball*. New York: Scribner's, 1973.

Rader, Benjamin G. *Baseball: A History of America's Game*. Chicago: University of Illinois Press, 1992.

Remini, Robert V. *Henry Clay: Statesman for the Union*. New York: W.W. Norton, 1991.

Riess, Steven A., ed. *Major Problems in American Sport History*. New York: Houghton Mifflin, 1997.

Richman, Jeffrey. *Brooklyn's Green-Wood Cemetery: New York's Buried Treasure*. Vermont: Stinehour Press, 1998.

Rotundo, E. Anthony. *American Manhood: Transformations in Masculinity from the Revolution to the Modern Era*. New York: Basic Books, 1993.

Ryczek, William J. *Blackguards and Redstockings: A History of Baseball's National Association, 1871–1875*. Jefferson, North Carolina: McFarland, 1999.

_____. *When Johnny Comes Sliding Home: The Post Civil War Boom, 1865–1870*. Jefferson, North Carolina: McFarland, 1995.

Schlossberg, Dan. *The Baseball Catalog*. New York: Jonathan David Publishers, 2000.

Schwarz, Alan. *The Numbers Game: Baseball's Lifelong Fascination with Statistics*. New York: St. Martin's Press, 2004.

Seymour, Harold. *Baseball, The People's Game*. New York: Oxford University Press, 1990.

Smith, Robert. *Baseball in America*. New York: Holt, Rinehart and Winston, 1961.

Snyder-Grenier, Ellen M. *Brooklyn! An Illustrated History for the Brooklyn Historical Society*. Philadelphia: Temple University Press, 1996.

Spalding, Albert Goodwill. *Base Ball: America's National Game, 1839–1915*. Revised and re-edited by Samm Coombs and Bob West. San Francisco: Halo Books, 1991.

Spink, Albert H. *The National Game*, 2nd Edition, foreword by Steven Gietschier. Carbondale: Southern Illinois University Press, 1999.

Sullivan, Dean A. *Early Innings: A Documentary History of Baseball, 1825–1908*. Lincoln, Nebraska: University of Nebraska Press, 1995.

Syrett, Harold Coffin. *The City of Brooklyn, 1865–1898: A Political History*. New York: Columbia University Press, 1944.

Thompson, E.P. *The Making of the English Working Class*. New York: Pantheon Books, 1964.

Turner, Frederick Jackson. *The Significance of the Frontier*. Mineola, New York: Dover Publications, 1996.

Tygiel, Jules. *Past Time: Baseball As History*. New York: Oxford University Press, 2000.

Voight, David Quentin. *American Baseball: From Gentleman's Sport to the Commissioner System*. Norman: University of Oklahoma Press, 1966.

Walters, Ronald G. *American Reformers, 1815–1860*. Gloucester, Massachusetts: Peter Smith Publisher, 1997.

White, G. Edward. *Creating the National Pastime: Baseball Transforms Itself.* Princeton, New Jersey: Princeton University Press, 1996.

Chadwick Collection of Peter Nash

"Baseball Devotion Cost Chadwick's Life: Refused Friend's Counsel." Source unknown, approximately April 21, 1908.

Chadwick, Henry. "The Game's Genesis: Rounders Developed into Base Ball in 1845." *Sporting News*, 1898.

"The Father of Baseball Dead in his 84th Year: Henry Chadwick Succumbs to Pneumonia and Heart Disease at His Home in Howard Avenue." *Standard Union*, April 20, 1908.

"Henry Chadwick Recalls Brooklyn 60 Years Ago: Sixty-Fourth Anniversary of the Eagle Puts the Father in Reminiscent Mood." *Brooklyn Eagle*, approx. November 2, 1905.

Guidebooks and Manuals

Chadwick, Henry. *Beadle's Dime Base-Ball Player.* New York: Beadle and Company, 1860.

_____. *Beadle's Dime Base-Ball Player.* New York: Beadle and Company, 1861.

_____. *Spalding's Official Base Ball Guide, 1907.* New York: American Sports Publishing Company, 1907.

_____, ed. *De Witt's Base-Ball Guide for 1879: A Complete Manual of the National Game.* New York: Clinton T. De Witt, Publisher, 1879.

_____, ed. *Spalding's Official Base-Ball Guide.* 1876.

Foster, John B. *Spalding's Official Base Ball Guide, 1909.* Chicago: A.G. Spalding and Bros., 1908.

Journal Articles

Betts, John Rickards. "Sporting Journalism in Nineteenth-Century America." *American Quarterly* (1953): 39–56.

_____. "The Technological Revolution and the Rise of Sport, 1850–1950." *The Mississippi Valley Historical Review* (1950): 231–256.

Chadwick, Henry. "Baseball in the Colleges." *Outing* (August 1888): 407–408.

Ivor-Campbell, Fred, et al., eds. "Henry Chadwick (Chad, Father of Base Ball)." *Baseball's First Stars* (1996).

Lamoreaux, David. "Baseball in the Late Nineteenth Century: The Source of Its Appeal." *Journal of Popular Culture II* (Winter 1977): 3–19.

Lewis, Robert M. "Cricket and the Beginnings of Organized Baseball in New York City." *The International Journal of History and Sport* (December 1987): 315–332.

Nugent, William Henry. "The Sports Section." *The American Mercury* (February 1929): 329–338.

Pesavento, Wilma J. "Sport and Recreation in the Pullman Experiment, 1880–1900." *Journal of Sport History* (Summer 1982): 38–62.

Schiff, Andrew J. "Baseball and Labor: A Historiography." *Clio: The History Journal of the Chi Delta Chapter of Phi Alpha Theta* 2 (Spring 1995).
Tassinari, Edward J. "Henry Chadwick: 'Father of Baseball,' Friend of Chess." *Lasker and His Contemporaries*, 5 (1997).

Magazine Articles

"In Memory of Henry Chadwick, 'Father of Baseball.'" *Baseball Magazine*, June 1908.
Ivor-Campbell, Fred. "Henry Chadwick." *Harvard Magazine*, September-October, 1987.

Manuscript Collections

Chadwick, Henry, Scrapbooks. Spalding Collection. New York Public Library.
Mills, Abraham G., Papers. New York Public Library, New York.

Newspapers

American Chronicle 1, February 29, 1868.
"Baseball, a Look Back." *Brooklyn Eagle*, 3, July, 1949, vol. 83: 129. *Base Ball Players' Chronicle*, August 22, 1867.
"Chad on the Eagle, Father of Baseball Will Write Exclusively for This Paper Hereafter." *Brooklyn Eagle*, 22, May 1907, vol. 144: 134.
Chadwick, Henry. "Old Time Games: Henry Chadwick's Recollections of Many Years Ago," *Brooklyn Eagle*, May 16, 1888.
_____. *Brooklyn Eagle*, June 6, 1868.
_____. *New York Clipper*, July 20, 1857.
_____. *New York Clipper*, July 27, 1858.
_____. *New York Clipper*, September 1, 1860.
_____. "The Model Base Ball Player," *New York Clipper*, September 1, 1860.
_____. *New York Daily Times*, July 10, 1856.
_____. *New York Daily Times*, July 20, 1856.
_____. "Chadwick's Chat," *Sporting News*, October 18, 1890.
_____. "Base-Ball Matters: The Grand Tournament," *Wilkes Spirit of the Times*, May 7, 1866.
Cook, K.D., and Joseph T. Basile, "Baseball Has Two Daddies: Here's a Story about the inception of the game that comes straight from Brooklyn, the borough of perpetual baseball mourning," *New York Newsday*, Monday, September 12, 2000.
"Father and Mrs. Chadwick Celebrate Their Fifty-eighth Anniversary of Their Wedding Day," August 25, 1906.
"'Father' Chadwick at Rest: Eulogized by Pastor of Church of Our Father," *Brooklyn Eagle*, April 23, 1908.
"Henry Chadwick — The Father of Baseball," *Washington Star*, July 2, 1906, vol. 18.
"Importance of Education," printed speech by Edward Everett, *New York Clipper*, July 5, 1856.

"Letter from Chadwick: Veteran Base Ball Writer on the Kicking Abuse," *Brooklyn Eagle*, April 1, 1901.

"Long Life Ended: Chadwick Called Out by Great Umpire," *Sporting News*, April 23, 1908.

Saunders, Allen. "The Father of Baseball," *Sporting Life*, 1906l *Sporting News*, April 21, 1908.

"Silver Ball Match: The Eckford Club Champions," *Brooklyn Eagle,* September 10, 1862.

Spalding, Albert Goodwill. "Spalding's Tribute to Father of Baseball: Noted Writer Had No Enemy," *San Diego Sun*, April 21, 1908.

"Their Golden Wedding: Mr. and Mrs. Henry Chadwick Will Celebrate Fifty Years of Wedded Life on August 19," *Brooklyn Eagle*, August, 8, 1898.

"Tombstone." *Brooklyn Eagle*, 17 Jan. 1932, vol. 9: 136.

Papers

"The Amateur Season of 1876." Vol. 3.

"Baseball: National League of Professional Clubs Formed — A Startling Coup d'E-tat." 1876, vol. 3.

"The Birthday of Baseball: Forty-Eight Years Ago Next Tuesday the First Game Was Played by the Knickerbockers and New Yorkers," June 12, 1894.

"Business and Recreation." 1871, vol. 2.

"An Early Base-Ball Reminiscence." 1895, vol. 3.

Judd, Jacob. "The History of Brooklyn, 1834–1855: Political and Administrative Aspects," Phd. Dissertation, New York University, April 1959.

Kimmel, Michael S., "Baseball and the Reconstitution of American Masculinity, 1880–1920," S.U.N.Y at Stony Brook.

Newman, Roberta, "The Pitch: Baseball, Advertising, and American Culture in the Late Nineteenth and Early Twentieth Centuries," unpublished manuscript as presented to the Society of American Baseball Research, Casey Stengal Chapter Regional, February 17, 2001.

Schiff, Andrew. "Baseball Brooklyn Style." Brooklyn College, 1988.

"Sports in Brooklyn: Henry Chadwick Talks About the Old Times." Vol. 2.

Index